Ethel Herr invests h  in an invitation to exp throne. *Lord, Show Me* blaze of unsurpassable, unimaginable glory." Ethel reveals more than a glimmer of His greatness. Feast on this book until you're wrapped, like Moses, in the afterglow of divine warmth. Prepare for a glorious invasion of your daily life.

—Janet Chester Bly
author of *Hope Lives Here*, *God Is Good All The Time*
and twenty-six other books

If you want to center your spiritual journey around the personality of God, Ethel Herr invites you to a week-by-week retreat-like experience of beholding the wise and engaging God who speaks to us.

—Jan Johnson
author of *When the Soul Listens*

You won't want to rush as you let Ethel Herr guide you into your own personal journey to the heart of God. In our "do-it-in-thirty-seconds-or-less" culture, we are often left with a longing to meet God more deeply. Now, through *Lord, Show Me Your Glory*, you can reflect on who God is and experience His presence in the depth of your soul.

—Roger Palms
former editor of *Decision* magazine
writer, teacher and speaker

This I know to be true: Ethel Herr has glimpsed the glory of the Lord. His Word permeates her prose. His presence hovers over her pages. *Lord, Show Me Your Glory* is filled with phrases so lyrical they not only speak to our hearts, they fairly *sing* to our Alpha and Omega God! As He clearly revealed Himself to Ethel, so does He reveal Himself to us through her writing. Often as I read, my mouth would drop open in wonder and my eyes would swim with tears of joy. If you want your devotional time to become an act of worship, trust Ethel to point you to the God of all glory.

—Liz Curtis Higgs
author of *Thorn in My Heart*

Ethel Herr's skill as a writer reaches a spectacular high in *Lord, Show Me Your Glory*. From personal experience Ethel paints pictures of God's glory in panoramas that attract a listless spiritual traveler toward an exciting adventure with the living God. This fine book is a tonic for all who want their daily routine transformed by the radiant presence of the Lord!

—**Ben Jennings**
international prayer coordinator
Campus Crusade for Christ

No one can doubt Ethel Herr's hunger for more of God in her life. She demonstrates this so well in her writing. Her enthusiasm for God spills over to encourage readers to join her in spiritual growth. In each chapter she emphasizes God's names, titles and attributes, offering a fresh, exciting way to open ourselves more fully to God.

—**Cecil Murphey**
author, coauthor or ghostwriter of ninety books
including *The God Who Pursues*

Knowing God's glory is really the purpose of this book. As revival breaks out, and I believe it is imminent, people will desperately hunger and truly need to understand the full measure of the God we serve. *Lord, Show Me Your Glory* answers and anticipates that need.

—**Tricia Rhodes**
speaker and author of *Soul at Rest*
and *Contemplating the Cross*

Lord, Show Me Your Glory

52 Weekly Meditations on the Majesty of God

Ethel Herr

CHRISTIAN PUBLICATIONS, INC.
CAMP HILL, PENNSYLVANIA

CHRISTIAN PUBLICATIONS, INC.

3825 Hartzdale Drive, Camp Hill, PA 17011
www.christianpublications.com

Faithful, biblical publishing since 1883

Lord, Show Me Your Glory
ISBN: 0-88965-215-5
LOC Control Number: 2003105205
© 2003 by Ethel Herr
All rights reserved
Printed in the United States of America

03 04 05 06 07   5 4 3 2

Contents

Glory is . . .

The glory of God is
thunder and lightning
and a timber-shivering storm
that swaths its jagged pathway
across the dailiness of our existence.

The glory of God is also
an inner calm
in the midst of terrifying wind and rain,
a sacred refuge in the hollow
of our Creator/Father's hand.

The glory of God is
Ten Hebrew characters
chiseled in the Rock of the Ages
forever circumscribing the borders of our conduct
by His eternal standard.

The glory of God is also
unnumbered heartbeats of the divine character
inscribed with a stylus of love
upon the fleshy tables of our souls
altering our passions
recreating us from within
to mirror
His radiant image
in a world tarnished
with rebellion.

Lord, Show Me Your Glory!

hile the hush and fresh dew of a newborn day hovered over the old mountain, Moses started his journey upward. In his arms he clutched the two stone tablets, a keen pain of remorse jabbing at his conscience. If only he had not destroyed the first ones.

Our God is a gracious God, he reminded himself and ascended into the thickening clouds. Remorse gave way to anticipation—an eagerness that caused his heart and feet to quicken up the craggy steeps. *Jehovah has promised to show me His glory!*

For the eighty long years of Moses' life, Jehovah had been pursuing him. Always, it seemed to him in retrospect, a fringe of tantalizing glory hovered nearby. Was it an accident that his life had been spared in the massacre of Hebrew babies? Or that he was raised in the sumptuous glory of Pharaoh's court and given the best education known to man? That he felt compelled to defend his people, then went about it in his own hotheaded way and had to flee into the obscurity of shepherding smelly sheep for forty years until he'd lost all the arrogance that had once fueled his efforts?

What about the burning bush being consumed with a dazzling, unearthly glory—yet never truly consumed? And the long, tension-filled days of pleas with Pharaoh and plagues and Passover and the Red Sea victory?

Moses sighed and paused to let the cloud engulf him totally—body, mind and spirit. Even now, the glory seemed to breathe in the mist about him. But it was not enough. He had to see more. He jabbed at the ground with his staff and remembered how the whole mountain had quaked. Lightning had rent the skies, an eerie trumpet sound had called to them from the fire and smoke above. The people had been terrified.

Ah, such wanton, wandering sheep, those people. Yet on their welfare rests the very glory of Jehovah in the eyes of all the peoples of the earth. Moses bowed his head, then dropped to one knee in the gravel and dry, scrubby grass.

"Great God, Jehovah," he cried out from an anguished soul. "Why will they never seek after Your eternal glory? Can they never know?"

For a long while, the gray-headed shepherd of Israel let his heart bleed on the side of the mountain. When he rose from the ground, thinking to go on, he sensed a presence that he had grown to recognize on his many trips up the mountain these past months.

"Oh, Lord God, Jehovah, You've come," he whispered into the cloud. "I confess I once thought that just to climb to the top and hear Your voice would satisfy the deep inner craving for eternal glory that ravaged my inner being. Instead it set such a hunger quivering within me that I must always have *more*. Is this the moment, LORD God, that time for which I was born and rescued from the Nile? Have You come to show me the fullness of Your glory?"

The silence that ensued held Moses in a state of suspended awe, even surpassing anything he had known before—not at the burning bush or at the Red Sea or at other times on the top of the mountain. As if moved by a power not his own, he backed into a cleft in the side of the rock. In a way that his physical senses could never experience, he heard, he saw, he felt the God of the universe passing by in front of him, darkening the opening of his shelter as it went.

Then suddenly the darkness vanished. A blaze of unsurpassable, unimaginable glory dazzled before him and a voice like the thundering of a thousand waterfalls called out:

"The LORD, the LORD God, compassionate and gracious, slow to anger, and abounding in lovingkindness and truth; who keeps lovingkindness for thousands, who forgives iniquity, transgression and sin; yet He will by no means leave the guilty unpunished, visiting the iniquity of fathers on the children and on the grandchildren to the third and fourth generations."

Moses fell instantly with his face to the earth, which vibrated with the echoes of the majestic voice. From his full, throbbing heart burst a volley of words so urgent he could scarcely get them out fast enough: "If now I have found favor in Your sight, O Lord, I pray, let the Lord go along in our midst, even though the people are so obstinate, and pardon our iniquity and our sin, and take us as Your own possession." In his moment of greatest wonder and intimacy with God, the moment he had longed for for a lifetime, his deepest passion was still for the people God had called him to shepherd.

For a long moment, Moses was wrapped in the warmth and afterglow of the glory he had witnessed. Then he heard the voice once more: "Behold, I am going to make a covenant. Before all your people I will perform miracles which have not been produced in all the earth nor among any of the nations; and all the people among whom you live will see the working of the LORD, for it is a fearful thing that I am going to perform with you."

God's words went on, carving the details of the covenant in the tablets of stone. For forty days and forty nights, Moses, the servant of Jehovah, lingered there with Him. He took neither water for drink nor food for nourishment, but feasted on the glory of God, preparing to carry it to his people, that they too might see a glimmer of its greatness.[1]

*   *   *

Does your heart cry out with Moses, "Show me Your glory!"?

You see glimpses of this glory in God's Creation, in His moral Law, in His Incarnation, in your own redemption and transformed life. But deep down in your heart, you are never satisfied with what you have experienced. Something tells you there is more!

In your hunger, you gather with His people for public worship through music, prayer and the reading, preaching and teaching of His Word. Or you sing, read your Bible and pray with your family or in secret.

But have you encountered God? Or do you simply give mental assent to some well-known facet of His glory? Worse yet, do you allow yourself to be manipulated into an emotional experience that never touches the heart of God? How often do you leave a worship service with an emptiness of spirit that you either fail to recognize or try to fill with something more accessible? How can you push the walls of tradition back to allow you to see and experience the "so much more" that your heart craves for?

It can be tough in our helter-skelter, rush-about world where earthly values distract and human schedules interrupt. Do you ever feel lost and wonder whether a real one-on-one encounter with God is even possible?

The glimpses into His glorious character that form the heart of this book will guide you in that direction. And you will find that to learn from experience who God is and what He is like is to be overwhelmed by His glory!

The meditations found in *Lord, Show Me Your Glory* are not Bible studies designed to teach you to interpret Scripture and apply it to your life. Nor are they short devotional readings you can grab in one hand, with a bagel in the other, on your way out the door each morning. Rather, think of this book as a consistent tap on the shoulder. Give it a priority place on your schedule. Allow it to usher you past the noise and confusion of daily life into His presence. There you will focus on Him and listen to whatever He says to you about your walk with Him and before others. And there you will have a daily encounter with the God of the universe.

Each of the fifty-two chapters in this book examines one facet of God's glorious character. While there are blank lines on the pages, the answers are not to be found by a simple reading of the assigned Scripture. Rather, you will use them to record your personal responses to the character of God as He reveals Himself to you.

Finally, I suggest that you read Moses' story often, along with the stories of other men in Scripture who walked with God. While we have no record of any other person ever asking God specifically, "Show me Your glory," they did seek after Him and He revealed much of His glory to them.

From Moses' experiences as recorded in the story on the previous pages, we find five guidelines for our own journey toward the heart of God. I pass them on to you, that you might be guided by them as well:

> When God first appeared atop Mount Sinai and called out to Moses, the people feared greatly, but *Moses went ahead into the cloud and the fire and the smoke.* He had a passion to follow after God that overcame whatever fears he may have felt. (Exodus 20:21)

> *Moses took time to wait in God's presence.* God's revelations of Himself could not be rushed, nor was Moses ready for them until his heart was totally quiet before Him. (24:16-18)

> *Moses listened with care to all of God's instructions* about how he was to take back to his people the message of His glory. God's glory must be revealed by God's patterns. (25-29)

> *Moses had a passion for God's reputation* and was ready to put his own life on the line to maintain that reputation. (32-33)

> *Moses craved the presence of God and His glory in his ministry.* He all but refused to go on serving God without it.

As a result, when he returned to the people, he carried the glow of that glory in his face. (33:12-23; 34:29-35)

The course you are about to embark upon may take you a year or more to complete. But the journey it helps you to begin will likely last the rest of your life. Like Moses, once you begin to encounter God, it will "spoil" you for life. The more you see of Him, the more you will yearn to see. The more you discover of Him, the more you will know there is yet to discover! The more you experience of His intimacy, the more you will sense how far you have yet to go to know Him perfectly! You can rest assured that God will never tire of hearing your repeated request to "Show me Your glory!"

* * *

The Glory of God is the biggest theme that can ever occupy our minds!

But to ponder God Himself! What, when I stop to think about it, could be more fascinating?[2]

The words that form the heart of this book fall into three categories: *names, titles* and *attributes.*

Names are God's own words for Himself. In Hebrew culture, names were chosen with care and communicated a specific meaning. When God revealed Himself by a name in that culture, He was identifying His person and character (e.g., in Genesis 17:1, "I am *El Shaddai*" meant "I am *God Almighty*" and spoke of His power and nurturing qualities).

Titles are usually metaphors that indicate God's character or office in relation to men and women. For example, "The LORD is my *light* and my *salvation*" (Psalm 27:1). "The LORD is my *shepherd*" (23:1).

Attributes are adjectives that describe the character of God, such as "O LORD my God, You are *very great*" (104:1).

This organized collection of God-prompters is designed to set you to thinking, meditating and chewing on the sort of meat that engenders spiritual growth. It consists of fifty-two chapters, one for each week of a calendar year. You may start it at any time. The meditations are planned so as to introduce the subject of God's glory and then bring it to a climactic summary.

Each chapter examines one facet of God's glorious character. It begins with a primary word—either a name, a title or an attribute of God—supported by one or two other words which speak to the same idea. Each supporting word presents a different nuance of the central theme (e.g., Creator is supported by Maker and Fashioner).

Helpful Suggestions for the Process

1. Set aside a specific place and an unhurried portion of time each day to pursue this adventure. Let nothing steal it from you. Aim for quietness in your soul and adequate time to meditate and worship. Give it whatever priority on your schedule is needed so it can grab your heart and enable you to see God's glory!

2. Begin by asking God to open your heart to learn all He wants to show you of Himself, to lead you into worship and to enable you to work these lessons out in your life. Next, read the Scriptures and the text provided and take time to meditate and ask God what He wants you to take away from this grand meditation.

3. Chapters are divided into sections by the individual names, titles and attributes that are used as a lens for viewing the concept for the week. Read and meditate at your own pace. Don't feel you have to complete an entire reading in a single day.

This book is planned in such a way that you can stay with each chapter for an entire week. Divide it up in whatever way your responses dictate to you. You may want to read the entire chapter one time through for an overview, then more slowly, one section at a sitting. Allow plenty of time to think deeply through all the implications of the Scriptures listed at the end of each section. You may repeat sections or even entire chapters if they seem to call you to spend more time.

4. At the end of each chapter, a question or statement is given to prompt your ongoing meditation, and blank lines are provided so you may record your responses to the readings.

5. In addition, you may wish to record other responses in a separate notebook. Such responses can reflect the musings of your heart. Some of the things you may want to record, in addition to others that come to you, are:

    -   What you are learning about the character of God, not simply from the text, but from God's voice moving in your heart and mind and from your consideration of the idea present in this book.

    -   Questions or subjects suggested that you want to pursue further.

    -   Instructions God gives you about applying the truth of His character to your life.

    -   Creative expressions of whatever you are learning, hearing or questioning.

6. Repeat these meditations as many times as you like. Feel free to take more than a year to work your way through them. You may want to repeat this book every year—in fact, you may find that these pictures of God lead you into a lifelong pattern of planning every day for a holy encounter with God.

His Name

Shout joyfully to God, all the earth;
Sing the glory of His name;
Make His praise glorious. (Psalm 66:1-2)

Name Personal attribution that opens a window into
an essential identity or personality.

The holy name of God! What is it? Finite beings that we
are, what can we shout or sing that would make the name
of our Creator glorious?

Can we ever hold a moonbeam in our hands and analyze its
wonder? Or can we conceive a description that encompasses the
vastness of a towering mountain range? Do we have a word in our
human tongue to describe the soul-stirring catharsis of the thundering sound of a spring waterfall?

If we fall tongue-tied before the majesties of the visible created
works all around us, what happens to our speech when we encounter the God of the universe? The most eloquent among us must
settle for stammered, inadequate expressions. Even the Spirit of
God speaking through the writers of Holy Scripture found no
words adequate to condense His endless fullness so that our finite
minds could comprehend it.

His name is like the golden rays of the sun shaken out upon
earth with an intensity too great for the human eye to behold. No

mere religious vocabulary or collection of metaphors can make of Him a familiar companion for our journey.

His name is an accommodation to our finite sensibilities and limited intellects. It takes hundreds of words to begin to give us a glimpse of all that is God. Creator, Judge, Savior, Wisdom, Love and Light . . . the list goes on and on. Each word reveals, in some small part, one more facet of this infinite diamond treasure that He is to our God-starved souls.

> God's name implies "the whole combination of divine perfections."[1]

The vast array of names and titles for God pulls back the veil to reveal to us a tantalizing view of Him, making us hungry always for more and more. They express His person, giving us clues to what He is like. They hint at His purposes, suggesting what it is that motivates His actions and words and what His overall goals may be. They embody His honor, showing us the majesty and exaltation of the esteem in which we mortals are designed to hold Him. They protect His authority, holding up for us a standard of the respect which is due to Him because of who He is in relation to all mankind and to His universe.

We see amazing glimmers of His glorious character shining out from each of these names of deity with holy radiance. Passionate to communicate Himself to us, He frames His names in words and images that open our eyes and touch our hearts and prepare us for His glorious invasion into our lives, invasions that become daily personal encounters.

How can we begin to sing such glory on earth? To pass it on?

One morning I heard the glory song when I stepped into a lingering Rocky Mountain mist just at dawn. In perfect silence, rising high above me, a window in the fog framed a glowing just-past-full moon. My ears heard nothing, but my heart picked up the strains of:

Glory! Glory be to God!

I looked around at a hundred trees, all pointing heavenward as they stood. Faint breezes rustled their yellowing leaves and sent them swirling in dizzy little eddies to the ground. What glorious miracles of God's unlimited artistic creativity, power and transcendence!

In that electric moment I knew that all nature sings the glory of the name Creator by simply being what God created it to be. It sings His glory by obeying His laws—laws that govern the smooth operation of our world, laws that no object of nature can either understand or resist at will.

Nature has no choice. Its voices must ring in every corner of our earth and God's infinite cosmos beyond. But the message is incomplete. It shows us only His creative fingers and their excellence in power, design and intricacy. Wonderful, marvelous, mind-staggering glimmers of the glory!

When it comes to men, women and children, God's crowning act of creation and self-expression, the glory potential explodes. Only we are fashioned in the very image and likeness of God. We alone among His works have hearts made to be attuned to the melodies He longs for us to create. We alone possess rare abilities to craft the songs we sing. And we alone are given the choice whether to sing the glory of God or to waste our lives playing at the production of ditties in our own honor.

The name of God, like His Person, is "good" (Psalm 52:9) and "lovely" (135:3). It is "everlasting" (135:13) and "majestic" (8:1, 9). It is "holy and awesome" (111:9) and "exalted" (148:13). We can know this incredible name, and when we do, we experience answers to prayer and deliverance from the powers of evil that surround us on earth (91:14-16). When God has defeated His last foe and all men stand before Him in judgment, "at the name of Jesus EVERY KNEE WILL BOW, of those who are in heaven and on earth and under the earth" (Philippians 2:10).

Jesus' tremendous name
Puts all our foes to flight
Jesus, the meek, the angry Lamb
A Lion is in fight.[2]

For further glimpses of the glorious Name of God, read: Psalm 20:1, 5, 7; 54:1; 72:19; 83:18; 96:8; Proverbs 18:10; Isaiah 26:8; Jeremiah 10:6; Ezekiel 36:20-23; Micah 5:4; Acts 4:10; Revelation 19:12; 22:4.

I AM

God said to Moses, "I AM WHO I AM." . . . This is My name forever, and this is My memorial-name to all generations. (Exodus 3:14-15)

Name indicating that God is totally self-existent, not dependent on any other beings for His being.

Hiding out in the backside of the Midianite desert, Moses had much to learn about the God of his fathers. Moses had run away from his people, married and settled down to a long, uneventful life in a non-Hebrew community. Little chance that there he would learn anything about the God of Abraham, Isaac and Jacob!

Then one day God broke through the endless sand dunes and cultural barriers and appeared to Moses in a most irregular way. The shepherd's attention was arrested dramatically by the sight of a desert bush on fire—burning and crackling, sending sparks heavenward, but never being consumed.

"I have come down to deliver [My people] from the power of the Egyptians, and to bring them up . . . to a good and spacious land . . . flowing with milk and honey," God said (Exodus 3:8).

Moses trembled, standing barefoot in the sand, listening, wondering. God was not through. "Come now, and I will send you to Pharaoh, so that you may bring My people . . . out of Egypt" (3:10).

He could not have heard the words right. He had already proven by experience that he was not the man to do the job. Confused, unbelieving, he stammered the first thing that came to mind: "Who am I, that I should go to Pharaoh, and that I should bring the sons of Israel out of Egypt? I am not Your man, God. I tried and failed. Surely in forty years' time, You could have found somebody much better qualified than I" (see 3:11).

If Moses was looking for a way out, he was mistaken. Or if he expected a pat on the back and a "Sure, Moses. You can do it," he was in for a disappointment. Almost as if ignoring Moses' question, God answered, "Certainly I will be with you . . . I who have sent you" (3:12).

Then the ludicrousness of the situation seized Moses. "Sure, God. Here I come in from a desert community Israel never heard of and claim the God of Israel's fathers has sent me to rescue them. They will sneer at me and challenge, 'What is the name of this *god* who sent you?' What shall I say?" (see 3:13).

The words from the bush came in clear, clean syllables that shook the holy ground on which Moses, already trembling, stood: "I AM WHO I AM. Tell them I AM sent you" (see 3:14).

Before Moses could put his tumbling thoughts into words, God was reminding him of what He had done for Israel's fathers. He promised again that He was going to lead them out of bondage. The message was clear and irresistible: "I AM. . . . I Have. . . . I Will. . . . Moses, get up and GO!"

At that point, Moses pulled out all his excuses: "What if they won't believe me?" "I am not eloquent." "Please send somebody else." Every time, God pointed the reluctant prophet away from his own inabilities and back to Himself.

"Throw your rod on the ground. When *I* turn it into a serpent, they will believe." "Who made your mouth, Moses? *I* will be with it." "*I'll* send your brother Aaron to help you, but you must do the job."

Moses finally picked up his staff and walked resolutely into the fire of Egyptian opposition. And God, whose whole identity lay in the simple name, I AM, made good on His promises.

Centuries later, when Jesus walked this earth, He touched five barley loaves and two small fish and fed a multitude. The next day when they came back for more, He fed them with bread for their souls. "*I am the bread of life*; he who comes to Me will not hunger" (John 6:35).

He made blind eyes to see and said, "*I am the Light of the world*; he who follows Me will not walk in the darkness" (8:12).

He spoke of His community of children and claimed: "*I am the door*; if anyone enters through Me, he will be saved, and . . . find pasture" (10:9). "*I am the good shepherd* . . . [who] lays down His life for the sheep" (10:11).

He wept with His dear friends, Martha and Mary, over the death of their brother Lazarus and assured them, "*I am the resurrection and the life*; he who believes in Me will live even if he dies" (11:25-26). Then He touched Lazarus and brought him back to life.

He warned His disciples that He was going away, then consoled their grief with the powerful words, "*I am the way, and the truth, and the life*; no one comes to the Father but through Me" (14:6).

Finally, on the way to Gethsemane, He taught His disciples, "*I am the vine*, you are the branches; he who abides in Me and I in him, he bears much fruit" (15:5).

The message comes back to us again and again. God's most basic and essential name is the great I AM. It is the ultimate rationale for everything He asks of us. It puts all else together and makes sense of it. He is, and we need never doubt it. He is all we need, and we can entrust our lives to the character of His being—His self-existent essence.

O Great I AM
Fix the gentle imprint
of Your perfectly contoured feet
into the moist gray sands
of my earthy being
That all who pass my way
may marvel
at the excellence of Your work of art—
sucking in great bellies full
of holy awe,
prostrating themselves
before Your forever Being,
enveloped with fadeless radiance
of your I AM Glory!

For further glimpses of the great I AM, read: Exodus 6:1-8; 20:1-2; Psalm 81:10; Isaiah 41:4, 10, 13; 42:6, 8; 43:3, 5, 10-11, 15, 25; 44:6, 24; 45:5-6, 18, 21-22; 51:15.

I am God, and there is no other. (Isaiah 46:9)

To Ponder

Begin to make a list of names by which your soul knows God. Meditate on each one, seeking to know the fullness of its significance for your life. _____

_____

_____

_____

Pray

Dear I AM, Self-Existent God, _____

_____

_____

_____

Alpha and Omega

I am the Alpha and the Omega, the first and the last, the beginning and the end. (Revelation 22:13)

Alpha and Omega First and last letters of the Greek alphabet. When used together as a phrase, they refer to the entire alphabet, not just the first letter and the last.

God is God at the beginning of the universe—powerful, omniscient Creator, Lawgiver. He will be God at the culmination of history—redemptive, omnipotent Judge, King of kings and Lord of lords. We see Him reflected in a million metaphors throughout the massive epochs of human existence in between—loving, gracious, nurturing, protective, provident, faithful. . . . Everything He does and says and creates expresses one or many facets of His character. The alphabet He has designed to communicate with us is His character. He is all the letters.

The great *Alpha and Omega* longs to be our first consideration, our first hope and our last—and everything in between. When we face uncertainties, He encourages us with the memory that He created us and assures us that He will take us into the communion of His heaven for eternity. He has also promised us daily sustenance, guidance, protection and comfort.

In human language, we cannot write words without using the letters in the alphabet. Like an enormous alphabet, God's multi-faceted character provides the essential boundaries and building blocks for every part of our lives. When we try to make sense of life's dilemmas without knowing what God is like and applying the principles His character outlines for us, our answers will be inadequate, confusing, erroneous and ultimately dangerous.

If, on the other hand, we dedicate our lives to becoming acquainted with each name, title and attribute of the great Alpha and Omega God, we shall find in Him all the resources we need for a fruitful life.

Alpha and Omega
encompasses our lives from beginning to end
enables us to bring
order out of our chaos,
clarity to our confusion,
a theme from our randomness,
meaning to our hopelessness.

"In Greek thinking, 'the beginning and the end' indicated the eternity of the highest God, an idea . . . reflected in the biblical image."[1]

I am the first and I am the last,
And there is no God besides Me. (Isaiah 44:6)

He will always be first and last—
Above His created works
Beyond the false gods
To whom men and women
So wantonly offer their
Worship
Allegiance
Passion.
Our God is the ever-present, the all-glorious,
The gracious and loving,

The overpowering, the sovereign
The only God!

"I am God and there is none besides Me!"

He was first in time, existing long before time began. He will transcend time—those endless eons of eternity. There has never been a time when He did not exist, nor will there be a time when His existence ceases. He initiated and created both time and our transition from time into eternity.

He is the ultimate cause and goal of all things.

> *The universe owes its origin to Him, was created by Him, and has its aim and purpose in Him. To Him be the glory throughout the Ages! Amen.* (Romans 11:36, Wey.)

He who spoke the vast unnumbered worlds of the universe into being has sustained them ever since. He alone has the wisdom and power to wrap up all of history into one grand and glorious finale.

> Happiness cannot perish as long as God lives; He is . . . the first of all delights, nothing before Him; the last of all pleasures, nothing beyond Him; a paradise of delights in every point, without a flaming sword.[2]

For further glimpses of the First and the Last, read: Isaiah 41:4; 43:10-11; 48:12; Revelation 1:8, 17.

Author and Perfecter

> *Let us run with endurance the race that is set before us, fixing our eyes on Jesus, the author and perfecter of faith, who for the joy set before Him endured the cross, despising the shame, and has sat down at the right hand of the throne of God.*

> (Hebrews 12:1-2)

Author

Creator of an original work of art.

Perfecter

One who polishes, refines and brings a work to an acceptable conclusion.

As Author, God planned and created the physical universe and all the rules that govern both that universe and the people who inhabit it. Then Adam and Eve rebelled and contaminated the entire human race. But He was not thwarted. He offered one more incredible plan, this time to redeem us from the disastrous consequences of our selfish rebellion and to bring us back to Himself. He authored the cross and our access to that cross for soul cleansing by faith.

Faith ushers us into a whole new pursuit—the recapture of the divine wholeness we lost when Adam and Eve sinned. The scars of sin lie deep, our minds have been severely twisted and as long as we live on this earth we are susceptible to the wiles of our spiritual enemy. The process of character reclamation we call salvation takes a lifetime. But God, our divine Author, has committed Himself to this salvation.

When an author creates a manuscript, it begins as a rough draft, which is most often in desperate need of cutting, rearranging and sometimes drastic altering to bring it to perfection. God authored us in His eternal mind, but we are flawed by our sin nature. So He works consistently and with unending patience to cut, rearrange, alter and polish us into a work of excellence that will bring glory to Him as our Creator/Redeemer.

His words in Hebrews 12:3-13 probe deeply into the painful mysteries of our life manuscript's sorrows and tough spots. They show us a loving Father who has borne us as His children and now pursues our growth and maturity into the very best He has created us to become. In His absolute wisdom as Author and Perfecter, He knows better than anyone else could know how our lives should be ordered for smoothness and fulfillment. He cares passionately about us and is prepared to use all that happens to us to accomplish the glory of His purposes for and through us.

> *Though I walk in the midst of trouble,*
>   *You will revive me;*
> *You will stretch forth Your hand against the wrath*
>   *of my enemies,*
> *And Your right hand will save me.*
> *The LORD will accomplish what concerns me;*
> *Your lovingkindness, O LORD, is everlasting;*
> *Do not forsake the works of Your hands.*

(Psalm 138:7-8)

If we nurture quietness in our souls and lean close to our great Alpha and Omega, First and Last and Finisher of the faith, we will hear His promise like an echo to our cry:

> *He who began a good work in you will perfect it until the day of Christ Jesus.* (Philippians 1:6)

For further glimpses of God as Author and Perfecter, read: Jeremiah 32:38-42; Ezekiel 37:26-28; Colossians 2:9-10; Hebrews 2:10.

> "Even if I turn out to be wrong, I shall bet my life on the assumption that this world is not idiotic, neither run by an absentee landlord, but that today, this very day, some stroke is being added to the cosmic canvas that in due course I shall understand with joy as a stroke made by the Architect who calls himself Alpha and Omega."[3]

To Ponder

Meditate on God's priority among all living beings in the earth, the universe and the realm of spiritual powers. _____

_____

_____

_____

Pray

Dear Lord of all Beginnings and Endings, _____

_____

_____

_____

Creator

Now Christ is the visible expression of the invisible God. He existed before creation began, for it was through him that every thing was made, whether spiritual or material, seen or unseen. Through him, and for him, also, were created power and dominion, ownership and authority. In fact, every single thing was created through, and for him. He is both the first principle and the upholding principle of the whole scheme of creation.

(Colossians 1:15-17, Phillips)

Creator

One who plans and makes something totally original and out of nothing.

God bursts into view in Genesis 1:1 in full action. He is not at all like the vast array of man-created gods, who are consumed with leisure, caprice and vengeance. The God of the Bible is the master Artist who expresses Himself through the purposeful action of mind and hands, in the creation of things of beauty, strength and usefulness. The Bible account of Creation fairly sparkles with an active artistry unparalleled anywhere in human history, fantasy or mythology.

Creation is . . .

God,
flexing His infinite mind

to dream up the farthest reaches of the seas,
the highest pinnacles of the mountain summits,
the minutest particles of sand
and atoms and cells
that swim in microscopic universes of life.

Creation is . . .

God,
shouting over vast empty echo chambers,
ageless chasms of cosmic "without form and void"
"Let there be light . . .
"Let there be firmament and waters . . .
"Let there be land and vegetation . . .
"Let there be sun and moon and stars . . .
"Let there be birds to fly and fish to swim . . .
"Let there be living creatures, great and small. . . ."

Creation is . . .

God,
stooping to the dampish sands,
dirtying celestial hands with the dust of a newly born earth,
shaping, forming, carving, smoothing, breathing,
birthing a creature unique
from every other voice-sparked being
already bringing
life and color and fascination
to the living sphere of His fond Father-heart
He'd set to spinning in a mighty palm.
Remarkable none-like-him created being
is as like Himself as if He gazed into a mirror
and watched it
reflect back to His sparkling eyes,
with senses to perceive it all,

powers of reason, intelligence and passion to enjoy and rule,
an urge for communion, purpose and
Creation!

Creation is . . .

God,
lullabying man,
this crowning act of workmanship,
into a deep slumber to numb all awareness,
then with fingers of a skilled surgeon,
removing a rib from next to a heart
that beats to the rhythm of the universe,
forming it into one more exquisite creature—
Woman—
wedding her
to a stammery-delighted Adam
for companionship and perpetuation
of a species too precious to imagine,
too valuable to let go.

Creation is . . .

God,
contemplating, surveying, deciding
"It is good—very, very good!"
Dancing the dance of holy celebration
in the meadows of Eden
then sitting,
enraptured,
on the circle of the earth,
resting on the seventh day

from all the works that He has crafted,
setting that day forever apart
to celebrate the wondrous joy of
Creation!

For further glimpses of God the Creator, read: Genesis 1-2; Psalm 51:10; Isaiah 40:28-29; 43-45; Malachi 2:10; John 1:1-3; Ephesians 2:10; 1 Peter 4:19.

"All His works are simply the spillover of His infinite exuberance for His own excellence."[1]

Maker / Fashioner

Thus says the LORD, your Redeemer, and the one who formed you from the womb,
"I, the LORD, am the maker of all things,
Stretching out the heavens by Myself,
And spreading out the earth all alone." (Isaiah 44:24)

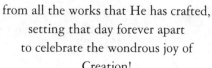

A craftsman who makes something, usually with his hands.

As a pattern for all creative acts of men and women, God used His own creative works to express the depths of His character. Author Ken Gire puts it this way in his book *Windows of the Soul*: "If we look with the right eyes, listen with the right ears, we will understand the natural creation as a form of sign language through which God expresses Himself."[2]

When we look at nature in search of the Creator, in all He has made, we see a purposeful fashioning, an incredible wisdom, a dazzling beauty, a profound goodness. Most of all, we see how He takes the raw materials of all kinds of life in its chaotic state and brings it into a masterful order.

The person who gives no thought to God will observe created works in a much different way. He may look at a mountain as an end in itself. Overcome by its beauty, power and size, he may feel controlled by it. A natural reaction is to worship the mountain. Or, in his fascination with the wondrous phenomenon before him, he may experience great fear and insecurity. Mountaineer and photographer Paul Schullery wrote, without any reference to God, that though he found the mountains beautiful and beckoning, he was forced to admit that they were harsh, remote, severe and unforgiving. "Mountains don't take a personal interest in us . . . ; all the caring, all the attachments and emotions, are ours."[3]

As worshipers of the God who created the mountain, we look with a wonder that feeds our faith and makes it grow. We recall the power of God and the dimensions of His concern for all the creatures finding shelter in the mountain. We remember how many and rich are earth's resources that arise from the mountains—resources that feed and protect our outer bodies and nurture the aesthetic and emotional senses of our inner beings.

In the intricacies of the fashionings of God's hands in creation, we see warmth, precision, beauty and balance—messages of mystery, warning and love. This is especially evident in His masterpiece of creative genius—the human body, mind and spirit. Every piece comes together to reveal to us an infinitely creative, caring and glorious God!

> You and I were fashioned from the clay of the earth and
> the kiss of His mouth.[4]

For further glimpses of God the Maker and Fashioner, read: Psalm 95:1-6; 100:1-5; 124:8; Proverbs 14:31; Isaiah 17:7; 44:24; Jeremiah 10:11-16.

To Ponder

We are His because He designed us, He created us and He continues to fashion us after His own image. Spend time thanking Him, praising Him and worshiping Him for the many faces of His creation. _____

_____

_____

_____

Pray

Dear Creator of the Universe, _____

_____

_____

_____

Carpenter

When the Sabbath came, He began to teach in the synagogue; and the many listeners were astonished, saying, "Where did this man get these things, and what is this wisdom given to Him, and such miracles as these performed by His hands? Is not this the carpenter, the son of Mary . . . ?" And they took offense at Him. (Mark 6:2-3)

One who works with wood, crafting articles with his hands.

God the Creator worked with His hands and fingers in the dirt. God the Redeemer/Son showed us what He is like through the life of a humble carpenter. For thirty years, Jesus showed us God working with His hands among the wood shavings, concerned about beauty and the modeling of excellence and the shaping of wood. In so doing, He gave dignity to the work of the common man and woman.

One day, He walked forever out the door of the carpenter shop and assumed His role as teacher, healer of diseased bodies and, finally, redeemer of a lost and hopeless mankind. His neighbors and most of His family resisted the slightest suggestion that this common laborer might be God. They missed the joy and wonder of one of the most incredible sights in history.

Ironically, His countrymen carried their rejection of Him so far that they hung their Carpenter on a rough wooden cross. There He completed for us His greatest work on earth—the purchase of our redemption.

He whose power had assumed fingers in order to sculpt us from earth's clay and a mouth to breathe into us the spirit of life now confined Himself to a human body where He could show us how to drive nails with a hammer into wood. Finally, with those same hands, He reached to our depths. He allowed men who neither understood nor cared what He was doing to break His hands with nails He chose not to control. With His expiring breath, He created for each of us new life.

As the crucified Carpenter, He showed us that every work of our hands—the sweeping of floors and the wiping of runny noses, the keeping of straight accounts and the manufacturing of electronic parts—every act can be a beautiful work of art in a mundane, tedious world. When once we come to view all of life in this light, we can share His eagerness to reproduce the beauty of His workmanship. We gain new reasons to strive in all our efforts to create beautifully grained, shaped and polished works that glow with the superb excellence of His glory!

We are God's work of art. (Ephesians 2:10, Jerusalem)

For further glimpses of God the Carpenter, read: Psalm 128:2; Ecclesiastes 5:12; Colossians 3:17, 23.

Potter

The LORD gave another message to Jeremiah. He said, "Go down to the shop where clay pots and jars are made. I will speak to you while you are there." So I did as he told me and found the potter working at his wheel. But the jar he was making did not turn out as he had hoped, so the potter squashed the jar into a lump of clay and started again.

> *Then the LORD gave me this message: "O Israel, can I not do to you as this potter has done to his clay? As the clay is in the potter's hand, so are you in my hand."* (Jeremiah 18:1-6, NLT)

Potter An artist who works with his hands to form objects out of clay.

The clay which a potter scrapes together is dull, unattractive, shapeless. To the untrained observer, it gives no hint of the beauty and design that the creator/potter envisions for it. Miraculously, the manipulations of skilled hands can transform the soggy, sloppy mass of mud into a work of art exquisite enough to draw accolades from the most discriminating of art lovers.

God likens us to the potter's clay.

> *But now, O LORD, You are our Father,*
> *We are the clay, and You our potter;*
> *And all of us are the work of Your hand.* (Isaiah 64:8)

Imperfect, rough-textured, filled with devastating air bubbles, we are totally useless outside of the Potter's hands. Left to our own designs, we should forever lie in a pit of unshapely, ugly, treacherous mud.

But God has the vision to see what can be made of us. He has the wisdom to know how to shape and scrape and etch His patterns into our hearts and lives. He never grows weary of squashing us when we refuse to yield up our bubbles and clods of hardened dirt and stone. He will start over again as many times as our stubborn refusal to be shaped demands.

God is the Creator, Maker, Potter. He has committed Himself to fashioning us into pots according to His own designs. And He will accomplish it, no matter how long or how many tries it takes.

In creation, God 'went public' with the glory that re-verberated joyfully between the Father and the Son![1]

For further glimpses of God the Potter, read: Isaiah 29:16; 45:9; Romans 9:20-21, 23.

> Master Potter,
>> keep this lump of clay
>> warm, moist,
>> supple to Your touch.
>
> Fashion it
>> a work of art
>> precision-planned
>> in Your eternal mind.
>
> Then angels,
>> pausing at the workshop door
>> to see
>> emerging vessel,
>> shall exclaim:
>
> "How skilled the Artisan!"[2]

Working God

What god is great like our God?
You are the God who works wonders. (Psalm 77:13-14)

A God who not only talks and demands worship, but who also works.

he God of the Bible is rare among gods worshiped by mankind. Pagan gods are, for the most part, lazy and inactive, serving only their own pleasures and waiting to be waited upon. Our God is active. He dirties His hands to perform great and mighty acts for the benefit of His creatures. He never ceases day and night to work in our lives, perfecting His glorious image in us.

Out of the agony of his ash heap of enforced inactivity, Job began to meditate on the God he had always served. And what he saw was an active God, a working God, a responsible God.

> *It is God who removes the mountains . . .*
> *Who shakes the earth out of its place,*
> *And its pillars tremble;*
> *Who commands the sun not to shine,*
> *And sets a seal upon the stars;*
> *Who alone stretches out the heavens*
> *And tramples down the waves of the sea . . .*
> *Who does great things, unfathomable,*
> *And wondrous works without number.* (Job 9:5-8, 10)

When God came to earth to live as a man, He moved about always doing good for the people—touching broken bodies, filling hungry stomachs, walking the length and breadth of the land to carry the good news of the kingdom to needy souls.

> *We must work the works of Him who sent Me.* (John 9:4)

When Jesus returned to heaven, He sent His Spirit to work with the men He had left behind to be His hands and feet. But He promised that He would never stop the work He had begun on earth.

> *I will build My church.* (Matthew 16:18)

Today in heaven, He continues to work as He prays for us here on earth. No matter what job we assume from His hand, He is still working with us. For our working, active God cannot be still.

> *He who began a good work in you will perfect it until the day*
> *of Christ Jesus.* (Philippians 1:6)

For further glimpses of our Working God, read: Genesis 2:2; Exodus 15:11; Psalm 19:1; 136; 145:5; Ecclesiastes 3:11; 7:13; Mark 16:20; Romans 8:28; 2 Corinthians 6:1.

On the glorious splendor of Your majesty
And on Your wonderful works, I will meditate.

(Psalm 145:5)

To Ponder

If our God is a working God, a creative craftsman, consider the many different ways we see evidences of His work in our world and in our lives. _____

_____

_____

_____

Pray

Dear Master Potter of this clay, _____

_____

_____

_____

faithful

I will sing of the lovingkindness of the LORD forever;
To all generations I will make known Your
faithfulness with my mouth. (Psalm 89:1)

faithful Firm, established, stable, steadfast, true and trustworthy.

very story in Scripture illustrates the faithfulness of our eternal God in some way. By contrast, it reveals the entire human race as subject to perpetual inconsistency and failure. All the steadfastness that we mortals wish we could exemplify in ourselves or find in each other, the Lord offers us in His eternally faithful and true character. He is completely loyal to us. He cares for us, stands by us, helps us along and forgives us—not because we are true to Him, but because He is, and ever will be, faithful and true.

Everything God asks of us or calls us to do for Him, He stands ready and faithful to help us accomplish in His power. *"Faithful is He who calls you, and He also will bring it to pass"* (1 Thessalonians 5:24).

He will always tower above us in moral achievement and spiritual power. Yet the moment we fail and look up to Him for forgiveness and restoration, we see Him bending over the cliff where we have fallen. Faithfully He stretches out a hand to lift us up and draw us back into the way He has planned for us.

Through His prophet, Jeremiah, God pleaded with the rebellious nation of Judah in gracious words that demonstrated the depths of His loyalty and faithfulness:

> *Thus says the LORD . . .*
> *"I have loved you with an everlasting love;*
> *Therefore I have drawn you with lovingkindness."*

> (Jeremiah 31:2-3)

Later, while mourning over the unheeding and persistent rebellion of the people, Jeremiah saw a glimpse of the heart of this loyal God who would always remain faithful and true. In awe, he broke into the midst of his prolonged and agonizing lamentation with these incredible words of hope:

> *It is of the LORD's mercies that we are not consumed, because his compassions fail not. They are new every morning: great is thy faithfulness.* (Lamentations 3:22-23, KJV)

In one of the final scenes of the book of Revelation, we see our faithful God in this same light. All through the ages, since before Adam and Eve disobeyed and introduced sin and the need for judgment into the human race, His faithfulness has never dimmed or waned or wavered. The same God who, in the opening lines of Genesis, said, "Let there be light," rides out of heaven in John's vision of Revelation 19:11, on a white horse, bearing the name "Faithful and True."

For further glimpses of a Faithful God, read: Deuteronomy 10:15; Psalm 36:5; 40:10; 119:90, 138; 138:2; 143:1; Isaiah 11:5; Hosea 2:20; Romans 3:3-4; 1 Corinthians 1:9; 2 Thessalonians 3:3; 2 Timothy 2:13; Hebrews 2:17; Revelation 1:5; 3:14.

Dependable

Trust in the LORD and do good;
Dwell in the land and {feed on His} faithfulness.

(Psalm 37:3)

Dependable One on whom you can count to do what is promised or expected.

While the word *dependable* does not appear in the text of Scripture, the concept is a strong outworking of faithfulness. Psalm 37:4-5 leads us on a delightful pathway of following ever after Him. Always, it reassures us, if we trust God fully, we need not fret but can depend on Him fully to reward our expectation by His faithfulness:

Delight yourself in the LORD;
And He will give you the desires of your heart.
Commit your way to the LORD,
Trust also in Him, and He will do it.

His actions are not always predictable. In our human weakness, we cannot always understand His ways, even as we often misunderstood our parents' ways when they guided us through our formative years. Our God is faithful to His Word, faithful to His purposes, faithful to His love for us. We can always absolutely depend on Him.

Trust in the LORD with all your heart
And do not lean on your own understanding.
In all your ways acknowledge Him,
And He will make your paths straight. (Proverbs 3:5-6)

There is no one else on earth or in this entire universe that we can count on so completely as we can count on Him. Only He is too wise to give us bad guidance and too dependable to let us down. In ways far more numerous than we can fathom, He is utterly, totally, infallibly, unchangeably dependable.

He will never let us down while we are looking up!

For further glimpses of a Dependable God, read: 1 Corinthians 10:13.

Infallible

> *Be strong and courageous, do not be afraid or tremble at them, for the LORD your God is the one who goes with you. He will not fail you or forsake you.* (Deuteronomy 31:6)

Incapable of failure or error.

Because God is not subject to our human frailties and inconsistencies, He will never fail in either judgments or intentions. He cannot fail to carry through on what He promises. He has no emotional flaws to hamper his actions, no moral lapses to short circuit His perfections. He can neither be tempted with evil nor lie nor cease to show us compassion.

God will not,
    does not fail,
        because He cannot fail!
It is contrary to His nature to fail
    In any way!

Even if our faith fails, He remains true—He cannot prove false to Himself. (2 Timothy 2:13, Wey.)

Human nature teaches us to measure ourselves by others. Such a standard is based on fallible creatures. It wavers with the pressure of circumstances, opinions, cultures or emotions and ceases to be a standard at all. Following such guidance can lead us to hopeless despair, dangerous self-righteousness or moral confusion.

God calls us to the measuring rod of His holy character. This is the ultimate standard against which all failure or success must be measured. He will not change, shift or alter even in the slightest detail. There is no way our infallible God can possibly fail to meet His own standard of excellence, purity and faithfulness.

We cannot measure up to such a high and noble standard. We all experience both abandonment and failure from those we depend upon in this life—including ourselves. But, in a world of disappointment and heartbreak, we know that He will never, never, no never, abandon us. His constant, abiding presence assures us that He will not fail in any way at all. In Hebrews 13:5, He speaks to us all where we are today in the simple, yet profound words:

I WILL NEVER DESERT YOU, NOR WILL I EVER FORSAKE YOU.

Because He does not fail, we need never faint!

For further glimpses of the Infallible God, read: Numbers 23:19; Joshua 1:5-9; 1 Chronicles 28:20; Psalm 27:9-10; Zephaniah 3:5; Titus 1:2; Hebrews 6:18; James 1:13.

Our faithful God is . . .

the Creator/Sustainer of an unbounded physical universe
the Maker and Keeper of eternal covenants
the Architect and Preserver of Noah's "ridiculous" boat on land
the Ruler of the Red Sea and the Jordan River
the Lover of an adulterous Gomer

the Restorer of Jerusalem's fallen wall
the Redeemer of Job, Mannaseh, Peter and Paul
the Master of angry waves on Galilee
the Dispenser of broken loaves and fishes
the Healer of lepers, demoniacs, prostitutes and mourners
the Sower and Reaper in all soils and seasons
the eager Father of the Prodigal
the Sacrificial Lamb and the Shepherd of lost sheep
the Rider on the white horse.
Great, O Lord, is Your faithfulness to all generations!

To Ponder

What things do we trust Him for? How has He proved Himself
faithful in these things? _____

_____

_____

_____

Pray

Dear Faithful, Infallible God, _____

_____

_____

_____

Good

According to Your lovingkindess remember me,
For Your goodness' sake, O LORD.
Good and upright is the LORD;
Therefore He instructs sinners in the way.
He leads the humble in justice,
And He teaches the humble His way.
All the paths of the LORD are lovingkindness and truth
To those who keep His covenant and His testimonies.

(Psalm 25:7-10)

Good "Having positive or desirable qualities . . . superior . . . beneficial . . . safe . . . bountiful . . . virtuous."[1]

Only God is:

> originally good. . . . All created goodness is a rivulet from this fountain, but Divine goodness hath no spring. . . . God only is infinitely good. A boundless goodness that knows no limits . . . not only good, but best. . . . All things else are but little particles of God, small sparks from this immense flame, sips of goodness to this fountain. . . . Nothing hath an absolutely perfect goodness but God. . . . The goodness of God is the measure and rule of goodness in everything else. . . . God is

so good, that he cannot be bad. . . . God always glitters in goodness. . . .[2]

God is so inherently good that He could never think a bad or unkind thought or have a motivation toward His creatures that is not good. Evil is totally foreign to Him; it is impossible for Him to do evil, speak evil, think evil or feel evil. All His actions toward us are motivated by goodness of heart and designed to bring about only good and beneficial results in our lives.

> *They shall be My people, and I will be their God; and I will give them one heart and one way, that they may fear Me always, for their own good. . . . I will make an everlasting covenant with them that I will not turn away from them, to do them good. . . . I will rejoice over them to do them good . . . with all My heart and with all My soul.* (Jeremiah 32:38-41)

Nothing pleases God's tender Creator/Father-heart like the wondrous privilege of doing good to us, His unique creatures. Each of us was created in His image and likeness, with the capacity to express His character for a watching universe to behold and wonder at His goodness.

> *So that the manifold wisdom of God might now be made known through the church to the rulers and the authorities in the heavenly places.* (Ephesians 3:10)

Oh, God of infinite goodness,
Eternal source of all good,
Measure of all good,
Dispenser of all good,
Motivator of all good,
Rewarder of all good,
Come, fill this empty vessel
With the fullness of Your good.

When things are going "bad" that does not mean God has stopped doing *good*. It means He is shifting things around to get them in place for more good, if you will go on loving Him. He works all things together for good for "those who love Him." (Romans 8:28, NIV)[3]

For further glimpses of a Good God, read: Genesis 50:20; Deuteronomy 8:6-16; Psalm 25:8; 65:4; 84:11; 86:5; 100:5; 106:1; 118:1, 29; 119:68; 136:1.

Men shall speak of the power of Your awesome acts;
And I will tell of Your greatness.
They shall {bubble over with} the memory of
      Your abundant goodness. (Psalm 145:6-7)

Bountiful

You have crowned the year with Your bounty,
And Your paths drip with fatness. (65:11)

Return to your rest, O my soul,
For the LORD has dealt bountifully with you. (116:7)

Bountiful Abundantly good and eager to share that goodness with others in need.

Our God is *boundless* in His goodness. His resources are transcendent, limitless, beyond anything that we mortals could ever begin to imagine or hope to see or understand or grasp hold of, even in a tiny way.

He is *bountiful* in His providence, ready to provide for all our needs in overabundant measure. He provides not only for those things essential for survival, but He goes beyond just the essential and does things in an artistic manner that satisfies our need for beauty and enjoyment.

He is *generous* in His heart, eager to give us all that will promote the best in our lives. His character is so generous that He can never give us enough to satisfy the urges of His love.

He is *abounding* in all the acts of His goodness, bubbling over with them like some perpetually self-renewing fountain, never running dry.

He is *lavish* in his affections. Like a doting Father overwhelmed with passion for His sons and daughters whom He has created in His image, He gives and gives again, and keeps on giving and promising gifts without end.

A million details and troubles in this life conspire to deceive us into thinking that God is stingy and delights only in our misery. Satan schemes in myriad ways to bring our eyes to focus on life's privations, problems and disappointments. He does not want us to look at our bountiful Father, to remember and bless the Lord. Much better to keep us feeling like cheated, abused paupers with no memory of a history of bounty.

But our God calls us to "sing to the LORD, because He has dealt bountifully with [us]" (Psalm 13:6).

The goodness of Your sovereign choice, Lord,
Lies beyond my puny powers of comprehension—
Totally beyond!
The bounty of Your lavish gifts, Lord,
Fills me up with wonder—
Up and over all the rims and boundaries!
I lie prostrate on the cobbles of Your holy temple, Lord,
Splashed with glass-hued light,
I praise Your utterly astounding blessedness—
Utterly incomprehensible!
Your bountiful heart
Chose me?

To come near,
Dwell in Your courts,
Settle down, be at home, draw sustenance
In the splendors of Your glorious presence?
Enfold me this day
In your bountiful sufficiency
This day and the next
Forevermore.

For further glimpses of a Bountiful God, read: Psalm 4:7-8; 116:12-14; 142:5-7; Matthew 7:7; 2 Corinthians 9:6; Ephesians 3:20; Philippians 4:19.

Amazing grace, how sweet the sound
    That saved a wretch like me!
I once was lost, but now am found—-
    Was blind, but now I see.

'Twas grace that taught my heart to fear,
    And grace my fears relieved;
How precious did that grace appear
    The hour I first believed.[4]

To Ponder

Begin keeping a list of all the ways God shows His goodness and bounty in the world. _____

_____

_____

_____

Pray

Dear Good and Bountiful God, _____

_____

_____

_____

Delight

One thing I have asked from the LORD, that I shall seek:
That I may dwell in the house of the LORD all the
days of my life,
To behold the {delightfulness}[1] of the LORD
And to meditate in His temple. (Psalm 27:4)

Delight Whatever brings great pleasure, gratification
or joy.

God created the human soul with an incredible capacity
and craving for delight. He also filled our world with an
enormous variety of created works and pursuits tailor-
made to bring us delight. We naturally seek after diversions, possessions and relationships to satisfy our deep God-given cravings
for pleasure and joy.

These things are not wrong. God gives them to us by way of
His creation, and He intends them for our delight. But they are
life's surface pleasures. He has other gifts that go deep enough to
feed our hungry spirits. Scripture overflows with promises of the
gifts God designs to bring us the deepest delight.

- The direction and security of His Law—Psalm 1:2; 119:77,
  92

- Abundance of all good things for the spirit—Psalm 36:8

47

- Opportunity to do what pleases Him—Psalm 40:8
- Confidence in His loving-kindness and acceptance—Psalm 90:14
- Joy that follows pain and suffering—Psalm 90:15
- His confirmation of the work of our hands—Psalm 90:17
- Consolations for our anxious souls—Psalm 94:14

Looming far above all other delights is the supreme delight of knowing and dwelling with God Himself. When we set our hearts on achieving this delight, He changes the bent of our hearts and gives us new desires—the kind that He stands eager to satisfy.

> *Delight yourself in the LORD;*
> *And He will give you the desires of your heart.*

> (Psalm 37:4)

He made us with the capacity and the need to turn wholeheartedly to Him, to seek after the delight which He alone can give to us.

> *If you return to the Almighty, you will be restored . . .*
> *Then the Almighty will be your gold*
> *And choice silver to you.*
> *For then you will delight in the Almighty*
> *And lift up your face to God.* (Job 22:23, 25-26)

Isaiah tells his people that if they put God and His wishes and desires first, "then you will take delight in the LORD" (Isaiah 58:14).

Like so many other spiritual benefits, delight goes around in circles. The God who offers us delight in Himself and in His ways also takes great delight in us, His redeemed followers. Let the incredible magnitude of this truth grip you as you mull it over and over.

> *He rescued me, because He delighted in me.* (Psalm 18:19)

You will also be a crown of beauty in the hand of the LORD,
And a royal diadem in the hand of your God. . . .
For the LORD delights in you. (Isaiah 62:3-4)

Who is a God like You, who pardons iniquity. . . .
Because He delights in unchanging love{?} (Micah 7:18)

God's highest glory consists in His securing our deepest happiness. What a God is this![2]

Like a passionate Father, He will ever delight in us as His children, while we seek our greatest delight in bringing delight to His heart by doing His will.

The joy of God's presence offers us a fullness of life unparalleled by anything of this world. Often, though, we turn back to weak substitutes, trying to seal our identity with activity and accomplishment. God continually woos us, reminding us that life is about the delight of knowing Him—nothing more and nothing less.[3]

For further glimpses of Him as our Delight, read: Isaiah 55:2.

Desire

Whom have I in heaven but You?
And besides You, I desire nothing on earth. (Psalm 73:25)

Desire A passionate craving, a longing so deeply pierced through and inscribed upon our hearts that it is entrenched in the very fiber of our beings.

e live in a world filled with all kinds of alluring things that attract our desires and send us chasing after rainbows and soap bubbles. Some of these fascinations are God's gifts, which are designed for our pleasure. Others are harmful attractions, which are designed by the enemy of our souls and presented in brightly colored packages that feign innocence.

No matter the source, anything can be dangerous. Whatever makes our heart beat with more passion than it does for God and His superior glory becomes a thorn in our sides. It may lead us to death or stunt our growth. At best, it deprives both us and God of the satisfying experiences of a moment-by-moment walk with Him.

In our raw humanness, why is it we seem content to settle for lesser desires and lower passions? We are pressured by a highly seductive world. Flashing lights, blaring noises, tantalizing textures, fragrances and taste adventures lure us constantly toward sensual pleasures. A host of emotional, mental and spiritual stimuli bombard our knowledge-hungry intellect and needy souls. The lower pathway is always attractive, accessible and difficult to resist.

By contrast, walking with God involves commitment and watchful obedience to His voice. Everything in our human nature urges us to follow our own purposes, not God's.

Unless we pray for a passion for God to motivate us, we will invariably settle for the fleeting pleasures offered by lesser things. The logic that leads us in this direction is flawed, as my friend, Tricia, reminded me when she said, "And to think, we could have had Glory instead!"

The more intently we gaze on His lovely face, the more desirable He becomes in our eyes. The more consistently we give to Him top priority on our schedules and in our affections, the more we desire to linger in His presence. The more we allow Him to draw us from gaudy baubles, camouflaged moral filth and self-exalting pursuits, the more we are overpowered with the pure desire to know Him better each day.

O God, You are my God; I shall seek You earnestly;
My soul thirsts for You, my flesh yearns for You,
In a dry and weary land where there is no water.

(Psalm 63:1)

For further glimpses of our Desirable God, read: Psalm 63; 73:21-28; 84:1-4; 119:20; Isaiah 26:9.

Altogether Lovely One

My beloved is white and ruddy,
Chief among ten thousand. . . .
His mouth is most sweet,
Yes, he is altogether lovely.
This is my beloved,
And this is my friend.

(Song of Solomon 5:10, 16, NKJV)

Totally flawless, with no imperfections to mar the absoluteness of His beauty.

In You, Lord God, can never be found
a hint, a shadow or trace
of ugliness or dull plainness—
not a speck of imperfection
to mar Your ravishing beauty
not a gaudy glittering bauble
to distract from
Your deep iridescent
loveliness—
not the faintest smudge

to destroy Your purity.
Rare, exquisite rosebud
gleaming in the sunlight
You have not a single misshapen or wilted petal
imperfection of form
insect-inflicted blemish—
no misblended hues
diseased textures
blighting, fading or dying away.
Translucent, delicate-yet-strong, breathtaking in beauty
Flawless, complete, unique—

You alone are the *Altogether Lovely One*
In whom my soul delights!

To Ponder

Of all the things in life that can bring you delight, what is it that
makes the Lord the highest and best and most beautiful of all?

_____

_____

_____

Pray

Dear, Delightful and Altogether Beautiful God, _____

_____

_____

_____

Balm in Gilead

For the brokenness of the daughter of my people I am broken;
I mourn, dismay has taken hold of me.
Is there no balm in Gilead?
Is there no physician there?
Why then has not the health of the daughter of my
      people been restored? (Jeremiah 8:21-22)

A healing salve created from a resinous gum which flowed from the pierced side of a tree or shrub found on the sunny slopes of Mount Gilead.

The "balm" is a beautiful symbol of Christ. The Mount Gilead, the tree, the pierced side, the stream thence issuing, and its mighty healing power—these send our thoughts to Mount Calvary, the cross, the pierced side of the Savior, the precious blood, and the unquestionable spiritual healing might there is therein. And Scripture is ever speaking of sin as a disease; of man as one whose health needs recovery. . . . Whilst we all are stricken with mortal disease, Christ is the Balm that surely heals.[1]

In order to heal a sickness so deadly as sin, God, our Great Physician, could neither escape from suffering nor spare His own life. He must offer up His blood as the balm for the healing of the souls of all mankind.

By His scourging {stripes}, we are healed. (Isaiah 53:5)

We gaze upon the raw open wounds of the stripes scoring Jesus' bleeding back, the nail holes defacing His hands and feet and those unthinkable thorn etchings upon His sweating brow. We allow the pain to penetrate our hearts with its awful, gut-wrenching power. Only here is the balm released that can bring about our healing.

We gaze again and marvel at the extravagance of divine grace and love displayed in such vivid color and with such immense flourishes. See how it stands out against the terrifying blackness of evil! We allow it to penetrate the wounds of our own souls and soothe away all the hurt and poison and loneliness produced by sin's pain.

> See, from His head, His hands, His feet,
>   Sorrow and love flow mingled down.
> Did e'er such love and sorrow meet
>   Or thorns compose so rich a crown?[2]

For further glimpses of the Balm in Gilead, read: Jeremiah 46:11.

> There is a balm in Gilead
>   that makes the wounded whole.
> There is a balm in Gilead
>   that heals the sin-sick soul.[3]

Restorer

Restore us to You, O LORD, that we may be restored;
Renew our days as of old. (Lamentations 5:21)

A healer who helps bring us back to sound health.

The nation of Israel had a fatal illness—or so it seemed. No matter what God did for His people, they persisted in following after the false gods and idols of their neighboring nations. Finally, in Isaiah 1, He issued a most depressing diagnosis:

> *Where will you be stricken again,*
> *As you continue in your rebellion?*
> *The whole head is sick*
> *And the whole heart is faint.*
> *From the sole of the foot even to the head*
> *There is nothing sound in it,*
> *Only bruises, welts and raw wounds,*
> *Not pressed out or bandaged,*
> *Nor softened with oil.* (1:5-6)

Repeatedly God offered to restore and heal them, if they would: "Wash yourselves, make yourselves clean" (1:16). Then He would warn them: "If you refuse and rebel, you will be devoured by the sword" (1:20).

Israel persisted in her rebellion, and God's warnings of judgment continued. But never did He threaten to destroy them. He seemed, rather, to be saying, "Though you refuse to follow my instruction for your healing, I cannot let you die. I love you far too much for that. Therefore, I must perform a radical surgery on you."

In Isaiah 35, He breaks into a chapters-long section of warning with a glorious vision of healing and restoration to come from the surgery. Like an unexpected rosebud bursting forth in the midst of the desert, this short chapter radiates with a Father/Healer's untiring love and passionate yearning:

> *The wilderness and the desert will be glad,*
> *And the Arabah will rejoice and blossom;*
> *Like the crocus*
> *It will blossom profusely*
> *And rejoice with rejoicing and shout of joy.*
> *The glory of Lebanon will be given to it,*
> *The majesty of Carmel and Sharon.*

> *They will see the glory of the LORD,*
> *The majesty of our God.* (35:1-2)

Like fragrant, healing herbs, the blossoms of His majesty and His glory cause hope to spring forth in this desert place. And the healing work begins:

> *Then the eyes of the blind will be opened*
> *And the ears of the deaf will be unstopped.*
> *Then the lame will leap like a deer,*
> *And the tongue of the mute will shout for joy.*
> *For waters will break forth in the wilderness*
> *And streams in the Arabah. . . .*
> *A highway will be there, a roadway,*
> *And it will be called the Highway of Holiness. . . .*
> *And the ransomed of the LORD will return*
> *And come with joyful shouting to Zion,*
> *With everlasting joy upon their heads.*
> *They will find gladness and joy,*
> *And sorrow and sighing will flee away.* (35:5-6, 8, 10)

The crowds of hurting, diseased and maimed penitents who have undergone the surgery are flocking to the Physician now. One by one He restores them, but their healing is a shared wonder. Opened eyes, unstopped ears, hart-like springing limbs and loosened tongues—all combine to create one incredible Hallelujah chorus! The dry and desolate desert, once strewn with invalid frames, has become a watered garden, alive with roses and fruit-laden trees with healing in their leaves. Restored men and women leap for joy and then bow in awed worship before their relentless Healer.

> *Restore to me the joy of Your salvation*
> *And sustain me with a willing spirit.* (Psalm 51:12)

For further glimpses of a Restoring God, read: Psalm 19:7; 23:3; 53:6; 80:3, 7, 19; 85:4-7; Isaiah 35; Jeremiah 12:14-17; 15:19; 33:7, 11; Joel 2:25.

Imperfect child
of a long line of fallen men and fallen women,
I am afflicted by
foul and festering places
deep, aching wounds
griefs and sorrows
daily imperfections
and inabilities to raise myself to Your standard,
O LORD OF RIGHTEOUSNESS!
Yet with unspeakable tenderness
You invite me to place them all
—each ugly, disgraceful sore—
in the palm of Your nail-scarred hand
that with Your freely gushing blood
You may cleanse,
purify,
heal,
restore to a fresh new wholeness,
reflecting Your eternal image
forevermore!

To Ponder

Meditate on all the ways the healing Balm of Gilead has soothed
and restored your needy soul. _____

_____

_____

_____

Pray

Dear God, my Balm and Restorer, _____

_____

_____

_____

Holy, Holy, Holy

Great and marvelous are Your works,
O Lord God, the Almighty;
Righteous and true are Your ways,
King of the nations!
Who will not fear, O Lord, and glorify Your name?
For You alone are holy. (Revelation 15:3-4)

Totally set apart from all that is tainted by human motivation or self-effort.

"A Hebrew idiom for the superlative, conveys the Israelite understanding of Yahweh as the most holy God."[1]

Holy! What a terrifying word! To the mind not yet redeemed and set free to see God as He truly is, the word *holiness* screams shrill messages of unreasonable restriction and the death of cherished freedoms and pleasures. Everything about the natural concept of holiness pinches everything that we are as human beings.

To the mind attuned to biblical truth it conjures up images of fire and smoke, lightning, thunder and trembling mountains. It recalls intimidating thrones and temples, frightening trumpet calls, doors that quake and fiery coals searing unclean lips.

We remember Sinai all afire and rumbling in the desert and God calling Moses to its summit to give him the laws which would govern His people forever.

We think of Isaiah the prophet "in the year of King Uzziah's death" (Isaiah 6:1). Uzziah had been a good king, in that he didn't follow after heathen gods. Yet he left pockets of disobedience unattended. He led his people into mediocrity. God prospered him politically, but Uzziah's heart grew arrogant. One day, he disregarded the holiness of God by rushing into the sacred temple chambers and offering incense, which only the priests were allowed to do. God struck him with leprosy, and he spent his final days in disgraceful isolation from his people (see 2 Chronicles 26).

God's temple had been violated and had to be cleansed. So, when the king died, God appeared to His prophet, Isaiah, "*sitting on a throne, lofty and exalted, with the train of His robe filling the temple*" (Isaiah 6:1).

Isaiah caught a fleeting glimpse of something his king had never helped him to see—the glory and holiness of God. He smelled the smoke of the divine presence consuming human sin, felt the trembling of the earth and heard the cherubims crying out:

> *Holy, Holy, Holy, is the* LORD *of hosts,*
> *The whole earth is full of His glory.* (Isaiah 6:3)

Completely stricken with awe in the face of such glory, he stammered:

> *Woe is me, for I am ruined!*
> *Because I am a man of unclean lips . . .*
> *For my eyes have seen the King, the* LORD *of hosts.*
>
> (Isaiah 6:5)

God had a mission for Isaiah: to carry the message of His holiness to a nation in mourning and poised on the brink of idolatry.

But first He had to cleanse Isaiah's unclean lips. One of the seraphim brought a live coal from the altar and touched it to Isaiah's lips. Through the searing pain, the prophet was cleansed and made holy for his divine mission.

> The holiness of God is His glory . . . His crown, and . . .
> the blessedness and nobleness of His nature.[2]

God's holiness sets Him forever apart from us, above us, beyond us. It is His most basic character trait, the thing that makes Him God. Out of the deep bubbling spring of His holiness flow all the other things we have learned to expect from Him—His love, power, wisdom and a million other glowing attributes which it will take us all of life and eternity to see and appreciate.

One clear glimpse of His holiness instills awe in our hearts. That mere glimpse bows our heads, bends our knees, puts a catch in our throats, subdues our wills. He touches our unclean lips with His live coals and sets us to singing His new song.

> Holy, Holy, Holy God!
> Absolutely holy!
> Immeasurably holy!
> Awesomely holy!
> Overwhelmingly holy!
> Unspeakably holy!

Someday we will join the heavenly hosts and the redeemed souls of all ages gathered around the throne of God with its lightning and thunder and sea of glass. Throughout the ages of eternity we will repeat the glorious theme:

> *HOLY, HOLY, HOLY is THE LORD GOD, THE ALMIGHTY,*
> *WHO WAS AND WHO IS AND WHO IS TO COME.*

(Revelation 4:8)

For further glimpses of a Holy God, read: Psalm 24:3-6; 29:2; 78:40-42; 99; 111:9; Isaiah 1:4; 6:1-7; 40:25; 48:17; Ezekiel 20:41; Luke 1:49; 1 Peter 1:16; Revelation 5:8-14; 15:2-4.

> *The LORD reigns, let the peoples tremble. . . .*
> *Holy is He. . . .*
> *Exalt the LORD our God*
> *And worship at His footstool;*
> *Holy is He. . . .*
> *Worship at His holy hill,*
> *For holy is the LORD our God.* (Psalm 99:1, 3, 5, 9)

Pure

> *Your eyes are too pure to approve evil,*
> *And You can not look on wickedness with favor.*

(Habakkuk 1:13)

Pure — Reflecting God's moral holiness; absolutely clean and free from contamination.

The holy, holy, holy God is unalterably pure. His character defines and sets the standards for purity of motives, ambitions, thoughts, words and actions.

The changelessly impeccable God demonstrates His purity for us in human terms in the earthly sojourn of His Son, Jesus Christ. How can we forget those graphic scenes from His temptation in the desert (see Matthew 4:1-11; Mark 1:12-13; Luke 4:1-13)?

Jesus spent forty days in that howling desert, all alone. He felt the pangs of physical hunger and the normal human cravings for creature comforts and satisfaction of appetites. Above all else, though, He was driven by a passion to see the kingdom and the glory of His Father established on earth. That was, after all, His reason for being born with a human body and walking on our soil.

Both Jesus and His tempter knew that the only way to achieve His goal was a way of pain and suffering and apparent defeat. Desperate to deflect this God-man from His goals, Satan gambled on the preposterous notion that, in His vulnerable human state, Jesus might be persuaded to act like any other man who walked in sandals and lived by bread and water and wine. In a manner so like his long-ago seduction of Eve in Eden, he hissed in Jesus' ear and gloated with an arrogant grin: "You want power? I have shortcuts. Come my way and you can have all your dreams—without the pain, the rejection, the dying. You have all the resources you need in yourself, you know. Use them for your comfort and fame. Turn these stones into bread, cast yourself down from the temple, fall down and worship me. You will have the whole world groveling at your feet in no time! And you won't have to endure suffering and rejection in order to accomplish it."

But Jesus was God, the Holy One. His thoughts were higher and nobler than any other man's. They were totally different, shaped by the laws and standards that ruled heaven. This once-in-the-history-of-the-world Man was absolutely pure in thought and motives. Earthly, temporary powers could not lure Him away from eternal purposes. He knew that all power was His, but only as He lived by His Father's patterns of holiness. This holy God incarnate resisted the deadly suggestions of evil and demonstrated the ultimate in holiness to a power-mad world.

Nowhere in all of Scripture does God ever tell us to "be powerful, for I am powerful." Our natural craving for power comes not from Him, but from the tempter whose great sin and temptation have always consisted in aspiring after God's power rather than His holiness.

Repeatedly God calls us to "*be holy, for I am holy!*" (see Leviticus 20:26; 1 Peter 1:16). When we obey this injunction, the fragrance of heaven pours out through our lives. But it is released only as we allow Him to crush all the selfish ambitions of our fallen nature and to reproduce His pure character in us instead.

For further glimpses of the Purity of God, read: Psalm 12:6; 119:140.

Glory is purity revealed with dazzling radiance!

To Ponder

Ask God to show You each day one more glimpse of what His holiness means in terms of moral purity. _____

_____

_____

_____

Pray

Dear Holy, Holy, Holy God, _____

_____

_____

_____

Sanctifier

May God Himself who gives peace, make you entirely holy.

(1 Thessalonians 5:23, Wey.)

Sanctify
To make holy, to set apart for some superior purpose and glory.

We are "made heirs, having been chosen . . . so that we should be devoted to the extolling of His glorious attributes" (Ephesians 1:11-12, Wey.).

What a calling! God has made us citizens of a heavenly kingdom. He has sanctified us to be different from a godless world:

- to see things in a different light;
- to do things for different reasons;
- to judge things on a different basis;
- to give ourselves in undivided, wholehearted loyalty to a different Master.

When Moses tended his father-in-law's sheep on the backside of the desert, God wanted to get his attention. He picked a most unlikely tool and sanctified one little wild bush for the job.

Richard Ellsworth Day, a devotional writer, once wrote that this little bush was nothing special—one bush among the millions out in that wild desert. Leafless and starved for water, it was totally ordinary. Why, then, was it chosen for this remarkable service? If it could talk, might it not say to us, "The King let *me* hold His fire in my branches"?

And, similar to the living sacrifices on the divine altar in these human temples that we are, it had no need to fear being burned "to a powdery heap of gray ashes, to be lost in the sands . . . [for it knew that] *He* does the burning and *He* does the shining; and it's not at my expense at all."[1]

How great the sacrifice God paid to build that fire and shine through us. He had to bear our sins in His body on the cross. This meant laying aside His own purity and, in the eyes of God, becoming the vilest of rebels against the laws that His holy nature had constructed. Wonder of wonders, He did this for us so He might free us from sin's awful power. Following a plan almost too costly to be believed, He sanctified us in His eternal mind long before we were born. Then He won us back to His original purposes and now daily enables us to "BE HOLY, FOR I AM HOLY" (1 Peter 1:16).

He continues day by day, circumstance by circumstance, to transform our thinking processes, our moral default settings and the affections of our hearts.

> Holiness means to be at God's disposal . . . the restoration of the image of God in man, the gradual assimilation of the believer to . . . the mind of Christ.[2]

For further glimpses of the Sanctifying God, read: Leviticus 22:31-33; Ezekiel 20:12; 37:28; 1 Corinthians 1:30; Ephesians 4:23-25, 29; Philippians 2:12-13; 1 Thessalonians 4:3-4; Titus 2:14; 1 Peter 1:2.

> *We are asking God that you may see things, as it were, from his point of view by being given spiritual insight and understanding.* (Colossians 1:9, Phillips)

Circumciser of the Heart

Moreover the LORD your God will circumcise your heart . . . to love the LORD your God with all your heart and with all your soul, so that you may live. (Deuteronomy 30:6)

Circumcision A ritual act performed on Jewish male babies as a physical sign of the spiritual act of cutting away all dependence on human ways of relating to God.

God called Abraham to be the father of a holy nation. He chose His people to be radically different from their neighbors—worshipers of an invisible God on whom they would rely for wisdom, strength, provision and character goodness.

As a sign of this relationship, God gave Abraham the physical ritual of circumcision, that pictured the cutting away of the excesses of the human flesh. This simple act didn't bestow grace on the people. It was, rather, a reminder that He was their God, committed to their protection and nurturing and that they were His people, committed to worship Him and obey His laws.

But Abraham's descendants became exceedingly proud of their distinctive rite, even while persisting in following after their neighbors' gods and lifestyles. God repeatedly sent His prophets to urge them to come to Him, not just with circumcisions and prescribed offerings, but with humble, contrite, devoted hearts. He spoke often of circumcising not their physical foreskins, but their spiritual hearts.

Today God calls us, His redeemed and heavenly people, to be circumcised in heart. Only as we allow Him to cut away everything in us that is worthless, flabby, self-centered and protesting His lordship, can He fulfill His purposes and make us holy, living images of His glory.

For we are the true circumcision—we who render to God a spiritual worship and make our boast in Christ Jesus and have no confidence in outward ceremonies. (Philippians 3:3, Wey.)

For further glimpses of the Circumciser of Our Hearts, read: Deuteronomy 7:7-9; 10:16; Jeremiah 4:4; Ezekiel 11:19; 36:26; Romans 2:28-29; Colossians 2:11.

Holiness is more important than my comfort,
my peace, my honor
or my victory!
On the Cross, Lord Jesus, You gave up all these things—
Your comfort, peace, honor, victory—-
You even laid aside your holiness
And picked up my filthy, ugly sins—
Just so You could share Your holiness with me!
Lord God of inexpressible holiness,
Forgive me when I despise Your priceless gift
And go searching instead for
My comforts and peace,
My honor and victory and so much more—
All rubbish beside
Your holy, holy, holiness
Purchased, for me, at such a cost!

To Ponder

Praise God for the wonder of His patience with us as He gives us His holiness. _____

_____

_____

_____

_____

Pray

Dear Circumciser of the Heart, _____

_____

_____

_____

Omniscient

*"Can a man hide himself in hiding places
So I do not see him?" declares the LORD.
"Do I not fill the heavens and the earth?"* (Jeremiah 23:24)

Now we know that You know all things. (John 16:30)

Omniscient Knowing all things—facts, ideas and motives—
with absolute completeness.

God is engineer, artist and maker of all things that ever
were or are or will be! He knows every minute detail of
the physical construction and interdependence of all
things upon each other. He knows all the secrets of behavior that
scientists search after and the rest of us puzzle over and struggle to
live with. As master of time, He knows the end from the beginning and the cause and effect of all things. As our God, He knows
our inner spirits and what is best for us.

Nothing takes Him by surprise—no illness or accident, no bad
turn of events or natural catastrophe, no loss of a loved one or heart-
breaking human failure. We can hide nothing from Him. We can
never lie to Him or deceive Him into expectations we fail to meet.
He may grieve over our actions when we choose to follow a path
other than the one chosen for us, but He can never be disappointed,

for He knows better than to anticipate something that will not happen.

God's omniscience encompasses the full range of all things that we either know or do not know or cannot know or imagine. He knows all things and all creatures from the inside out.

> *O LORD, You have searched me and known me.*
> *You know when I sit down and when I rise up;*
> *You understand my thought from afar.*
> *You scrutinize my path and my lying down,*
> *And are intimately acquainted with all my ways.*

> (Psalm 139:1-3)

Our God knows all there is to know about our motivations, fears and dreams, our every move and activity. He knows the real truth about us, things we do not know about ourselves—our deepest thoughts and every word before it reaches our tongues. He scrutinizes our spiritual journey and sees every rest stop and stumbling step along the way. He hedges us about and lays His hand upon us for our protection in every danger.

David meditated on all this and exclaimed, with knee bowed to the earth and hand covering his mouth:

> *Such knowledge is too wonderful for me.* (139:6)

Then, he prayed a most remarkable prayer:

> *Search me, O God, and know my heart;*
> *Try me and know my anxious thoughts;*
> *And see if there be any hurtful way in me.* (139:23-24)

Incredibly, he was inviting this all-knowing God to reveal to him the things he did not yet know about himself. Mostly, these would be incriminating things, shortcomings, weaknesses, the kinds of things that threatened to drag him into trouble. How could he open himself up to such an examination?

The answer lies in his expression of faith in the final line of the psalm:

And lead me along the path of everlasting life. (139:24, NLT)

David knew God would lead him on because he had learned the secret that made openness before an omniscient God endurable— grace.

If, in our pride, we try to search our own hearts, we may make excuses for the wrongs we discover. Then we neither confess them as sins nor experience forgiveness for them. We grow progressively callous toward the sin and wander far from God. Or, we might indeed acknowledge each sin as sin. But in our diligence to uncover the last offensive thing, we often indulge in an unhealthy self-focus. This leads to graceless condemnation, guilt, agony and depression. Without the grace that forgives and leads into His way, recognition of God's omniscience can be terrifying.

At the same time, grace without God's omniscience would be as elusive as a hollow wind whistling through the broken window panes of an empty church. For grace must know and accept us as rebellious sinners, hopelessly flawed and damaged by that sin. Otherwise, there is nothing to forgive, and we are forced to dismiss the hurts of our lives simply as incurable tricks of fate.

Only God dispenses true grace in a way that lifts us up to walk in the light of His glory. He is equally omniscient and gracious.

For further glimpses of an All-knowing, Omniscient God, read: 1 Chronicles 28:9; Job 28:10, 24; 36:4; 37:16; Psalm 1:6; 33:13-15; 147:4-5; Proverbs 15:3; Isaiah 40:13-14, 26-27; Matthew 6:8; 7:11; John 10:14, 27; Hebrews 4:13.

O God of Omniscience,
None of the things that make sense to me
can ever exempt me from
the demands of Your laws
that will always surpass

my greatest powers of comprehension.
In Your presence, Lord,
the best and highest of my store of knowledge
and the full repertoire of my cleverness
crumble into an unsightly heap
of ignorance
and selfish incompetence.

Wisdom

The LORD is exalted, for He dwells on high . . .
And He will be the stability of your times,
A wealth of salvation, wisdom and knowledge.

(Isaiah 33:5-6)

Wise in heart and mighty in strength . . .
Who does great things, unfathomable,
And wondrous works without number. (Job 9:4, 10)

Wisdom The ability to apply knowledge to life's needs with an eternal perspective. It demonstrates long-term thinking and sound judgment in ways that benefit others.

God is capable of greater wisdom than any human being. But His other attributes make their contributions to His incomparable wisdom as well. His love and compassion enable Him to see beyond the moment and to care about the lifelong effects of every scrap of knowledge on His human creatures. His transcendent nature takes Him out of the realm of the here and now and lets

Him function toward us in terms of eternal values. His holiness gives Him a different viewpoint of the facts and realities He knows, and He always uses knowledge with wisdom.

Creative beings create new things. Sometimes they make sense and sometimes they dart out beyond boundaries of logic and artistic design. When God created our universe, He did not do it as some wild, experimental, helter-skelter forming of every sort of creature and physical structure He was capable of creating with His unlimited power. God the Creator is not a mindless, power-driven machine gone berserk.

> *It is He who made the earth by His power,*
> *Who established the world by His wisdom,*
> *And by His understanding He stretched out the heavens.*

(Jeremiah 51:15)

The God of wisdom made all things according to a constructive design. Each creature, each rock, each wind current, each color and shape is made, with jigsaw precision, to fit into its own ecological niche.

Wisdom is . . .

the Ultimate Craftsman
musing on the circle of the earth,
"How can I fill my crowning art works,
my image-reflecting creatures,
with enough fresh newness to keep them alive
enough mystery to keep them wondering
enough nourishment to keep them feasting
enough dazzling beauty to keep them ever seeking
for My glory?"
For His colors stretch in ribboned rainbows
into the unmapped reaches of eternity
His sketch books spill out

beyond the windows and walls
of every library in heaven
and His passion for our delight
exceeds our capacities and days
by the immeasurable multiples of
artistic infinity.

No matter how great God's wisdom may be, it often looks like foolishness to our earthbound minds. Who of us would have planned a cross for the Messiah? So devastating, so painful, so shameful, so risky! If God had consulted with and heeded the priests in Jerusalem, Calvary never would have happened—nor our redemption!

> *For the word of the cross is foolishness to those who are perishing. . . . But we preach Christ crucified, to Jews a stumbling block and to Gentiles foolishness, but to those who are the called . . . the power of God and the wisdom of God.*
>
> (1 Corinthians 1:18, 23-24)

God imparts His wisdom to us when we sense our need and ask. It is one of the inestimably valuable gifts He gives to us when we accept His Son as our Savior.

> *By His doing you are in Christ Jesus, who became to us wisdom from God.* (1 Corinthians 1:30)

He gives us wisdom only as we have need of it for the moments of our days. We must continually go to Him, laying aside any prideful notions that we can ever gain it all. We bow before Him, overwhelmed by the mystery of His vast reservoir of wisdom. The moment we lose sight of the wonder, we begin to shrivel up in pursuit of our own foolish ways.

> Openness before the mystery of God is the hallmark of a humble spirit, coupled with certain confidence that the end of human wisdom is the beginning of God's clarity.[1]

Blind unbelief is sure to err,
And scan His work in vain;
God is His own interpreter,
And He will make it plain.[2]

To the only wise God, through Jesus Christ, be the glory forever. Amen. (Romans 16:27)

For further glimpses of the Wisdom of God, read: Job 12:16; 28:12, 20, 23-28; 38:36-37; Psalm 104:24; Jeremiah 10:7, 12; Luke 21:15; Ephesians 3:10; James 3:17; Revelation 7:12.

To Ponder

Consider the ways that God's wisdom is superior to man's.

_____

_____

_____

_____

Pray

Dear Omniscient and All-Wise God, _____

_____

_____

_____

Living Bread

"God's bread . . . comes down out of Heaven and gives Life to the world."

"Sir," they said, "always give us that bread."

"I am the bread of Life," replied Jesus; "he who comes to me shall never hunger, and he who believes in me shall never, never thirst." (John 6:33-35, Wey.)

Food for the nourishment of the body, mind, emotions and spirit.

In the intricacy of divine ecology, God created men and women with bodies that must have bread. Without it, we would cease to grow, to be healthy, to function or to think. We would die! So He created grains—wheat, rye, barley, oats and rice! Vegetables—soy, beans and corn. Fruits and nuts and meats and milk and . . . Ah, but the menu is endless!

He gave Adam and Eve a hunger that only His vast array of foods could satisfy. Then He put them in a garden called Earth and taught them to till the soil and harvest its bounties and turn them into delicacies to lighten the eyes, strengthen bone and brain and delight the palate.

At the same time, He provided "bread" for the spirit. This holy bread came from His heart. He dispensed it as the words of His mouth and the sweetness of His presence. But often His people cared only about food for their bodies. They grew increasingly enamored with their own abilities to provide for all their needs. Failing to feed their souls at His banquet table, they lost their appetite and their souls shriveled and died.

How God grieved over the shortsightedness and earth-centeredness of His people! How He yearned to fill them with His real food, created to meet their deepest needs! He wept as He watched them fall into a state of spiritual apathy, malnutrition and starvation.

> *Oh that My people would listen to Me,*
> *That Israel would walk in My ways! . . .*
> *I would feed you with the finest of the wheat,*
> *And with honey from the rock I would satisfy you.*

> (Psalm 81:13, 16)

In the New Testament, Jesus burst onto the human scene— God's Bread in human flesh. But before He could offer Himself to a starving people, He had to spend thirty years incarnating a whole, God-nurtured spirit. Then God sent Him into a desert wasteland (see Matthew 4:1-11). For forty days and forty nights, He went without food for His body that He might experience the genuine bodily hunger of those He came to feed with spiritual bread.

Wearied and weakened by hunger, He was assailed by the tempter of men's souls. Satan came to Him with a temptation so timely it must have held an incredible enticement.

"If you are the Son of God," he hissed into His ear, "command that these stones become bread" (4:3).

Firsthand now, Jesus knew the tug of body against spirit. All around Him on the ground lay huge stones in the shape and like-ness of the very kind of loaves of bread His mother had fed to Him for the past thirty years. He must have felt the contractions of hunger in His stomach, the flow of saliva in His mouth, the weak-ness in His limbs. All He had to do was speak the word and His hunger would end.

"*But,*" the Scriptures say, "*He answered and said, 'It is written, "MAN SHALL NOT LIVE ON BREAD ALONE, BUT ON EVERY WORD THAT PROCEEDS OUT OF THE MOUTH OF GOD" ' *" (4:4).

He overcame the evil one and earned the full right to say, months later, on the shores of Galilee, "*I am the bread of life*" (John 6:48).

He who knew the physical hunger of His audience was eager to show them His compassion and His power. He fed them by the thousands with two small fish and five small loaves of bread. But the next day, when they sought Him out and begged for one more spectacular dole, He revealed to them the underlying purpose for His miracle.

"Do not work for the food which perishes," He told them, "but for the food which endures to eternal life, which the Son of Man will give to you. . . . This is the work of God, that you believe in Him whom He has sent. . . . I am the bread of life" (6:27, 29, 48).

His message was revolutionary to the hearts of a people accustomed to living by the dictates of their daily physical needs.

- His bread was not temporary, but enduring, giving life to their eternal souls.
- His bread was heavenly, a gift from God.
- He was the Bread of heavenly life—the only source of food which their souls were created to eat and to thrive on and be filled. (6:48-58)

On His last night with His disciples, Jesus took bread, blessed it and broke it and shared with them one more secret of the broken bread, the shared bread, the life-giving bread:

> *This is My body which is given for you; do this in remembrance of Me.* (Luke 22:19)

Though they did not understand His meaning then, they did as He told them. After He had gone back to heaven, they went on celebrating His death. As they ate, their understanding grew, and their spiritual satisfaction and their passion were fed.

All men and women experience a deep spiritual hunger. Not all recognize what that hunger is for. Many try with frantic abandon to fill it with all kinds of things. But whatever is not of God is but chunks of dry, lifeless styrofoam.

"Our bond with God is such a deep one—being created in His image—that we don't find meaning except in Him."[1]

Come to the Living Bread

Listen to His life-giving words

Forsake your pseudo-meals with their gaudy appeal

Seek the satisfaction only He can give

Feast on Heaven's Bread

And LIVE!

For further glimpses of God, the Living Bread, read: Psalm 34:8-10; 107:5-9; Isaiah 25:6-9; Matthew 5:6; Luke 14:15-24; Revelation 7:16.

Manna

> *You shall remember all the way which the LORD your God has led you in the wilderness these forty years. . . . He humbled you and let you be hungry, and fed you with manna which you did not know, nor did your fathers know, that He might make you understand that man does not live by bread alone, but man lives by everything that proceeds out of the mouth of the LORD.*
>
> (Deuteronomy 8:2-3)

Manna Bread from heaven, sent by God to feed Israel in the wilderness.

God did a miracle of gigantic proportions when He delivered Israel out of slavery in Egypt. But once He got them out in the Sinai desert—3 million people, all with the scent of freedom in their nostrils and visions of the Promised Land dangling like sugarplums before their eyes—the call for miracles had just begun.

In no time, the people began to complain. With little real concept of what God had delivered them from or where He was taking them, they cried out to Moses:

> *Would that we had died by the LORD's hand in the land of Egypt, when we sat by the pots of meat, when we ate bread to the full; for you have brought us out into this wilderness to kill this whole assembly with hunger.* (Exodus 16:3)

Moses had no idea how he was going to feed all those people. But God, who had called him in a heavenly way out of the midst of a burning bush, had a heavenly solution for this problem too. One morning, He sent them a gift from heaven. It rained upon the camp and "lay cushioned on the dew; morsels of food, opal grey like gems of precious bdellium making the desert look like a vast tray of jewels."[2]

When the sons of Israel saw it, they said to one another, "What is it?"[3]

And Moses said to them, "It is the bread which the LORD has given you to eat" (16:15).

This unique "bread of angels" (Psalm 78:25) was specially formulated to meet all their nutritional needs. God dispensed it in such a way as to teach them utter dependence on Him. Every day for the next forty years, He fed His people with the manna. He always came through! Yet they never fully appreciated what they had. Often they complained. Always slow to learn what God wanted to teach them, "they had Egyptian appetites, wave-lengthed for leeks and onions and garlics!"[4]

What about my appetite today? In a world filled with "Egyptian appetites," how easily do I settle for less than the truly satisfying manna from heaven?

Holy Manna
Heavenly Bread
Feed me fully, daily, amply
With the glorious wonders of Yourself!
Revive my heavenly appetites
Teach me to feast on You—
Feast, not nibble,
Feast with a passion
And insatiable appetite always for
MORE
Holy Manna!
Heavenly Bread!

For further glimpses of God, the heavenly Manna, read: Exodus 16; Numbers 11; Joshua 5:12; Nehemiah 9:15, 20; Revelation 2:17.

To Ponder

Consider how God Himself can satisfy all the cravings of your heart. _____

_____

_____

_____

Pray

Dear Living Bread and Heavenly Manna, _____

_____

_____

_____

Everlasting God

Lord, You have been our dwelling place in all generations.
Before the mountains were born
Or You gave birth to the earth and the world,
Even from everlasting to everlasting,
{from vanishing point to vanishing point}
You are God. (Psalm 90:1-2)

God without beginning or ending; infinitely beyond human measurement.

Our everlasting God has always been. He stretches out behind us far past anything we can conceive. Past all the generations of ancestors we can trace, past creation, past whatever time when He sat in the throne room of heaven and planned our universe, our world, our unique personalities and our redemption.

His plans, His works—our God preceded them all!

He is the solid rock basis for all things—the sure foundation and frame of reference for our deepest thoughts and our most trivial whims and everything else about us in between. Try as we might, we cannot imagine a time or a place when or where He was not!

This same God stretches out before us into the unending eons of time and timelessness yet to come.

Endless, infinite, enduring God is He—
the God who will always
elicit our wonder
exceed our grasp
yet never cease to be!

Time-bound and earthbound creatures that we are, something in this mind-boggling image of God tugs at our hearts and imaginations. It is challenging, yet it entices us, urges us to try to understand Him more and more. Passionate to know, we take up the challenge. But always we discover that He goes beyond the vanishing point where the horizons of our mental and emotional abilities blur off into the blinding glory of His everlastingness.

Overwhelmed, we can but bow in awe before Him—the great everlasting Father, everlasting King, the God of everlasting loving-kindness and strength, the incredible Forever One!

> *May grace be granted to you, and peace, from Him who is and was and evermore will be. . . . To Him who loves us and has freed us from our sins with His own blood, and has formed us into a Kingdom, to be priests to God, His Father—to Him be ascribed the glory and the power until the Ages of the Ages. Amen.* (Revelation 1:4-6, Wey.)

For further glimpses of the Everlasting God, read: Genesis 21:33; Psalm 45:6; 93:2; 102:24-27; 136; Isaiah 9:6-7; 26:4; 40:28; Lamentations 5:19; Daniel 2:44; 4:34; 7:14, 18, 27; Habakkuk 1:12; Luke 1:32-33; Revelation 10:6; 16:5.

Timeless

> *For a thousand years in Your sight*
> *Are like yesterday when it passes by,*
> *Or as a watch in the night. (Psalm 90:4)*

With the Lord one day is like a thousand years, and a thousand years like one day. (2 Peter 3:8)

Timeless Being totally above and outside of all limitations of time.

The God who has lived outside of time created time and will one day bring it to an end. He fashioned the universe, this world and everything in it with time limitations and constraints. Time is a vital part of the grand ecological scheme of His creation.

The paradox of God's timelessness and His involvement with time staggers the time-dependent human mind. Our trivially oriented souls live in constant, desperate need of stopping to meditate on the meaning of it all. We must open ourselves up to let this concept expand our adoration of a God far too big to be grasped by His creatures.

The timeless God
whose holy essence
transcends eons and millennia,
shaped, with skillful fingers,
a world clocked by seasons and cycles
and men with heart rhythms, anniversaries and schedules.
What high and sacred awe these works inspire,
smoky mirrors all,
of the vast array
of His artistry and glory.
And why?
For unfathomable purposes
cherished, cloistered, obscured
in the great
eternal, timeless
heart of God!

Only He who transcends time, manages time, directs time, limits time, is capable of giving to our lives and our deeds a meaning and purpose that crosses the barriers of time. Through His everlasting working together of all things in gracious concert, our words said and our deeds done today have significance for all eternity.

> *There is an appointed time for everything . . . for every event*
> *   under heaven—*
> *A time to give birth and a time to die;*
> *A time to plant and a time to uproot what is planted.*
> *A time to kill and a time to heal;*
> *A time to tear down and a time to build up.*
> *A time to weep and a time to laugh;*
> *A time to mourn and a time to dance.*
> *A time to throw stones and a time to gather stones;*
> *A time to embrace and a time to shun embracing.*
> *A time to search and a time to give up as lost;*
> *A time to keep and a time to throw away.*
> *A time to tear apart and a time to sew together;*
> *A time to be silent and a time to speak.*
> *A time to love and a time to hate;*
> *A time for war and a time for peace. . . .*
> *He has made everything appropriate in its time.*
>
> (Ecclesiastes 3:1-8, 11)

Eternal God

> *Now to the King eternal, immortal, invisible, the only God, be*
> *honor and glory forever and ever. Amen.* (1 Timothy 1:17)

A God who stretches beyond our finite concept of time and our earthly perspectives.

Our Eternal God turns all of life into a rare and precious gem, sparkling in the glory of eternal light. He gives us a new heavenly perspective on what perplexes us today. He shows us that nothing in life on earth is without purpose in heaven.

The eternal God can never be old-fashioned or out-of-date. Granted, His values and standards will clash with what is fashionable among men and women of every generation. The reason, however, has nothing to do with the passage of time. It has everything to do with the eternal quality of life, the heavenly perspective, the holy otherness of God.

Through eyes set to a heavenly compass, He sees every storm that batters our faith and leaves us asking, "Why?" With a heart warmed in heaven's streets, He feels the frustrations that force us to put life on hold. With a sensitivity sharpened by heaven's compassion, He suffers with our pain.

He reminds us that He is the eternal God who designed our lives and orders them and offers us hope. Each time we respond and seek Him for comfort, for help, for understanding, He opens one of His rooms and shows us a glimpse of eternal glory. This we would never stop long enough to see if everything moved according to our clocks.

The eternal God who works all things for His glory and our good delights in transforming our anxious moments into personal adventures with Himself.

"Be still," He coaxes us. "Sit down, be quiet, relax, let go of all your time-sensitive frazzeledness. *Be still, and know that I am God; I will be exalted among the nations, I will be exalted in the earth*" (Psalm 46:10, NIV).

He knows that we will always find ourselves backed into tight corners with no way to go but up. He knows that doubts will always assail us and hang a cloud between us and His glorious face. He knows that fears will always torment, dangers will always be real. Most of all, He knows the strong pull of the temptation we feel to "play God" with our difficulties and doubts and fears and to try to do for ourselves what only He is capable of doing for us.

But this all-knowing God is God—now and tomorrow, for always and forever.

> *The eternal God is a dwelling place,*
> *And underneath are the everlasting arms.*

(Deuteronomy 33:27)

For further glimpses of the Eternal God, read: Exodus 3:15; 1 Chronicles 16:36; 29:10; Psalm 9:7; 92:8; Isaiah 43:13; 57:15; Hebrews 9:12, 14; 1 Peter 5:10; Revelation 4:8-10.

To Ponder

Give your mind and heart to much meditation of the wonders of heavenly perspectives on earthly life. _____

_____

_____

_____

Pray

Dear Everlasting, Timeless and Eternal God, _____

_____

_____

_____

Captain of the LORD of Hosts

*He said . . . "I indeed come now as captain of the host of the
LORD. . . . Remove your sandals from your feet, for the place
where you are standing is holy." (Joshua 5:14-15)*

Leader of all of God's armies in the heavenly
realms.

In the quiet space at the end of a day on the Promised Land
side of Jordan, Joshua slipped out of camp alone. He crept
to a spot where he could view Jericho. The city glared
down at his smallness and prodded his heart to beat with something akin to fear.

He knew the God of Abraham, Jacob and Moses had brought
him, as leader of the vast company of His people, across the Jordan. The spies he had sent into the city came back with a good re-
port: "All the inhabitants of the land have melted away before us"
(Joshua 2:24).

Joshua looked at the city, shut up tightly as a green rosebud, and
pondered.

Repeatedly, he had heard God's voice saying, "Fear not, be of
good courage. As I was with Moses, so I will be with you." But
when it came to instructions for how to go about the "assured"
battle, that same God remained silent. Joshua stared at the city,

waiting. The stillness of the air was eerie. Not even a sentry moved about outside the walls, and the desert sounds were soft, muted and haunting.

Then he saw the man. He hadn't seen him come or heard his approaching footsteps. Just suddenly, he was there, legs spread apart in an aggressive stance, sword drawn and glinting in the few last rays of the setting sun.

"Are you for us," Joshua stammered, trying to sound threatening, "or for our adversaries?" (5:13). His hand went to his own sword and his fingers gripped the handle.

"No," came the answer, "rather I indeed come now as captain of the host of the LORD" (5:14).

His Commander-in-Chief! A strange presence overpowered Joshua. With neither fear nor bravado, he fell on his face to the earth and heard himself asking, "What has my lord to say to his servant?" (5:14). He dared not miss a single word.

"Remove your sandals from your feet," came the voice of unquestionable authority, "for the place where you are standing is holy" (5:15).

Joshua shivered in the evening warmth. Rising from his prone position, yet staying low to the ground, he unlatched first one sandal, then the other, and slipped them off. The sands, still burning with the day's fierce heat, stung at his feet.

Bowing once more, his heart cried out, though his lips never parted: "O mighty LORD of hosts, my Captain!"

* * *

Leading God's people can be a heady experience. We are often terrified to do the thing God asks of us, and so we seek out wisdom for our task in our own shallow wells rather than from the bottomless vastness of God's wisdom. Each victory along the way bolsters our human pride and deafens our ears further to the higher ways of the Commander-in-Chief.

God knew all this. So when He came to give Joshua his battle orders, He first made sure that Joshua knew who was in charge. In the culture of the raw desert, the act of standing one's ground made the bold statement, "This is my turf. I am in control here. My sandals protect me from the ravages of the elements and enable me to be strong."

Joshua bowed, in recognition of his Lord's superiority. He removed his sandals in the presence of Jehovah as the holy One who alone could protect him in the heat of battle.

> LORD GOD of Hosts
> Sole source of power
> in every struggle against evil,
> thank You for the multitude of ways
> You bring me to my face in the sand at Your feet,
> protecting Your honor,
> unfurling Your banners,
> assuring Your victory,
> conquering me with
> a million wonders
> in the glorious revelation
> of who You are!

For further glimpses of the Lord of Hosts at work, read: Exodus 17:8-16; 2 Chronicles 13:12; 14:1-15; 20:1-30; 32:1-23; Psalm 20:5; Isaiah 5:13-16; Jeremiah 9:7-9, 12-16; Amos 4:13; 5:14-15.

> "Devote yourself to God and you will find God fights the battles of a will resigned."[1]

Lion of the Tribe of Judah

Stop weeping; behold, the Lion that is from the tribe of Judah, the Root of David, has overcome. (Revelation 5:5)

Lion of the Tribe of Judah

The battle standard of Jesus Christ, which identifies Him with the Jewish royal line when He comes as God's King over all spiritual realms.

Lion! King of beasts, captain of all the conquering, destroying hosts of the earth's animal kingdom! What sort of symbol is this of the LORD of Hosts? He is the picture of strength and ferocity, and we both fear and admire Him. For he carries Himself with a majestic demeanor that also speaks of dignity and authority. Nobility is here and we cannot escape its draw. Yet when we dare to come close enough to stand before Him, we see the fire in His eyes. The heat and power of His breath wither whatever arrogance we have not shed. Everything in our sinful human nature trembles under the gaze of His overwhelming purity.

Like Joshua before his visitor outside the walls of Jericho, we fall on our faces and cry out for mercy. His presence strips us of our sandals, and our toes burn in the sand. In the honest depths of our spirits, we know we deserve nothing from Him but to be torn by His gigantic paws, mauled and maimed, even consumed by a just and holy appetite for revenge.

When at last we dare to lift our eyes, the sight that greets us shatters us with even greater impact than the vision of His Majesty, the Lion of the Tribe of Judah. Gone is the Lion, and in His place, a Lamb looks down upon us. The picture of innocence, patience, tenderness and sacrificial submission, He has a mortal wound in His breast.

A heavenly chorus is singing around us a new song:

> *Worthy is the Lamb that was slain to receive power and riches and wisdom and might and honor and glory and blessing.*

(Revelation 5:12)

Then, just as the wonder begins to grab us, the entire heavens explode in one voice:

> *To Him who sits on the throne, and to the Lamb, be blessing*
> *and honor and glory and dominion forever and ever. . . .*
> *Amen.* (5:13-14)

We are singing with the numberless throng. Our faces are awash with tears of joy!

> In the presence of God's holy Lion,
> Captain of the LORD of Hosts,
> appointed to settle sin's awful score,
> we must always tremble.
> Before the Lamb whose sacrificial obedience
> took the death-blows we deserve,
> we come in brokenness
> and rise—stripped of our sandals,
> toes burning in the sand—
> forgiven!

For further glimpses of God as the Lion, read: Genesis 49:9; Jeremiah 4:7; 49:19; 50:44; Hosea 5:14-15; 11:10; 13:7.

To Ponder

Think on the power of God to destroy all enemies of His Spirit and our souls. Breathe your praises. _____

_____

_____

_____

Pray

Dear LORD GOD of Hosts, _____

_____

_____

_____

Stiller of Storms

By awesome deeds You answer us in righteousness,
O God of our salvation. . . .
Who stills the roaring of the seas,
The roaring of their waves,
And the tumult of the peoples.
They who dwell in the ends of the earth stand in
awe of Your signs;
You make the dawn and the sunset shout for joy.

(Psalm 65:5, 7-8)

Stiller of Storms. One with supernatural power to quiet a storm and bring peace to the landscape or to our souls.

On a night in ancient Galilee, the Son of God got into a boat with His twelve apprentices in faith. He promptly curled up on a pillow in the bow of the ship and fell fast asleep. They rowed the boat toward the opposite shore and no doubt talked about all kinds of things.

Then a storm began to brew. Some of these men were fishermen, from this very lake. Panic gripped their hearts, for they knew the capricious ways of the sea all too well. Never could they face a Galilean storm with quiet confidence in their own abilities to bring a craft through it unscathed.

In their terror, the men suddenly remembered that their Rabbi and Master was with them. But He was sleeping in perfect calm while they cried out in terror.

"Rabbi, don't You care that we all perish?" They screamed above the howl of the wind, as they shook Him awake. "Save us!"

What frantic visions must have darted through their brains? Overturned boats? Desperate clinging to bits and pieces of wood? But there was one thing they did not seem to anticipate, one thing their Rabbi did before their unbelieving eyes. He stood up in the topsy-turvy boat, stretched out His hand over the threatening waves and spoke into the wind: "Hush, be still!"

The men held their breath, and so did the world around them. As suddenly as the wind had begun, it ceased—"a perfect calm set in" (Mark 4:39, Wey.).

"Who then is this?" someone gasped. Then as if with one voice, they mumbled in awe: "Even the wind and sea obey Him" (see Mark 4:35-41).

This was God, who specializes in the kinds of rescue that catch us unaware. So often He seems not to be paying attention to our distress. At best we think He lies sleeping in the corner of our boat and we nearly miss the miracle that can calm even the most violent of storms.

Why all this needless pain and stress?

> "Poets have wronged poor storms: such days are best;
> They purge the air without, within the breast."[1]

Out of each storm, no matter how disastrous the results seem to be, God brings something incredibly beautiful. The issue is not the storm, but our faith. Faith scours the beaches of our souls after each violent and terrifying storm for some of life's most priceless treasures:

- an alteration in the channel of our lives;
- a cooling refreshment for our weary souls;
- a display of God's power to encourage our wilting hearts;
- fresh growth in some area of our daily walk;
- a cleansing of the air about us and a bright new vision of truth;

- the destruction of something we have been leaning upon in place of God;
- a rainbow of promise for the way ahead.

Oh, what joy when we allow every circumstance in life to bow in subservience to the Master of earth and sea and calm and storm. Even when He does not still the storm, but leaves us floating for days on a scrap of battered boat, He can still the storm that rages in our hearts, with the assurance that He owns it all and will never cease to rule.

For further glimpses of the Stiller of Storms, read: Psalm 89:9; 93:3-4; 107:23-32; Matthew 8:23-27; 14:22-33; Luke 8:22-25.

Let go, relax, "cease striving and know that I am God."

(Psalm 46:10)

Hope

O Hope of Israel,
Its Savior in time of distress . . .
We are called by Your name;
Do not forsake us! (Jeremiah 14:8-9)

The riches of the glory of this mystery among the Gentiles,
which is Christ in you, the hope of glory. (Colossians 1:27)

Assurance, trust, confidence; that for which I wait with anticipation, tarry/have patience for.

Bless the LORD! He has fashioned us for a hopeful end!

e are born trusting others, hoping for the best to come. We crave a hopeful word. We are easily led to hope in those who offer us good things. We stake our lives on threads of hope, no matter how thin or flimsy they may be.

But in this life hope is often nothing more than a rainbow-hued soap bubble. Tantalizing, glorious, yet it is light as air, carried away by the slightest breeze—elusive, evading our grasp, bursting in our faces. The word of the promiser proves false. The power we trust proves weak. Our dreams lack substance. People disappoint, our bodies fail, circumstances destroy the thing we expect with such eagerness. After repeated experiences of unfulfilled hope, the despair of disillusionment and bitterness may set in. Cynicism is born; hope flounders. When we cease to hope, we cease to live.

The God who created us to look for hope, however, can Himself be trusted. God of hope and hope of glory, He will come through, even when we must endure disappointments, delayed promises and dreadful reversals.

"Though He slay me, I will hope in Him," cried Job in his darkest hour when hope had completely disappeared over all his horizons (Job 13:15).

As long as our hope rests on the solid rock of the goodness and mercy and graciousness of a holy God, we can wait long, even though with great sorrow, for the best to be ours. How beautiful the hope that makes it possible to wait!

For further glimpses of the God of Hope, read: Psalm 38:15; 71:5; 130; 131:3; Jeremiah 14:22; 17:13; 50:7; Romans 15:13; 1 Timothy 1:1; Hebrews 6:19-20; 1 Peter 1:3.

> Wait at His door with prayer . . . at His foot with humility . . . at His table with service . . . at His window with expectancy.[2]

To Ponder

What can you recall about the character of God that causes you to have hope when you face difficult situations? _____

_____

_____

_____

Pray

Dear God of Hope, Stiller of my Storms, _____

_____

_____

_____

Incomparable

For who in the skies is comparable to the LORD?
Who among the sons of the mighty is like the LORD,
A God greatly feared in the council of the holy ones,
And awesome above all those who are around Him?
O LORD God of hosts, who is like You, O mighty LORD?

(Psalm 89:6-8)

Incomparable Beyond all comparisons, without equal, unsur-
passed, peerless.

With the LORD God Jehovah, *no* comparisons
are possible—only contrasts!

As Deliverer of the needy from affliction
None compares with You, O God.
In great and mighty deeds and incredible wonders
None compares with You, O God.
In show of strength and power
or demonstration of pure righteousness
None compares with You, O God.
In acts of compassion and humble condescension
to raise up those that are fallen,
None compares with You, O God.

> Majestic in holiness,
> awesome in praises,
> enthroned on high, far, far above all others,
> *None compares with You, O God.*

God Himself has given to us hundreds of metaphors to teach us about His nature—things we could never glimpse in any other way. None of these can adequately reveal the depths of His person or His character. Perhaps when all the metaphors are taken together, they might begin to represent something approximating the whole—as multiple facets in a large diamond.

Yet even this cannot tell it all, for the God we worship holds a million mysteries in His being. A diamond so large we cannot estimate its size, He sparkles into the far reaches of eternity with an infinity of facets that will always tantalize and stagger the imagination. When we have searched all the metaphors we know or can imagine, this God is incomparably beyond the greatest and most profound picture in our universe.

> *O LORD, the God of Israel, there is no God like You in heaven above or on earth beneath. . . . The LORD is God; there is no one else.* (1 Kings 8:23, 60)

In every category of life, He is totally unequaled. None can measure up to Him in ability or creativity or passion. He excels them all in performance of noteworthy deeds as well as in moral excellence.

In Isaiah 43-46 God has hung for us an incredible gallery of pictures of Himself as the God who stands far and above all others. He has no equals, no rivals! He is Creator and King.

> *I am the LORD, your Holy One,*
> *The Creator of Israel, your King.* (Isaiah 43:15)

He is present with us and protects His people.

> *When you pass through the waters, I will be with you;*
> *And through the rivers, they will not overflow you.*

When you walk through the fire, you will not be scorched,
Nor will the flame burn you.
For I am the LORD your God. (Isaiah 43:2-3)

He is our forgiver and redeemer.

I have wiped out your transgressions like a thick cloud
And your sins like a heavy mist.
Return to Me, for I have redeemed you. (44:22)

He is ultimate Lord of all the earth.

Turn to Me and be saved, all the ends of the earth;
For I am God, and there is no other. . . .
To Me every knee will bow, every tongue will swear allegiance.
They will say of Me, "Only in the LORD are righteousness
and strength." (45:22-24)

Towering high in the clouds above all His grasping pretenders, God alone can reach down to earth and right the wrongs. Some He rights in this life; others await His action in eternity. But He alone is the perfect and final balancer, leveler and restorer of both justice and perspective.

I am God, and there is no other.[1]

For further glimpses of the Incomparable God, read: Exodus 15:11; 1 Samuel 2:2; 2 Samuel 7:22; Psalm 35:10; 40:5; 71:19; 86:8; 113:5-9; Isaiah 37:16; 40:18-20; 44:6-8; 46:9; Jeremiah 10:6-7; Revelation 15:4.

Unique

There is no one like You among the gods, O Lord,
Nor are there any works like Yours.
All nations whom You have made shall come and worship
before You, O Lord

And they shall glorify Your name.
For You are great and do wondrous deeds;
You alone are God. (Psalm 86:8-10)

Unique

One of a kind.

Far above the horde of supernatural beings and so-called gods, the God of Scripture stands out. There is none like Him—not in earth beneath nor in the heavenly realms above. Other gods are created by the hands of men and women. *The God of the universe creates all things* (see Jeremiah 10:6-16).

Other gods are foolish and senseless. *The God of the universe is all-wise* (see Isaiah 40:12-20).

Other gods live lives of wantonness and debauchery. *The God of the universe is absolutely holy and righteous* (see Revelation 15:4).

Other gods are feared and placated for their anger and capricious acts of revenge. *The God of the universe is compassionate, forgiving all who believe and call upon Him for mercy* (see Micah 7:18).

Other gods demand that their subjects serve them as slaves. *The God of the universe serves for and with all those who wait for Him* (see Isaiah 64:4).

Other gods have no control over either life or death. *The God of the universe holds the keys of death and resurrection life. He wounds or allows us to be wounded, then heals our festering and otherwise mortal wounds* (see Deuteronomy 32:39).

Every man, woman and child on earth is an individual expression of God's great handiwork—unique in some way. But the God who planned and fashioned us all is totally unique from all other living, personal beings in the universe. While He has placed within each of us faint shadow images of His character, they are nothing more than reflections of His own excellent uniqueness.

God alone is absolutely, unquestionably unique among all living beings.

Unique in creative energy, power and wisdom
Infinity and authority
Tirelessness, beauty and purity
Majesty, glory and mystery
Justice, tender strength and redemptive compassion!

For further glimpses of the Unique God, read: Exodus 8:10; 9:14; 15:11; Deuteronomy 32:39; Psalm 115:1-8; Isaiah 43:11.

Only God

But to Him who is able to keep you safe from stumbling, and cause you to stand in the presence of His glory free from blemish and full of exultant joy—to the only God our Saviour—through Jesus Christ our Lord, be ascribed glory, majesty, might, and authority, as it was before all time, is now, and shall be to all the Ages! Amen. (Jude 24-25, Wey.)

Only God

The one true and living God.

How surrounded we are, with a plethora of false, so-called gods. Pleasures, work, possessions, ambitions, causes and people—these are all forces for good when controlled by our passion for the God of the universe. But, in the earthiness of daily life in a polluted world, these things creep subtly into our hearts. Little by little, we allow them to consume our time, energies and resources and hold us in their grip. They divert our worship and rape our spiritual purity.

Dear God,
deliver us from the allure of all that beckons,

> pretending to explain Your depths,
> while serving to obscure You
> with some lesser being,
> object or concept!

We have exchanged the glory of God for something else: for images of glory, like a new home or car or VCR or computers or vacation days or impressive resumes or whatever makes our ticker tick more than the wonder of God's glory.[2]

How sterile the life given over to empty worship of such false gods! How rich the life where God the LORD is God alone!

> *This is eternal life, that they may know You, the only true God, and Jesus Christ whom You have sent.* (John 17:3)

> *I am the LORD, that is My name;*
> *I will not give My glory to another.* (Isaiah 42:8)

The only living God has every right, and all authority, to ask of us our absolute allegiance—our spiritual chastity. In exchange, He gives to us joys unimaginable in ever deepening visions of His Glory.

> *My soul waits in silence for God only;*
> *From Him is my salvation.*
> *He only is my rock and my salvation,*
> *My stronghold; I shall not be greatly shaken.*

> (Psalm 62:1-2)

For further glimpses of the Only God, read: Deuteronomy 6:4; 32:39; 2 Kings 19:15, 19; Nehemiah 9:6; Jeremiah 10:6-7; Zechariah 14:9; John 5:44; 1 Timothy 1:17; 6:15.

To Ponder

Think on each of the ways that God is unique and let your soul be enlarged, nurtured and transported into realms of incredible glory.

_____

_____

_____

_____

Pray

Dear Unparalleled, Unique and Only God, _____

_____

_____

_____

Tear Catcher

Behold, the tabernacle of God is among men, and He will
dwell among them, and they shall be His people, and God
Himself will be among them, and He will wipe away every
tear from their eyes; and there will no longer be any death;
there will no longer be any mourning, or crying, or pain.

(Revelation 21:3-4)

Catcher of Tears

One who sees our tears, catches them, turns
them into good, often wipes them away and
fills us with joy in place of sorrow.

Tears of the Sufferer (Genesis 21)

In the heat of an arid desert—the wilderness of Beersheba—
the sun beat down and the silence was broken by human
sobs. Across the crumpled body of a teenage boy, the scanty
shade of a shrub fell. "God heard the lad crying."

About a bowshot away, just out of sight but not totally out of
hearing, his mother sat hugging her skirts in the shade of another
bush. She lifted up her voice and wept. "Do not let me see my boy
die," she cried, scarcely knowing to whom she spoke.

With a suddenness that startled the grieving woman, a voice
spoke to her from the heavens above:

"What is the matter with you, Hagar?"

Who was this calling to her? How did He know her name? Her tears stopped and she gasped, but offered no words in reply. Surely He could see why she grieved.

"Do not fear, for God has heard the voice of the lad where he is."

The words flowed over her soul like soothing oil. Dare she believe enough to give up her fears? He went on: "Arise, lift up the lad, and hold him by the hand, for I will make a great nation of him."

A great nation? It was what she had always hoped for, but that was while Ishmael lived in Abraham's tent—before Isaac had been born. Must he mock her so? Her stomach clenched in pain and she stifled the urge to retch into the sand. At that moment, even the prospect of her son becoming a "great nation" seemed so inconsequential. How could God not know that the only thing she needed was water? Without that, nothing else would matter.

Refusing to lift her eyes to the heavens from whence came this mockery of a voice, she stared straight into the clump of rocks that separated her from her son. Then, suddenly, something sparkled in the sunlight and her ears picked up the faint sound of a trickle. Could it be? She blinked, then leaned forward, and she saw it so clearly there could be no mistake—a flow of water, gushing from the rock!

This same God, who delivered Hagar and her son, Ishmael, from certain death in the desert, hears our cries, sees our tears, feels our pain and hopelessness. He has Himself shed tears of deep anguish and pain and He knows how they feel. It is the Man of Sorrows who comes to us in our despair and speaks away our fears. He opens our eyes to see the abundance of His wells of water gushing just where and when we need them to sustain life. He promises a future blessedness and lifts us up, strengthened to face our deserts and grow.

> *When I am afraid,*
> *I will put my trust in You. . . .*
> *You have taken account of my wanderings;*

Put my tears in Your bottle.
Are they not in Your book?
Then my enemies will turn back in the day when I call;
This I know, that God is for me.
In God, whose word I praise,
In the LORD, whose word I praise,
In God I have put my trust, I shall not be afraid.
What can man do to me? (Psalm 56:3, 8-11)

For further glimpses of the God Who Dries Tears of Suffering,
read: 2 Kings 20:5; Psalm 6; 116:8.

Tears of Penitence (Luke 7:36-50)

Lounging at the dining table in the house of Simon the Phari-
see, Jesus was the guest of honor. All the doors and windows stood
open, and a parade of spectators strolled by, some stopping to peer
across the courtyard.

But when the well-known street woman came to the spot, she
did not pass by. She turned and passed through the doorway,
crossed the courtyard and dared to enter into the very room in
which Jesus sat. She was aware of stares and gasps all around. It
was nothing new to her; she endured stares and gasps on a daily
basis. It was a part of her way of living.

The one man in the company who neither stared nor gasped
was Jesus. She walked straight for His couch, then stopped and
knelt at His feet. Blinking back a thickening curtain of hot tears
and reaching into the folds of her garments, she pulled out an ala-
baster vial. It was cool and smooth to her touch as she uncorked it
and began pouring out its precious contents onto His feet. Her
tears flowed freely now, falling with the ointment. Bending over
Him, she pursed her lips and kissed His feet, then wiped at them
with the long, silken tresses of her hair. Again and again she mur-

mured soft words of broken anguish: "Forgive me, I am a sinner. Oh, Lord, forgive, forgive. . . ."

For a long moment, silence reigned in the room. Then she heard the voice of Simon. She did not listen to his words, only the tone of scathing accusation. When Jesus replied, she heard His rebuke of the religious man with the gorgeous robes and jealously guarded reputation: "Do you see this woman? . . . Her sins, which are many, have been forgiven, for she loved much; but he who is forgiven little, loves little" (7:44, 47).

She trembled and shivered, the coolness of her dampened hair wrapped around the beloved feet of the one man she loved in a different way than any she had pretended to love before. Then He spoke to her: "Your sins have been forgiven."

Fresh tears of joy rolled down her face. Then she looked up into His eyes and felt all of her tears forever washed away. "Your faith has saved you," He said. "Go in peace."

He who shed tears of intense grief over our sins searches the world over for tears of humble, broken penitence. There is nothing He longs to do more than to forgive our sin, heal our guilt, dry our tears and fill us with the joy of redemption.

> *Be gracious to me, O God, according to Your lovingkindness;*
> *According to the greatness of Your compassion blot out my*
>   *transgressions.*
> *Wash me thoroughly from my iniquity*
> *And cleanse me from my sin. . . .*
> *Create in me a clean heart, O God,*
> *And renew a steadfast spirit within me.*
> *Do not cast me away from Your presence*
> *And do not take Your Holy Spirit from me.*
> *Restore to me the joy of Your salvation. . . .*
> *The sacrifices of God are a broken spirit;*
> *A broken and a contrite heart, O God, You will not despise.*
>
> (Psalm 51:1-2, 10-12, 17)

For further glimpses of the God Who Dries Tears of Penitence, read: Psalm 30:5; 39:11-13; 51; Isaiah 25:8; Joel 2:12-13.

Tears of Disappointment
(John 20:1-2, 11-18)

Mary, once a wild woman of Magdala, from whom Jesus had cast out seven demons, lingered in the dew-blessed garden alone after all the others had gone. Life had had no meaning until Jesus came and rescued her and dried her tears. She thought she would never weep again.

How could it be that He had allowed them to kill Him, take Him from her, smash her dreams? She'd come here to stay as close as possible to what was left of Him. There was no hope anywhere else. And now, even His body was gone!

Tears flooded her face, saturated her hair, wet her robe and shawl. Her entire spirit had turned to soggy, dreary anguish. Where could she go? What could she do? She must forever bow here and let the tears flow.

The voice that intruded on her intimate and heart-wrenching solitude twisted like a spear in her gut. "Why are you weeping, woman?"

Why indeed? "Sir, if you have carried Him away, tell me where you have laid Him, and I will take Him away."

The gardener whom she had addressed hovered over her bowed form. She felt His presence and held her breath while the tears continued to stream.

"Mary!"

That voice! It was no gardener. His voice had spoken her name! Her tears suddenly stopped and she turned to see with her own eyes what could not be. It was her Lord!

"Rabboni!" The word rose upward from a heart lightened in an instant.

He spoke to her something about going to His Father. Then He was gone. She flew back into the town, shouting all the way, "I have seen the LORD!" No, she would never cry that kind of tears again. Never!

Life is filled with disappointments that bring tears. So often we have heard His promises, counted on them, then watched our visions of their fulfillment drop away, falling out of sight. And when our eyes run with tears, He hears, He comes, He speaks our name in ways that only He can speak it. He dries our tears, restores our hope, shows us the true fulfillment of His promises.

> *When the LORD brought back the captive ones of Zion,*
> *We were like those who dream.*
> *Then our mouth was filled with laughter*
> *And our tongue with joyful shouting;*
> *Then they said among the nations,*
> *"The LORD had done great things for them."*
> *The LORD has done great things for us;*
> *We are glad.*
> *Restore our captivity, O LORD,*
> *As the streams in the South.*
> *Those who sow in tears shall reap with joyful shouting.*
> *He who goes to and fro weeping, carrying his bag of seed,*
> *Shall indeed come again with a shout of joy, bringing his*
>   *sheaves with him.* (Psalm 126)

For further glimpses of the God Who Dries Our Tears of Disappointment, read: Isaiah 65:19; Jeremiah 31:16; John 11:33, 35; Hebrews 5:7.

> *They will hunger no longer, nor thirst anymore; nor will the*
> *sun beat down on them, nor any heat; for the Lamb in the cen-*
> *ter of the throne will be their shepherd, and will guide them to*
> *springs of the water of life; and God will wipe every tear from*
> *their eyes.* (Revelation 7:16-17)

To Ponder

Jesus, in the prophetic passage of Isaiah 53:3, was called "a man of sorrows and acquainted with grief." How did His experiences with tears qualify Him to dry our tears? _____

_____

_____

_____

Pray

Dear God, who shed hot tears for me and who promises to dry my tears, _____

_____

_____

_____

Resurrection and the Life

Jesus said to her, "I am the resurrection and the life; he who be-lieves in Me will live even if he dies." (John 11:25)

Resurrection

Restoration to new life of one who has died.

We love the word *resurrection*. It conjures up bright, colorful images of spring flowers, singing birds, feather-light butterflies and Christ with a body that could move through locked doors. It speaks to us of new beginnings, exciting discoveries, soul-stirring mysteries and a golden sun rising on the horizons of our world.

So easily we forget that without a death there can be no resurrection.

Like Mary and Martha of Bethany, we trust in Jesus, the Great Physician. Eagerly we bring Him our wounded, emaciated and threatened dreams and selves. We count on His love for us and do not doubt His power to heal. So, when He chooses to let our dreams die so He can give us a resurrection rather than a healing, we sometimes feel abandoned. We think to ourselves, *Surely God doesn't want us to suffer the anguish of death! He wants our dreams to come true, our ills to be healed, our joy to be full! What kind of place, then, is the valley of the shadow of death for the God of quickening, renewal and revival?*

Well, where else can resurrection occur? Jesus said it about Himself before He went to the cross: *"Unless a grain of wheat falls into the earth and dies, it remains alone; but if it dies, it bears much fruit"* (John 12:24).

> The beauty and awesomeness of what I see hints of One who watches and waits, one who allows the pain of crucifixion but transmutes it into new life.[1]

In Colossians 3 we can trace the process——on our knees, with bleeding hearts. There we see how deep the pain goes, how contrary to all that our human natures hold dear:

> *If however you have risen with Christ, seek the things that are above, where Christ is, enthroned at God's right hand. Give your minds to the things that are above, not to the things that are on the earth. For you have died, and your life is hidden with Christ in God. When Christ appears—He is our true Life—then you also will appear with Him in glory. Therefore put to death your earthward inclinations . . . rid yourselves of every kind of sin.* (3:1-5, 8, Wey.)

Must we indeed humble ourselves, confess our sins, die with Him, consider ourselves dead and powerless? Can't we simply reform ourselves by choosing to live righteous and holy lives?

> *I have been crucified with Christ; and it is no longer I who live, but Christ lives in me; and the life which I now live in the flesh I live by faith in the Son of God, who loved me and gave Himself up for me.* (Galatians 2:20)

The best we can do on our own is nothing more than a pale and deadly imitation of God's life. Only the resurrection life of Christ is pure and holy and truly new. His life in us makes us *"God's picked representatives of the new humanity, purified and beloved of God himself"* (Colossians 3:12, Phillips).

For further glimpses of God as the Resurrection and the Life, read: Ezekiel 37:1-14; John 6:35-40, 53-58; 11:1-45; Romans 6:4; 8:11-13.

Dear Quickening God,
our world is plagued by death . . .
obsessed with death . . .
in fear of death!
You have come and quickened us—
given us Your life.
Forgive us that we move about
among the grave slabs of our culture,
forgetting to appreciate how precious
is the life we have!

Transformer

And all of us, with unveiled faces, reflecting like bright mirrors the glory of the Lord, are being transformed into the same likeness, from one degree of radiant holiness to another, even as derived from the Lord the Spirit. (2 Corinthians 3:18, Wey.)

Transformer

One who radically alters the old sinful nature, infusing it with a life focused on godly priorities and possibilities.

A resurrected life is a glorious phenomenon! Transformed by the God of life, it breathes across the staleness and the stench of a dying world, offering something fresh and new and fragrant.

Like the gift of a bridegroom coming to his bride, this is much more than an exquisitely wrapped package marked "Life." It is not something we could open and enjoy, either with or without His presence and companionship, like the sun that He has suspended in the sky or the food that He causes to grow from our earth. Rather, He is eager to claim us as His willing Bride. The life that He gives to our impoverished and hopeless spirits is the treasured gift of His person. When we open it, we are transformed:

- from depraved human souls with selfish agendas into God-reflectors-in-process;
- from slaves to sin into His beloved children with a family resemblance;
- from instruments for the destruction of others to passion-ate rescuers of a lost mankind.

We need hearts that see as God sees.[2]

For further glimpses of the Transformer God, read: Leviticus 26:11-13; Jeremiah 32:37-40; Ezekiel 36:22-28; Romans 8:29; 2 Corinthians 3:18; Titus 3:4-7.

> *So that if any one is in Christ, he is a new creature: the old state of things has passed away; a new state of things has come into existence.* (2 Corinthians 5:17, Wey.)

Renewer/Reviver

> *They that wait upon the LORD shall renew their strength; they shall mount up with wings as eagles; they shall run, and not be weary; and they shall walk, and not faint.*
>
> (Isaiah 40:31, KJV)

> *O LORD, revive Your work in the midst of the years, In the midst of the years make it known; In wrath remember mercy.* (Habakkuk 3:2)

Renewer
One who restores, repairs, renovates, makes new.

Reviver
One who revitalizes, restores, recovers.

Even when we have been quickened and our orientation to life has been transformed by the indwelling presence of the God of the universe, we are still far from perfect specimens of the new life we possess. Everything in this mundane, physical world where we live out our days has the effect of tarnishing that beautiful, transformed image of God in us.

Our sin-ridden society pressures and entices us to walk in godless ways. Our bodies grow weary and feeble and tempt us to resort to human ways of dealing with our problems. Our minds and emotions are bombarded with thousands of bits of information and images daily, all calculated to lead us backward into the ways of death. Busyness and confusion fill our days and cool the ardor of our devotion to God.

But God has committed Himself to the never-ending task of transforming us. So, each day He comes to us with offers of renewal and revival:

- forgiveness for our sins and coldness of heart;
- words of assurance and encouragement;
- insights into resources we never dreamed were ours for the claiming;
- fresh fire from His altar to reignite our passion for Himself.

God desperately desires for us to succeed
at the lifelong business
of growing into His likeness!

He will do whatever it takes
to revive and renew us through and through.

He knows the process will take time. In love, He walks with us and shows us the way and strengthens our hearts. He is patient with our stumblings, always heeding our cries for grace and mercy and lifting us up to go on.

Renewal and revival come into our lives when we give Him increased access to the deepest parts of our being. The more we open up to Him, the more incomprehensibly wonderful He seems to us. Awe swells within our bosoms and worship lifts us up into the arms of His glory. His mystery draws us deeper and closer, and we yearn more and more for daily renewal—that we may have more and more of Him.

> If Jesus has come afresh into the central place, be assured it is revival; and who knows where this will end if we go on walking with Him?[3]

As we focus our lives on watching Him, learning from Him, yielding to His control, He transforms us bit by bit and piece by piece. Not until we see Him in heaven and are finally free from the influence of sin will the process be complete. Then, *we shall be like him; for we shall see him as he is*" (1 John 3:2, KJV).

For further glimpses of God our Renewer/Reviver, read: Psalm 51:10; 80:18; 85:6; 119:50, 93, 159; 138:7; Romans 12:1-2; 2 Corinthians 4:16; Ephesians 4:22-24; Titus 3:5.

> *For thus says the high and exalted One*
> *Who lives forever, whose name is Holy,*
> *"I dwell on a high and holy place,*
> *And also with the contrite and lowly of spirit*
> *In order to revive the spirit of the lowly*
> *And to revive the heart of the contrite."* (Isaiah 57:15)

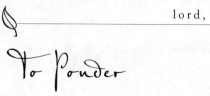

To Ponder

Meditate on the beauties of the life of God and ask Him to transform your own life to make it like His. _____

_____

_____

_____

Pray

Dear Resurrection- and Life-Giving God, _____

_____

_____

_____

father

For this reason I bow my knees before the Father, from whom every family in heaven and on earth derives its name, that He would grant you, according to the riches of His glory, to be strengthened with power through His Spirit in the inner man.

(Ephesians 3:14-16)

father A male parent, responsible for conception, care and nurturing of a child.

e are all born with needs that only a father can meet. Nothing runs deeper in the human heart than the desperate need for a father and mother. We yearn for the roots and stability provided by parents who care for us, accept us, love us, nurture us. We need a father with authority to confront us when we fail and act foolishly—to guide us, discipline us and hold us accountable for our actions. Above and beyond all else, we need the sort of parents we can be proud of because they model maturity, high morality and worthy goals for us to emulate.

No human parent can quite measure up to this standard. Even the best have frailties and imperfections. Not a one can function adequately to meet all our emotional, psychological and spiritual needs. We all suffer in some way because of the inevitable failures of our parents. Who has not known the anguish of trying to make excuses for a parent's mistakes?

121

But the God who planned families has not left us as orphans just because our parents are not perfect. He gives us a hope of rescue and restoration. God is Himself our ultimate Father, the perfect parent. With a pure and heavenly passion He fathers each one of us into existence. He willed that we should be born, that we should bear a heavenly family likeness and serve as a channel through which He might express His magnificent glory in the universe. *We, above all His works of creation, are His treasure!*

God is the perfect, flawless parent! He represents everything we could possibly desire, and many things we never imagined to desire. His perfections are so dazzling that we call them His glory. Just to meditate on His parental virtues can bring us untold ecstasy and assurance.

- He never makes mistakes, but always has our best interest at heart. (Psalm 138:8)

- He understands and sympathizes with us as no other ever could. (Psalm 103:11-14)

- He is patient with us beyond imagination. (Malachi 3:17)

- He will never forget us or let us down. (Isaiah 49:15-16)

- He guides us when we ask for help. (James 1:5-6)

- He is dependable to give us freely all the good things we need. (James 1:17)

- He pursues us when we rebel. (Luke 15:11-32)

- He comforts us in our tough times. (2 Corinthians 1:3-5)

- He heals the deepest wounds of our spirits. (Isaiah 53:3-5)

  We don't have to live in permanent emotional pain. Because of our heavenly Father's love for us and because Jesus has suffered in our place, we don't have to carry our wounds with us all our life. We can be healed and set free to live in the joy of His love.[1]

- He delivers us from our fears. (Psalm 56:3)

- He delights in us, His children. (Zephaniah 3:17)

God our Father never makes us ashamed. We can confidently extol Him from every angle. He will never disappoint our lifelong expectations of pure, unmitigated glory.

> *O my God, in You I trust,*
> *Do not let me be ashamed. . . .*
> *Indeed, none of those who wait for You will be ashamed.*
>
> (Psalm 25:2-3)

We call God *Abba*, father—that is of immense importance, an incredible concept of God: someone who holds space and time and eternity in his hands and yet invites us to pray to him as our father. That seems to me the heart of Christianity.[2]

For further glimpses of God the Father, read: Deuteronomy 1:31; 32:6-14; Psalm 68:5; Isaiah 63:8; 64:8; Jeremiah 31:9; Malachi 2:10; Matthew 6:25-34; Luke 11:11-13; 1 John 3:1.

> *Our Father which art in heaven, Hallowed be thy name. Thy kingdom come. Thy will be done in earth, as it is in heaven. Give us this day our daily bread. And forgive us our debts, as we forgive our debtors. And lead us not into temptation, but deliver us from evil: For thine is the kingdom, and the power, and the glory, for ever. Amen.* (Matthew 6:9-13, KJV)

Son of God

> *For God so loved the world, that He gave His only begotten Son, that whoever believes in Him shall not perish, but have eternal life.* (John 3:16)

Son of God

Role of Jesus in the Trinity as the physical expression of God, submissive to fulfill the redemptive plans and purposes of His Father.

ather is a fearful word to many people. Bruised and battered by an abusive earthly father or father figure, they
shrink back in terror from a name that speaks to them of
unspeakable injustice and evil.

"God the Father would always be too much for us to handle," said
one such woman, then added, "without Jesus Christ to interpret
Him." Jesus, the Son, came to earth to express the limitlessness of divine love and to make our heavenly Father accessible to us. He made
a way so the demands of God's just wrath against our sin could be
satisfied and we could be invited in to share the Father's heart. First,
He spent thirty years walking on our soil, confining Himself to the
constraints of time and space and hunger. As He walked and
adapted heavenly truths to the scaled-down concepts embodied in
human language and relationships, He modeled a Father-Son relationship such as the world had never seen—nor shall ever see again.

The Father's love for the world made it necessary for Him to
send His only Son on the great redemptive mission. The Son's
great love for the Father and His single purpose to see His glory
expressed prompted Him to obey.

Before Jesus began His active ministry, He was driven by the
Spirit of God into the wilderness. There Satan taunted Him with
His title, Son of God. "If indeed that's who you are, then turn
these stones into bread . . . cast yourself down from the temple . . .
bow Your knee and worship me." In every case the temptation
was to use His identity as the Son of God to make a shortcut to get
the things His Father planned for Him to have. But in each situation, He would have to disobey the Father. To Him that was un-

thinkable. He resisted, then spent the rest of His human life pleasing His Father, waiting for the Father's timing and methods to bring about His goals (Matthew 4:1-11).

You are My beloved Son, in You I am well-pleased.

(Mark 1:11)

I speak these things as the Father taught Me. . . . For I always do the things that are pleasing to Him. (John 8:28-29)

All through the Gospels, Jesus spoke of God as His Father. It expressed the strong identity He carried with Him every day of His earthly life. In the Garden of Gethsemane, where He went to pray before He faced the awfulness of the cross, He cried out in the most intimate term possible, to "Abba (Daddy), Father" (see Mark 14:36).

His biographers record how, repeatedly throughout the years of His ministry, Jesus slipped away from the crowds and from His friends to be alone with His Father. Again and again He sought solace, strength, wisdom and intimacy with His Father (Mark 1:35; 6:46; Luke 6:12).

In the end, when He stood before His enemies on trial for His life, He refused to answer any false accusations hurled at Him. Rather, only when they asked Him if He claimed to be the Son of God did He speak. Then, He said the three words that alone could condemn Him: "Yes, I am" (Luke 22:70).

> The most important priority
> of the Son of God
> was the overpowering Glory
> of His Father!
> As God's blood-bought child,
> what is my most important priority
> today?

For further glimpses of the Son of God, read: Matthew 14:33; 16:16; 27:39-43; Mark 5:7; John 1:34, 49; 20:21.

Peace be with you; as the Father has sent Me, I also send you.

(John 20:21)

To Ponder

Meditate on all of the ways that God functions as a good Father.

_____

_____

_____

_____

Pray

Dear Father God, _____

_____

_____

_____

Discipliner

MY SON, DO NOT REGARD LIGHTLY THE DISCIPLINE OF
   THE LORD,
NOR FAINT WHEN YOU ARE REPROVED BY HIM;
FOR THOSE WHOM THE LORD LOVES HE DISCIPLINES,
AND HE SCOURGES EVERY SON WHOM HE RECEIVES.

(Hebrews 12:5-6)

Discipliner One who corrects and trains another who is under his tutelage by use of systematic rules and/or punishment.

In our heart of hearts we know that firm and compassionate discipline is one mark of an excellent father, teacher or master. Our earthly instructors and fathers, however, often disappoint us. Some lash out in anger or as an expression of self-centeredness. They may inflict a punishment that does not fit either the child's temperament or his misbehavior. At times, they may turn soft when they should be tough or even discipline the wrong child.

God, on the other hand, administers discipline with a wisdom that we, His children and disciples, can rarely fathom. When He withholds the thing we ask for or allows us to suffer some apparently undeserved pain, it comes quite naturally to think it is God's retribution for our sins. This is not always so.

Dear Job, God's faithful servant among men, learned this truth through a trial of unspeakable pain and apparent injustice. Bereaved of his children, stripped of his wealth, the tormented man sat on a heap of ashes, scraping oozing boils with broken bits of pottery. He cried out to God, protesting that he was righteous. What had he done to deserve this sort of treatment?

Enter his three "friends"—berating him, telling him exactly what evil he had done. But their words were false and revealed a shallow concept of God. God let them go on talking until they had run out of windy words and simplistic answers. Then He stepped in and revealed His Father heart. He never accused Job of any evil. Rather He challenged him to recognize his own place of humility before a holy, perfect God. In the end, Job confessed, *"I have heard of You by the hearing of the ear; but now my eye sees You; therefore I retract, and I repent in dust and ashes"* (Job 42:5-6).

When God wants to reveal the deep places of His heart and character to us, He often takes us through pain too penetrating for simple answers. His discipline is designed to increase our dependence on Him. It sets us to crying out to Him for mercy or simply for intimacy. It weans us away from junk food for the soul and increases our appetites for the healthy nourishment that will cause us to grow more and more like Him.

> He *disciplines us for our good, so that we may share His holiness.* (Hebrews 12:10)

That we may share His holiness? To be like Him? To represent Him with a crystal clarity that will dazzle this dark world and give promise of light to all who languish around us? Can it really be that He cares enough about us to make us more and more *unlike* the world around us and change us to be more and more *like* Himself instead? It is enough to stop us dead in our tracks with awe.

What wonder! Amazing Father love!

As if that were not enough, He surrounds us with a spiritual family to help the process. When the rod falls on one of us, we are to rally round and *"strengthen the hands that are weak and the knees that are feeble, and make straight paths for your feet, so that the limb which is lame may not be put out of joint, but rather be healed"* (Hebrews 12:12-13).

> Bastards may escape the rod
>> Sunk in earthly vain delight;
> But the true-born child of God,
>> Must not, would not, if he might.[1]

For further glimpses of God the Discipliner, read: Job 5:17-18; Psalm 94:12-14; 118:5, 18; Proverbs 3:11-12; Isaiah 1:10-20; John 16:8; 2 Timothy 3:16-17; Hebrews 12:1-13.

> Come, holy Father,
> overwhelm me with Your radiant glory,
> overpower me with Your indestructible love,
> peel back the layers of self-absorption and mediocrity,
> and set my heart to swelling
> with unending praises for
> the disciplinary compassion of
> my Lord and my God,
> my Father.

Teacher/Master

He, your Teacher will no longer hide Himself, but your eyes will behold your Teacher. Your ears will hear a word behind you, "This is the way, walk in it," whenever you turn to the right or to the left. (Isaiah 30:20-21)

One who instructs and guides students with the intent of passing on knowledge and facilitating growth.

every pathway of life spreads out before us with unknown twists and turns, untested terrain, challenging mountain peaks and unexpected intrusions. We are equipped with an amazing ability to learn and adapt to these unmapped adventures. Our instincts for survival are strong. But the strongest of us is still so vulnerable, so unlearned and so in need of help and guidance.

> Dear God,
> When I lack knowledge
> Impart to me Your truth.
> When I do not know how to apply what
> I have learned to life's perplexities,
> Teach me the way to go.
> When life demands new habit patterns and lifestyles,
> Train me to be Your godly child.
> When I cannot see the path before me,
> Be my Guide, my Teacher,
> My Master.

For further glimpses of God our Teacher, read: Psalm 25:4-15; 71:17; 86:11.

Teach me Your way, O LORD,
And lead me in a level path. (Psalm 27:11)

Rabbi/Rabboni

Nathanael answered {Jesus}, "Rabbi, You are the Son of God; You are the King of Israel." (John 1:49)

Rabbi Hebrew term for teacher, implying both authority and mastership.

Rabboni

Term of address used for a teacher who is particularly revered.

Rabbis in Jesus' day gathered disciples around them to read and interpret the Law. Disciples questioned the rabbi's statements and discussed them with him at length until they understood both the intention and the application of the Law.

We can easily imagine the astonishment of the rabbis who found themselves in discussion with a twelve-year-old boy named Jesus. No child of that tender age could ask the questions He asked or give the answers He gave. But it was only a beginning. All through His life on earth Jesus gained a hearing with the common folk who recognized in His words a rare authority.

> *They were amazed at His teaching; for He was teaching them as one having authority.* (Mark 1:22)

> *Never has a man spoken the way this man speaks.* (John 7:46)

Jesus' disciples called Him "Rabbi." Nicodemus called Him "Rabbi." The multitudes whom He had fed miraculously with one boy's small lunch called Him "Rabbi."

But on two occasions, Rabbi did not suffice. Two needy people were so overwhelmed by not only His authority and wisdom, but by His mastery as well, that they used a superlative form of the word *rabbi*: Rabboni!

A blind man sitting beside a crowded city street called out into the confusion, "Jesus, Son of David, have mercy on me!"

Jesus stopped the procession that thronged around him and asked him, "What do you want me to do for you?"

Trembling with anticipation and awe in the presence of a God who cared for him personally, the man cried out, "Rabboni (My Master)! I want to regain my sight."

In his heart, blind Bartimaeus was already smitten with the greatness and authority of this heavenly Man. He had crowned Him as Master and King and was ready to cast himself totally on His mercy and follow Him for the rest of his days (see Mark 10:46-52).

On the day of His resurrection, Jesus crept up behind Mary of Magdalene in the garden and asked her why she wept. She supposed he was the gardener and poured out her anguish on him. Jesus had captured her heart, and nothing could change her passion to have Him back, alive—or dead. He was indeed her Rabbi—teacher, master, object of holy reverence and awe.

Then He spoke her name in a way that only Jesus could speak it: "Mary!"

With an instantaneous flash of recognition, she turned and gasped and uttered the only word that sprang from her heart: "Rabboni!" (see John 20:11-16).

Rabboni is
the worshipful, awestruck "Hallelujah!"
uttered in willing and overpowered response
to an authoritative,
but also benevolent, and worthy
Master Teacher.
No slavery here,
imposed by some clever despot.
Your love
and Your glory
have won my heart,
Rabboni!

For further glimpses of God as Rabbi/Master, read: Matthew 7:28-29; 13:54; 22:33; 23:7-8; Mark 1:22; 11:18; Luke 4:32; John 1:38, 49; 3:2; 4:31; 6:25.

To Ponder

What does God's use of discipline in our lives teach us about the perfection of His skills as a Master/Teacher? _____

_____

_____

_____

Pray

Dear Master, Teacher, Rabbi, _____

_____

_____

_____

Inexhaustible

Oh, how inexhaustible are God's resources and God's wisdom and God's knowledge! How impossible it is to search into His decrees or trace His footsteps! . . . For the universe owes its origin to Him, was created by Him, and has its aim and purpose in Him. (Romans 11:33, 36, Wey.)

Inexhaustible
Incapable of being exhausted or used up.

The God of the Always-More stretches out beyond us into a soundless ocean of never-ceasing resources. Like a bottomless well, He staggers our thirsty souls almost into disbelief, for the deepest, finest springs of our own holiness so quickly run dry. Our hardiest roots are nothing more than shallow runners lying barely beneath the surface.

> Is it not the beginning of perfection to lament your imperfections?[1]

We have no power in ourselves to strengthen or commend or to cause us to endure. All we have, God has given to us. All that counts for eternity, He has done through us—and at an unthinkable cost.

When Christ hung on the cross, He laid aside all the resources that could have rescued Him—the angels, the clever answers, the forceful power of His presence, the authority of heaven at His disposal. In obedience to His Father's plan, He submitted to an ordeal of inhumane suffering, which lies beyond the experience or imagination of the keenest human mind.

In history's darkest hour, heaven's crown Prince was cut off from the sustaining presence of the Father who had sent Him to the cross. For three long days and nights, Jesus allowed His reservoir to be drained.

Through this supreme sacrifice, He opened the gates of heaven's eternal reservoir to us. With eager tenderness, He invites us to come draw on His forever inexhaustible supply of strength, wisdom and every conceivable virtue needed for our sustenance and continuance in the faith.

> The Father as Source [of power] is inexhaustible riches,
> a treasure of grace made incarnate in the Word and applied by the Spirit.[2]

Our day-to-day strength begins when we come to Him in our need and exchange our depletedness for His great riches. It is maintained only as we cherish a sense of wondering awe and admiring worship for Him whose reservoir will always remain too deep for us to plumb and too inexhaustible for us to drain dry.

If ever I turn the spigot
in my parched soul
and am greeted
with the hiss of dry air passing through my empty pipes,
remind me, Lord,
that either You are teaching me some new lesson in waiting,
or I have not been careful in maintaining the pipes.
Grant to me the gracious humbleness
to take care to clear the channels to my heart
of all debris
of self-sufficiency, fretfulness, rebellion and unconfessed sin.
Teach me the art of learning from Your eternal timing.
Keep my ears open to Your voice calling me
to come moment-by-moment,
for Your generous supply

and bask in holy awe
at the ever-abundance
of Your merciful provision.
Amen.

For further glimpses of the Inexhaustible God, read: Isaiah 9:7; Lamentations 5:19; Ephesians 3:8-19.

The best return for one like me,
So wretched and so poor,
Is from His gifts to draw a plea
And ask Him still for more.[3]

Boundless

"Do I not fill the heavens and the earth?" declares the LORD.

(Jeremiah 23:24)

Boundless Having no boundaries, no limits.

With little effort, we can imagine things or living beings that are better, stronger, larger, older, more perfect than ourselves. But to imagine any being with no boundaries, no limits to his power, no end to his wisdom? That passes all the lines that define the way our human minds have been constructed.

No matter how deeply we dig into the wonders of science or philosophy or art, we can never learn enough to put a fence around God and say, "So far and no farther." In fact, the more we learn, the more we know there is to elude our grasp. An honest seeker after truth and knowledge will admit that God alone has set whatever boundaries exist.

Boundless in power and wisdom, indeed. But that is not the half. He is also boundless in character—purity, integrity, authority, justice, faithfulness, beauty. . . . The list goes on until words fail us to describe Him or we have no more mind to conceive the half of His boundless wonders.

The most treasured of all His boundless characteristics is that of everlasting love, expressed in grace. We cannot imagine any length to which He will not go to rescue a human soul. The breadth of His love is so wide, it takes in every human being ever created. We will spend eternity plumbing the depths to which He yearns to bring us in our relationship with Himself. The heights which His love enables us to scale are enough to keep us soaring for eternity.

Incredibly, His love is so vast that absolutely nothing can separate us from it: "*Neither death, nor life, nor angels, nor principalities, nor things present, nor things to come, nor powers, nor height, nor depth, nor any other created thing*" (Romans 8:38-39).

This is the God who stoops to rescue every soul who hears His voice and cries out to Him in desperate faith.

> *Heaven is My throne and the earth is My footstool. . . .*
> *But to this one I will look,*
> *To him who is humble and contrite of spirit, and who trembles*
>   *at My word.* (Isaiah 66:1-2)

For further glimpses of the Boundless God, read: 1 Kings 8:26-27; Jeremiah 31:3; 2 Timothy 2:7.

> Oh the deep, deep love of Jesus,
>   Vast, unmeasured, boundless, free!
> Rolling as a mighty ocean
>   In its fullness over me!
> Underneath me, all around me,
>   Is the current of Thy love—
> Leading onward, leading homeward,
>   To Thy glorious rest above![4]

Unwearied

*The Everlasting God, the LORD, the Creator of the ends of the
     earth
Does not become weary or tired.
His understanding is inscrutable.
He gives strength to the weary,
And to him who lacks might He increases power.
Though youths grow weary and tired,
And vigorous young men stumble badly,
Yet those who wait for the LORD
Will gain new strength;
They will mount up with wings like eagles,
They will run and not get tired,
They will walk and not become weary.* (Isaiah 40:28-31)

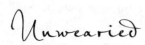 Not experiencing tiredness, weariness or fatigue.

Our abounding God never grows weary of listening to
our praises or our pain. He never tires of answering our
prayers, forgiving our sins, picking us up when we
stumble. Tirelessly, He reminds us of His commandments and
watches over us in all our ways—the good and pleasant and the
difficult and dangerous.

Yet He who knew no weariness learned it in His incarnation. In
order to show us His Father, He assumed a body that grew weary
and needed rest. He experienced the pain of living with limitations.
He took on a mind that met the challenges of learning new things.
On the way to Calvary, His back and head were bleeding. His whole
mind and body cried out for rest and food and relief from pain. He

stumbled under the load of the cross and had to let another carry it for Him. He submitted as the weak one to those who were stronger than He and let them nail and spear Him. Finally, He surrendered to the last enemy, Death, giving up His life in an act that looked like total weakness.

But the One who has learned weariness and submissive weakness stands ready to share with us His everlasting unwearyingness and strength in our time of need. Now in the heavens, His enemies defeated, His reservoir is filled again, and He is praying for us, watching out for us, carrying us over the rough terrain of our lives. For He is eternally unwearied, abounding, boundless and inexhaustible.

> O weary not of me, most blessed Comforter, who am often weary of myself. My only hope is in Thy love, which loves to the uttermost. Gird Thyself yet once again, and wash my soiled life. Thou will not quench the smoking flax nor break the bruised reed.[5]

For further glimpses of the Unwearied God, read: Psalm 121:3-4; Matthew 11:28-30; Galatians 6:9; Hebrews 2:14-18.

> If God were for a moment to "faint" or "be weary," to "slumber" or "sleep," the whole fabric of nature would fail and disappear, universal chaos would set in, all moral order would cease.[6]

To Ponder

Think on all the ways God shows His inexhaustibility and power never to grow weary. _____

_____

_____

_____

Pray

Dear Inexhaustible, Boundless and Unwearying God, _____

_____

_____

_____

_____

Very Present Help

God is our refuge and strength,
A very present help in trouble.
Therefore we will not fear, though the earth should change
And though the mountains slip into the heart of the sea;
Though its waters roar and foam,
Though the mountains quake at its swelling pride.

(Psalm 46:1-3)

Very Present Help Means of deliverance from trouble, available just when we need it.

God is our Protector! The message leaps at us from every corner of His Book. The words He uses to paint the picture and reassure our hearts are myriad—helper, keeper, defender, preserver, deliverer. . . . Metaphors abound, making the concept concrete—shield, rock, fortress, bulwark, refuge, tower, stronghold. . . .

In the margin of my Bible I found a translation of "very present help" so profound that I recite it over and over again: "abundantly available for help in tight places."[1]

- *Abundantly*: not just adequately, but over and beyond the basic or the minimum needed to sustain life. The inexhaustible God does things in an abundant way.

- *Available*: ours for the taking, not shut up in some safe deposit box with no key in our hands to unlock it. God is always more eager to provide for our deliverances than we are to receive them.

- *For help*: assistance, making a difference, deliverance from all the evil things that would otherwise destroy us.

- *In tight places*: impossible, intolerable situations where we are powerless and falling apart and cannot begin to see any wisdom to deal with them. When we reach that tight place, we are like a scared rabbit cowering at the end of a long, narrow tunnel with no exit.

God's protection is not always obvious. At times He seems not to deliver us from physical or emotional trauma, but allows us to suffer many difficulties. We are tempted to think He has forsaken us.

Like a long line of suffering saints that have gone before us, we must learn the art of clinging to God and His repeated promises. Failing to trust makes us quick to accuse God of injustice. Like Job in the famous story in the Old Testament, we struggle to defend ourselves before God, reminding Him that we are too righteous to deserve such mistreatment. Also as with Job, God must bring us to the end of all our misplaced self-confidences where we will be willing to put all our trust in Him.

Only as we learn to believe in His passionate concern for us and His inexhaustible resources to back His promises can we come to the place where Job was when he cried out, *"Though He slay me, I will hope in Him"* (Job 13:15).

> God cradles my life. . . . This is a God who surrounds
> and enfolds my every coming and going.[2]

The God of the "very present help" we worship met a lot of biblical characters in their tight places. He met Joseph in an Egyptian dungeon (see Genesis 39:14-41:57), Elijah on Mount Carmel (see 1 Kings 18), Daniel's three friends in the midst of a raging fiery furnace (see Daniel 3), the Apostle Paul beneath a pile of stones outside the city of Lystra (see Acts 14). He met His own Son in Gethsemane, sending angels to encourage Him in His darkest hour. Even though the Father forsook His Son while He carried all our sins, He was giving Him the strength to go through with the ordeal rather than putting His divine power into play to provide an escape.

Places in my life will always be tight.
Doubts will always assail when
deliverance does not come swiftly.
Dangers will always be real.
Fears will always grip my heart.
Temptations to play God will never cease to come.
But my Very Present Help
will ever—and forever—be
the mighty God:
calm, unperplexed,
in full control,
defending to the end!

For further glimpses of the Very Present Help, read: Psalm 46:1-11; 73:21-28; Isaiah 41:10; Matthew 28:19-20.

My help comes from the LORD,
Who made heaven and earth.
He will not allow your foot to slip;
He who keeps you will not slumber.
Behold, He who keeps Israel
Will neither slumber nor sleep.
The LORD is your keeper;
The LORD is your shade on your right hand.
The sun will not smite you by day,
Nor the moon by night.
The LORD will protect you from all evil;
He will keep your soul.

*The LORD will guard your going out and your coming in
From this time forth and forever.* (Psalm 121:2-8)

Tower (fortress, Stronghold)

*From the end of the earth will I cry unto thee, when my heart is
overwhelmed: lead me to the rock that is higher than I. For
thou hast been a shelter for me, and a strong tower from the enemy. I will abide in thy tabernacle for ever: I will trust in the
covert of thy wings.* (Psalm 61:2-4, KJV)

A fortified enclosure to keep us safe from our
enemies.

David could have said over and over, "God is my strong
protector in every time of need." Instead, he used powerful visual images, charged with emotional impact. As he
writes we sense ourselves running across an arid desert toward a distant tower, pursued by a whole troop of fierce armed soldiers. We
hear their weapons clanging, their voices shouting terrifying threats.
The gap between us is closing rapidly. The tower looms closer, more
distinct, firmly built of impregnable stones, and hope spurs us on.

We reach the tower to discover it is perched atop an inaccessibly
high crag of a rock. We have no choice but to stop dead in our tracks.
By now, we smell the sulfurous breath of our pursuers, feel it on the
back of our necks. In an agony of helplessness, we cry out for mercy.
Have we come so far to be destroyed at the foot of the tower that has
offered us vain hope all these weary miles?

Then, of a sudden, a golden cloud of glory encloses the tower like a
canopy. Stunned by its blinding rays, our enemies fall back. We hear

above us a hopeful creaking of hinges. The gate opens just a wee crack and a strong arm reaches out over the edge of the rock and pulls us inside. The gate closes behind us and we hear the bolt fall into place, keeping us forever safe inside with the King of Glory, our great champion.

The name of the LORD is a strong tower;
The righteous runs into it and is safe. (Proverbs 18:10)

For further glimpses of God as our Tower, Stronghold and Fortress, read: 2 Samuel 22:2-3; Psalm 46:7-11; 48:3; 59:9, 16-17; 62:1-8; 144:2; Jeremiah 16:19; Joel 3:16; Nahum 1:7.

In the tower of the protector God
We see the world from His point of view,
We feel His strong arms about us,
We learn to war against the enemies of our souls,
We hold up high a witness in the deserts of
spiritual desolation and hopelessness!

To Ponder

What kinds of protection does God offer to our endangered souls?

_____

_____

_____

_____

Pray

Dear Helper, Defender and Tower of Protection and Strength,

_____

_____

_____

Shield

You are my hiding place and my shield;
I wait for Your word. (Psalm 119:114)

Shield A piece of protective armor used to cover the warrior in the face of enemy fire.

As lovers of peace and quietness, most of us are battle shy. Any day, we'd opt to flee rather than stand and face a serious challenge, be it of an enemy or of a brother in need of confrontation. When trouble comes, we yearn to flee to God and be gathered into His secure tower. But many are the times when He leaves us in the thick of the battle and protects us by covering us with a shield. Large enough to hide our vital parts, strong enough to quench all the fiery darts of the enemy, whatever He provides will always be more than adequate.

We think of David as a strong warrior who never feared the struggle as we do. But, in Psalm 55, we detect a truly kindred spirit:

Oh, that I had wings like a dove!
I would fly away and be at rest. . . .
I would hasten to my place of refuge
From the stormy wind and tempest. (55:6, 8)

"Lord, get me out of here!" is David's cry. At the end of the psalm, after he has poured out his heart's bitter anguish and looked at the Redeemer of his soul, this once-fearful man changes his tune:

> *Cast {what He has given you} upon the LORD and He will*
> *   sustain you;*
> *He will never allow the righteous to be shaken.* (55:22)

He has heard the Protector's answer: "I will not take you out, but I *will* carry you through."

A lifetime of difficulties and treasured times in the presence of his God taught the godly man David something essential. Sometimes God is our "hiding place"—our tent on the edge of the battlefield where we can sit in safety with the Commander. On other occasions, He is our "shield"—our protector out in the thick of the battle.

> *Blessed be the LORD, my rock,*
> *Who trains my hands for war,*
> *And my fingers for battle;*
> *My lovingkindness and my fortress,*
> *My stronghold and my deliverer*
> *My shield and He in whom I take refuge.* (144:1-2)

In ancient times, a shield was a common metaphor for a deity whom the people trusted to win their battles for them. Our God will always be a symbol for us—of strength, protection, deliverance. Whether He uses a cave to hide us, a tent on the edge of the battlefield or a shield in the thick of battle, He Himself will shelter and protect us.

For further glimpses of God as our Shield, read: Genesis 15:1; Deuteronomy 33:29; Psalm 28:7; 59:11; 89:18; 91:4; Ephesians 6:16.

> We rest on Thee, our Shield and our Defender!
> We go not forth alone against the foe;

Strong in Thy strength, safe in Thy keeping tender,
We rest on Thee, and in Thy name we go.[1]

Preserver

> *O LORD God of heaven, the great and awesome God, who pre-*
> *serves the covenant and lovingkindness for those who love Him*
> *and keep His commandments.* (Nehemiah 1:5)

Preserver

One who guards, protects, attends to and keeps
us safe from danger.

All the vast resources of the limitless strength of God lie like a sword within our reach, ready to protect us in whatever circumstances may threaten us. He has promised this protection in many vivid images designed to touch our hearts and encourage our trust.

> *And they will never perish; and no one will snatch them out of*
> *My hand.* (John 10:28)

We are fragile vessels, bearing the precious treasure of God's presence in this world. We are in continual danger from a million sources of strength that exceed our own, all set on destroying both us and our treasure. But we are preserved by God's ways and words. As they take possession of our beings, we are kept in absolute safety and security—protected and cherished in His *Almighty hand.*

> *How precious is Your lovingkindness, O God!*
> *And the children of men take refuge in the shadow*
> *of Your wings.* (Psalm 36:7)

In a quiet, often-dark place, where we cannot see either what is happening or the face of our Protector, we may feel cut off and helpless. But these words remind us that we are being held near to His breast. Here He would warm us with His love and teach us the rhythms of His heart. And none of the enemies we fear can touch us in this sacred place, under the *shadow of His wings*.

> *O Savior of those who take refuge at Your right hand*
> *From those who rise up against them.*
> *Keep me as the apple of the eye.* (Psalm 17:7-8)

Like the pupil of the eye, we are exceedingly valuable to our God, and He cherishes us. In the words of one of His prophets, *"He who touches you, touches the apple of His eye"* (Zechariah 2:8). Because we are weak and vulnerable, He provides for our protection with an eye socket constructed of a strong, *protruding bony ridge* in the skull.

> *You are my hiding place;*
> *You hedge me about as with thorns,*
> *Preserving me from trouble.* (Psalm 32:7, author paraphrase)

Like a gigantic *hedge of menacing thorns*, God keeps our enemies at bay. Any person or force for evil that would take us on must first cut through that hedge. Foreboding, threatening in absolute power and skill, He stands between us and all that would destroy us.

> *"For I,"* declares the LORD, *"will be a wall of fire around her,*
> *and I will be the glory in her midst."* (Zechariah 2:5)

Inside a blazing *wall of consuming fire* He shelters us from all the forces of evil that would sap our spiritual vitality and effectiveness. But that wall is His glory, not our own.

He has dedicated Himself to our protection but He will not ride roughshod over our wills. We must choose to accept His protection and rest in the shelter His glory provides. When we let our love grow cold and our lives grow unholy and we no longer live in a righteous or godly manner, His glory departs. With the glory goes our hedge of thorns, our covering wing, our wall of fire. How vulnerable we are in a pagan world when all we have left for our protection is the sham of our own glory!

For further glimpses of God our Preserver, read: Joshua 24:17; 2 Kings 6:8-19; Job 10:12; Psalm 16:1; 37:28; Proverbs 2:6-8; Isaiah 4:5; 60:1-3, 17-18.

To Ponder

Meditate on the many ways God has protected you and what each one shows of His great attributes. _____

_____

_____

_____

Pray

Dear God, my Shield and Protector, _____

_____

_____

_____

Treasure

But store up for yourselves treasures in heaven, where neither moth nor rust destroys, and where thieves do not break in or steal; for where your treasure is, there your heart will be also.

(Matthew 6:20-21)

Treasure
What we hold dear enough to give our lives for.

How wealthy we are in earthly benefits! Lavishly loaded with visible, tangible treasures, things that gratify our senses, stimulate our intellects and buoy up our emotions, we rarely lack either for basic necessities or for extravagant pleasures. What marvelous gifts! An abundant outpouring of the generosity of our loving Father.

Yet what is the greater treasure? These good gifts with their temporary appeal to physical and emotional creature comfort? Or the sheer joy of spending an hour in the presence of the Father Himself, pouring out our souls to Him, listening to the soft whispers of His loving voice? How far do we live from the passion of the prophet Habakkuk?

Though the fig tree should not blossom
And there be no fruit on the vines,
Though the yield of the olive should fail
And the fields produce no food,
Though the flock should be cut off from the fold
And there be no cattle in the stalls,

> *Yet I will exult in the LORD,*
> *I will rejoice in the God of my salvation.*

> (Habakkuk 3:17-18)

God calls us to pant after Him as a deer running through a desolate desert pants for the infrequent tiny brook of trickling water (see Psalm 42:1-2). Or as the traveler in a thirsty land where no water is (see Psalm 63:1-2). He longs for us to seek after Him as a treasure buried in a field and long forsaken (see Matthew 13:44). He wants us to enjoy Him with the ecstasy of a lover who treasures His companionship above all else life has to offer (see Song of Solomon).

> *Whatever things were gain to me, those things I counted as loss for*
> *the sake of Christ. . . . I count all things to be loss in view of the*
> *surpassing value of knowing Christ Jesus my Lord.*

> (Philippians 3:7-8)

For further glimpses of God as our Treasure, read: Exodus 33:18; Psalm 73:25-28; Philippians 3:7-10.

Above the madness

Of this world's vast array

Of gaudy gold and silver plate

And multi-colored shreds of tinsel,

O God, You shine forth,

Paling the brightest, most splendorous

Of earthly treasures

Into tarnished insignificance.

What a treasure You are!

Prize

> *This one thing I do—forgetting everything which is past and*
> *stretching forward to what lies in front of me, with my eyes*

fixed on the goal I push on to secure the prize of God's heaven-
ward call in Christ Jesus. (Philippians 3:13-14, Wey.)

Prize A reward given at the end of a contest, a treasured acquisition.

Jesus Christ is the Way to God, the racetrack which we must
follow. And God Himself, in His absolute holiness and
shimmering majesty, will always be the prize at race's end.

The glorious truth is that He is Himself not only the Way
to blessing, but the needed blessing *itself;* not only the
Way to power but our *power;* not only the Way to victory
but our *victory;* not only the Way to sanctification but our
sanctification; not only the Way to healing but our *healing;*
not only the Way to revival but our *revival;* and so on for
everything else. *He is Himself . . . what we need.* In Him
dwells all the fullness of the Godhead bodily, as Paul says,
and we are complete in Him (Colossians 2:10).[1]

The goal He has set for us is far and high and wide and will always
elude our grasp. Our finest achievements—past, present and future—must all fall short. No matter how faithfully we serve or how
diligently we obey His leading, His highest prize still lies out ahead
of us. It is His great upward, heavenward calling in Christ Jesus.

Everything in our world pressures us to chase after lesser prizes.
These are false gods. Like the idols that lured Israel away from her
worship of Jehovah again and again, they rob us of God's prize.
Worse, they leave us mocked, with empty, defiled hands into
which God cannot place His prize.

> The world is poor because
> her fortune is buried in the sky

and all her treasure maps
    are of the earth.[2]

When God is our dearest treasure, we will ignore the false, insisting only on the true. For there is no way we can be content until we have claimed the prize—walked with Him, felt the warmth of His smile, known the glow of intimacy with Him.

> We must break the habit of treasuring our treasures, and develop the habit of treasuring the abundance of God's grace.[3]

For further glimpses of God our Prize, read: 1 Corinthians 9:24-27; 1 Timothy 2:3-7.

> *Let us fling aside every encumbrance and the sin that so readily entangles our feet. And let us run with patient endurance the race that lies before us, simply fixing our gaze upon Jesus, our Prince Leader in the faith, who will also award us the prize. He, for the sake of the joy which lay before Him, patiently endured the cross, looking with contempt upon its shame, and afterwards seated Himself—where He still sits—at the right hand of the throne of God. (Hebrews 12:1-2, Wey.)*

To Ponder

What about Jesus Christ would you consider to be your dearest treasure? _____

_____

_____

_____

Pray

Dear God, my Treasure and Prize, _____

_____

_____

_____

Precious

How precious is Your lovingkindness, O God!
And the children of men . . .
Drink their fill of the abundance of Your house.

(Psalm 36:7-8)

Precious

Heavy, valuable, costly, dear and rare.

Infinitely more precious than earth's costliest and most radiant jewels is God, our treasure and our prize. He is a source of adornment and unsullied beauty. His wealth and power are unmatched. He has royal authority and evokes a sense of holiness and worship. He is of the permanent, "transcendent, heavenly realm."[1] What could be more precious?

Like a chain of glittering jewels and precious stones, all the connecting links between us and God are also precious:

- His thoughts to us are precious;
- His word to us is precious;
- His foundations beneath us are precious;
- His blood cleansing us is precious;
- His redemption of our souls is precious;
- His music of praise in our hearts is precious.

All He plans and does and offers us is precious because every gift of God comes directly from His yearning heart. Each gift expresses the full, wide and endless range of His rare and glorious character.

O God, my God,
Tune the strings that lace my heart
To create rich chords
In sacred tribute to Yourself,
My highest and best,
Dearest and most precious
Heavenly keynote.
How precious You are!

For further glimpses of God as Precious, read: 1 Samuel 3:1; Psalm 40:5; 139:17-18; Isaiah 28:16; Philippians 3:8.

No creature can love God according to His worth.[2]

Pearl of Great Price

Again, the kingdom of heaven is like a merchant seeking fine pearls, and upon finding one pearl of great value, he went and sold all that he had and bought it. (Matthew 13:45-46)

A gem so rare and exquisite that it can command the top price in all the jewel markets of the world.

When Jesus wanted to give us a picture of the intense worth of our relationship with Himself, He told a story about a man who was an expert in pearls. He had seen thousands of them and studied their deep-down beauty. In the process, He had developed a passion for

lord, show me your glory

finding the best and most beautiful of all pearls on earth. Nothing could stop him till he found it.

And when he did, he went to the mad extreme of selling everything he owned—everything! He bankrupted himself in order to lay it all on the counter and purchase the exquisite jewel for himself.

In relaying this one-sentence story, Jesus said two things about treasures:

- You and I are a treasure so profound that no price could be too great for Him to purchase us for Himself.
- God is a treasure so dear and enviable that no price could be too great for us to pay to know Him and enjoy His intimacy.

When we have stretched our imaginations to their finite limits and ventured to peer out beyond those borders into His fathomlessness, we still must shake our heads in wonder. We shall always fail to see the pearl in ourselves as He sees it.

Nugget

And who am I? A lump, a clod?
No, less—a piece of grit,
A pebble in an unfenced field,
A chip of gravel.

And who is this
Exploring here,
With Geiger counter held
For careful searching back and forth?

His fingers brush my flint,
Unyielding, cutting.
He picks me up and turns me over,
Fingers dripping red.

His tender glance discerns my blush.
He puts me in his pocket.

Why does he rush to make me His?
At such a cost!
Me?[3]

For the LORD takes pleasure in His people;
He will beautify the afflicted ones with salvation.

(Psalm 149:4)

Marked with so high a price tag by the Creator of the finest jewels in the universe, how can we ever count any price half too high to maintain the intimacy with Him He offers in those blood-stained hands?

Christ Himself, in whom are hidden all the treasures of wisdom and knowledge. (Colossians 2:2-3)

Passion, treasures and pearls all speak of a special gift almost above all others from our Father's hand. The inner restlessness, the unquenchable thirst, the disarray of melodic strains—all of these things prod and torment us until we have found Him and cast aside all lesser gems so that we may possess Him in His fullness, beauty and glory.

Don't cling to cheap, painted fragments of glass when the pearl of great price is being offered.[4]

To Ponder

What things has God done in your life that demonstrate to you that you are His treasure? How have you demonstrated His value to you?

_____

_____

_____

_____

Pray

Dear God, my Treasure and Pearl of Great Price, _____

_____

_____

_____

Humble

Who is like the LORD our God,
Who is enthroned on high,
Who humbles Himself to behold
The things that are in heaven and in the earth?
He raises the poor from the dust
And lifts the needy from the ash heap. . . .
Praise the LORD! (Psalm 113:5-7, 9)

Humble Giving up a high estate which one deserves and condescending to a lower estate for the benefit of one who is powerless to help himself.

How absurd it seems to think that the mighty, majestic and exalted God of the universe—King of kings and Lord of lords—would humble Himself. Yet He did! In the person of Jesus Christ He redefined humility once and for all, in terms that glow with compassion and grace.

Humility, in God, means:

- creating a world, then dirtying His hands with simple clay in order to people the globe with a race of creatures He could share His heart and mind with.

- stooping down to involve Himself in the affairs of a mankind in rebellion against His laws and pleasures.

- accommodating Himself to our limited understanding in order to lift us up to His fellowship. When He speaks our language, at our level of comprehension, He must leave so much unsaid.

- forgoing what is His own by right in order to serve us in our desperate neediness.

- giving up all He has—reputation, wealth, glory, infinite wisdom, absolute holiness of character. This self-emptying expressed itself most fully when He let sinful men nail Him to a cross.

- delighting to dwell with all who are broken and contrite of heart over their sinfulness, and never tiring of shaping us into creatures that reflect His image and His glory in the universe.

Jesus Christ,
Holy Son
of the God of all Glory,
had no sins to confess,
no flaws to compensate for,
nothing to prove or cover up
or regret!
Yet
perfect, sinless, never-failing One—
our pattern of righteousness,
our guide in the way of holiness,
our protector from the darts of the evil one,
HE HUMBLED HIMSELF
to live in our messiness,
to lift us up from the rotting trash heap,
and seat us in the heavenlies
WITH HIM!
Great and humble God of the universe,

come, indwell this trembling,
broken soul,
touch with Your unlimited grace,
make of me a showplace of
Your divine humility.

For further glimpses of our Humble God, read: Psalm 34:18; Isaiah 57:15; 66:1-2; Luke 18:9-14; Philippians 2:5-11.

Meek and Lowly

Rejoice greatly, O daughter of Zion!
Shout in triumph, O daughter of Jerusalem!
Behold, your king is coming to you;
He is just and endowed with salvation,
Humble, and mounted on a donkey,
Even on a colt, the foal of a donkey. . . .
And He will speak peace to the nations;
And His dominion will be from sea to sea.

(Zechariah 9:9-10)

Meek. Retiring, submissive, chaste in spirit.

Lowly. Not exalted, of lower rank, not having an inflated opinion of one's self.

In the Scriptures, when God comes riding on a horse He comes for war and judgment, vindicating His holy name and establishing His exalted position as King. When He rides on a donkey, He comes as recognized King and bringer of peace. Warriors ride horses to conquer. Reigning kings ride donkeys to receive homage and praise from their already loyal subjects.

As His people, His bride, we come to meet Him in submissiveness and joy, and He comes as the meek and lowly Bridegroom to greet us in peace.

Meekness and weakness do not share a shred of meaning. To be lowly and submissive rather than quarrelsome and arrogant in a world that sets dominion as its goal takes a superhuman strength.

> Meekness is the strength of a wild animal tamed and under control.[1]

- Meekness may correct a brother in error, but it always speaks with restoration in view. (2 Timothy 2:25)

- Meekness is never contentious, but constantly manifests an unselfish and forgiving spirit. (Titus 3:2)

- Meekness accepts reproof and instruction with a teachable spirit. (James 1:21; 3:13)

- Meekness shuns arrogance, seeks for a lowly attitude of one's own self. (Colossians 3:12)

- Meekness is a winning way. Meek people have been called unaggressive victors. (Matthew 5:5)

> The unassertive person gains what the pushy person finally forfeits.[2]

For further glimpses of a Meek and Lowly God, read: Matthew 11:28-30; Galatians 5:22-23; Ephesians 4:2.

To Ponder

How would God define humility and meekness? _____

_____

_____

_____

_____

Pray

Dear Humble, Meek and Lowly God, _____

_____

_____

_____

Gentle

You have also given me the shield of Your salvation,
And Your right hand upholds me;
And Your gentleness makes me great. (Psalm 18:35)

Gentle: Characterized by a kindness born of redemptive compassion and grace.

Heathen gods are proud, harsh, repressive and vindictive in nature. They rule with an iron hand and motivate their subjects to faithful loyalty by means of constant fear. How different the immeasurable grace of our God! That grace, applied to our hopeless depravity, is always gentle, even when it must cause pain. Like a whispered power, it thunders irresistibly in the soul and melts away all opposition and hindrances to the exuberant bursting forth of His magnificent glory.

An old fable paints a vivid picture of this. The sun and the wind had a contest one day to see which could make a traveling man take off his jacket. The wind blew first, whipping at the tails of the jacket, determined to wrest it from the man's body. But the more it blew, the more tightly the man wrapped himself in his garment, refusing to let it go. Then the sun took his turn, shining down upon the scene. The man felt the gentle warmth and quickly removed his jacket.

No matter how difficult our God may allow our lives to become, He will always deal with us in gentleness. Even a stern voice directed to our rebellious attitudes comes from a gentle heart. He is bent on making us into an instrument of His love in a world of hate.

A bruised reed He will not break. (Isaiah 42:3)

The prophet Isaiah's picture in this pastoral metaphor softens the heart with a gentle warmth. He shows us a shepherd picking up a reed in order to play a tune on it. But the reed is bruised and crushed, incapable of producing the music he desires. If he is a human shepherd, he will most likely toss it out and continue searching for a flawless reed.

If He is God, however, He will not discard it, no matter how bruised or crushed. Rather, He works with it to heal the wounds and restore it to wholeness. He keeps massaging and trimming and re-shaping until His chosen reed yields itself to allow Him to waft His sweet music across the hillsides and into the heavenlies beyond.

God's gentleness doesn't assail us from without, but transforms us from within. He never forces instant maturity on us, but grows us up step by step. Gentleness is one of the fruits of the Holy Spirit, clustered on His living, growing branch. Such growth comes quietly and reveals the surpassing goodness of the character of God.

Have patience, O my soul,
Relax in the hand of your God.
Be still, still, still,
midst the rush and noise and clamor.
For underneath, in the subterranean channels of the heart
run deep streams of His untiring gentle love.
His gentleness will make you great.

For further glimpses of a Gentle God, read: Exodus 2:1-4:18; 1 Kings 17; Isaiah 40:1-11; 42:1-3; Matthew 11:28-30; Luke 7:36-50; Romans 2:4; Hebrews 2:14-18.

Servant

Although from the beginning He had the nature of God He did not reckon His equality with God a treasure to be tightly grasped. Nay, He stripped Himself of His glory, and took on Him the nature of a bondservant by becoming a man. . . . He humbled Himself and even stooped to die; yes, to die on a cross.

(Philippians 2:6-8, Wey.)

Servant One who gives himself/herself to meeting the needs of another.

Humility always manifests itself in an eagerness to serve, a willingness if need be, to suffer.[1]

At the most crucial moment in the earthly life of Jesus, He was facing the excruciating events of His arrest, a mock and inhumane trial and that most disgraceful of all forms of capital punishment—death by crucifixion. He knew it was the pinnacle event in the eternal purpose of His incarnation. He spent His last hours of freedom sharing Passover with His disciples, preparing both Himself and His friends for the grueling torture that lay before Him.

As they entered the room, the men were having an argument about who was going to be the greatest among them in Jesus' kingdom, which they expected Him to establish on Jewish soil very soon. Like petulant kindergartners, not a one of them was willing to do the common menial act of service—the washing of their dusty feet.

Jesus heard the petulance in their hearts even before they expressed it with their lips. He also knew the lateness of the hour in God's timetable. In light of these facts, the Son of God did something radically out of the ordinary.

> *{He} rose from table* [left His deserved comfort zone as the Master] *threw off His upper garments, and took a towel and tied it round Him* [assumed the identity of servant]. *Then He poured water into a basin* [did the whole job in the most menial way] *and proceeded to wash the feet of the disciples and to wipe them with the towel which He had put round Him* [marked them with His servant identity and left them clean, warm and dry]. (John 13:4-5, Wey.)

In this one startling act of humble, gentle servitude, the Son of God summarized a truth He had been demonstrating for thirty-three years. It was His eternal purpose to serve the creatures He had created for His glory and whom He sought to instruct to be His leaders.

At the moment when He had the most to fear from the things He knew lay ahead for Him, and when He needed the support of His disciples the most, He put His own needs behind Him. He stooped to meet their mundane needs and in so doing, He rebuked their selfishness. If they could catch the connection, He was reminding them of the revolutionary words He had spoken to them on another occasion when their desire for self-advancement had gotten out of hand:

> *You know that the rulers of the Gentiles lord it over them, and their great men exercise authority over them. Not so shall it be among you; but whoever desires to be great among you shall be your servant, and whoever desires to be first among you shall be your bondservant: just as the Son of Man came not to be served but to serve, and to give His life as the redemption-price for many.* (Matthew 20:25-28, Wey.)

The King of the universe sets a clear example for us. He serves His creatures day and night without ceasing and enjoins us *"through love {to} serve one another"* (Galatians 5:13).

Towels

He took a towel,
Not a star
Or galaxy,
But a towel.
Was it fluffy yellow,
Or gray and frayed
From common use?
I take a towel, too.
I like to keep mine
New.[2]

For further glimpses of the Servant God, read: Isaiah 42:1-4; 52:13-53:12; Mark 10:42-45; Acts 3:26; 4:27.

In submitting to death as a servant, Jesus acted like God.
Had He held onto His prerogatives as God,
Refusing to let them go,
He would have been acting like men.

To Ponder

What is the relationship between a gentle spirit and a willingness to serve the needs of others? _____

_____

_____

_____

Pray

Dear Gentle Servant-God, _____

_____

_____

_____

True Vine

> *I am the Vine—the True Vine. . . . I am the Vine, you are the branches. He who continues in me and in whom I continue bears abundant fruit, for apart from me you can do nothing.*

(John 15:1, 5, Wey.)

True Vine

Source of all genuine spiritual life, beauty and fruitfulness.

Vine and branches! No allegory is at once more earthy and more mystical. Like the grapevine that grows in our earthly soil, we have only one function. We were not planted in order to provide shade or lumber or even good firewood. God created the vine to bear fruit that we might nourish one another's spiritual hunger, bring merriment to our souls and honor the Vinedresser.

Also like the grapevine, the process involves an unhindered union of vine and branches. Both branches and fruit are produced by the free flow of sap from the vine.

> The vine may live without the branches . . . but the branches cannot live without the vine.[1]

Our arrogant human nature deceives us into fancying that we are our own vines, capable of producing God's kind of fruit on our own initiative. Like the Israelites living by the dictates of the Old Testament law, we hold ourselves accountable to keep the sap flowing, to bear the fruit of obedience to a myriad divine statutes. But serving God and doing good is strenuous activity for the unassisted human nature. Our branches wither and our best efforts produce little more than wild grapes—sour, shriveled and unnourishing.

> *Israel is a {degenerate} vine;*
> *He produces fruit for himself.* (Hosea 10:1)

How refreshingly different the picture Jesus paints for us! He is our Vine; we are His branches, united with Him in life and redemptive mission. An outgrowth of His vine-sap life, we form the connecting link through which He produces spiritual fruit.

> All over this world which He redeemed at the cost of
> His blood, Jesus the Vine is bringing forth His fruit for
> the healing of the nations—and dying sinners, tasting
> of that fruit, live.[2]

> Jesus, my Life, my Vine,
> Sacred source of divine energy
> And fruitful sweetness of the Father's nature,
> Come, claim my waking thoughts and passions
> All for Yourself.
> Teach me to abide in You
> Till new life courses freely
> And fruit hangs in lush profusion
> From this chosen branch
> Heavy with Your
> Virile presence and delight.

> Our power to do reaches exactly so far as our abiding in
> Christ and His abiding in us.[3]

For further glimpses of Jesus as the Vine, read: John 15:1-11; Galatians 2:20.

Celestial Vine! Pour Thy vital sap through all the arteries of my soul, that I may bear much fruit for Thy glory.[4]

Vinedresser

{Jehovah} had a vineyard on a fertile hill.
He dug it all around, removed its stones,
And planted it with the choicest vine.
And He built a tower in the middle of it
And also hewed out a wine vat in it;
Then He expected it to produce good grapes. (Isaiah 5:1-2)

The planter, caretaker and protector of a vineyard.

"I am the true vine," said Jesus, adding quickly, "My Father is the vinedresser" (John 15:1).

Nothing so pleased Jesus in His life on earth as to point men and women to His Father. Even now, on center stage Himself as the Vine, the source of life and growth, He wants us to know the stabilizing truth. He and His Father are in this thing together. God is both owner and caretaker of this vineyard we call the Body of Christ.

He buys and prepares the land. "He engrafts the plants into the vine, as He supports and guards the vine itself."[5]

He sorts and tests the branches and weeds out those that are not attached to the vine (Isaiah 5:3-7; John 15:2). When He sees fruit, he prunes back the excess greenery, forcing the life of the vine to produce more fruit (John 15:2).

> Pruning is a drastic process, which often looks cruel, as
> the bush is cut right back and left jagged and almost
> naked. But when the spring and summer come round
> again, there is much fruit.[6]

Few if any other domestic plants demand so much continuing
attention as the grapevine. The heavenly Vinedresser must watch
over us without a moment's slumber or a day's vacation. With inexhaustible tenderness and care,

> The same love and delight with which the Father watched
> over the beloved Son Himself, watch over every member
> of His body, every one who is in Christ Jesus.[7]

And when the fruit is gathered in and the waiting universe joins
in the celebration of harvest, all the honor and glory for a success-
ful, fruitful vineyard will go to God the Vinedresser.

For further glimpses of God the Vinedresser, read: Psalm
80:8-19; Jeremiah 31:4-6; Ezekiel 15:1-7; 19:10-14; Amos
9:13-15.

Wheat and Grapes

Bluff Point farmers sow their wheat
Close against their Concord vines,
Where purple goblets hold the wines
That rain and sunshine pour so sweet.

Bluff Point farmers see it right—
That wheat and vineyards should unite,
Since bread and wine fulfill this union
In the serving of Communion.[8]

Nurturer

Every branch in Me . . . that bears fruit, He prunes it so that it may bear more fruit. . . . You did not choose Me but I chose you, and appointed you that you would go and bear fruit, and that your fruit would remain. (John 15:2, 16)

One who feeds and cares for those in His charge with an eye to their well-being and growth.

Bearing fruit is a supernatural experience and something that comes to us and through us. There is not something we must do; there is something we must be and someone we must know.[9]

Ever so subtly, the idea of giving our lives to serve God may appeal to the arrogance in us. We seem ever to be looking for ways to be our own vine. Eager to do something that will impress God and a watching world, we may spend our whole lives striving to do all the right things, say all the right words, reach all the right people. But while we busy ourselves with much serving, our branch may wither and die. The fruit God looks for on these branches is His character incarnated in our daily lives. Oh, for the deep supernatural work that will cause people around us to turn their heads and inquire about the source of our moral strength!

The fruit of the Spirit is love, joy, peace, patience, kindness, goodness, faithfulness, gentleness, self-control.

(Galatians 5:22-23)

Such a list can only intimidate us when we have allowed ourselves to become detached from the Vine. Or if we look at it today and expect it to become an accurate description of us tomorrow, like some sort of a God-zapping wonder, it can totally devastate us.

Using the imagery of branches growing out of a living Vine under the patient care of an all-wise, all-powerful, all-loving Vinedresser, Jesus assures us that producing fruit in our lives is the miracle of a slow growth toward God.

Spurts of glory
produce no lasting fruit.
Like fireworks in the heavens,
they explode,
dazzling and filled with promise,
then vanish into the night sky,
leaving a ghostly trail
of smoke
to dissipate
upon the breeze.

God is limitless and . . . this has implications for conversion.[10]

Only an incomprehensibly vast God would care enough to:

take such imperfect, immature creatures
and pour so much of Himself into us,
risk so much, promise so much,
then experience so much delight just to see us
beginning to bear fruit on our weak little attached
branches.

For further glimpses of God the Nurturer, read: Jeremiah 31:9-14; Ezekiel 34:11-16; Micah 5:4; 1 Corinthians 3:6-9.

From eternity Christ and I were ordained for each other;
  inseparably we belong to each other;
it is God's will;
  I shall abide in Christ.[11]

To Ponder

How can we be assured that we are abiding in the Vine?

_____

_____

_____

_____

Pray

Dear Vine and Vinedresser, _____

_____

_____

_____

Lawgiver

For the LORD is our judge,
The LORD is our lawgiver,
The LORD is our king;
He will save us. (Isaiah 33:22)

Lawgiver One who creates and establishes the laws for the governing of a society.

When God spoke the world into existence and His great hands scooped clay and carved a rib to shape Adam and Eve in that faraway, long-ago garden, He had passion in His heart.

"I love you!"

He whisper-shouted into the echo chambers of space.
His consuming, irresistible message
was woven into the brilliance of the stars He flung
across the gaping heavens.
It shimmered in each field of dew-drenched grass.
It enticed human appetites in each succulent
peach hanging from a tree.
It sighed in the wind-blown majesty of each
snow-draped mountain peak.

It laughed and teased in the playful antics of
each baby creature romping through earth's
landscapes, seascapes, skyscapes. . . .
And with each fathering-forth breath of His creative Spirit,
He pronounced eternal, unbreakable laws—
Laws of structure and design,
laws of sowing and harvest,
laws of ecological arrangement,
laws of social order . . .
Each in its own unique and winsome way
reflecting the radiance of His glory,
suggesting hints of the staggering proportions
of His incomprehensibly vast character.

Like an instruction manual that comes with a new appliance, He gave to Moses on the trembling mountain of His holy presence two stone tablets. On each tablet He had engraved with His own fingers the moral instructions by which mankind, His masterpiece of created art, was designed to function and thrive and be at peace.

Along with the laws, God gave this incredible promise to His people through Moses:

> *If you will indeed obey My voice and keep My covenant, then you shall be My own possession {My special treasure} among all the peoples . . . and you shall be to Me a kingdom of priests and a holy nation.* (Exodus 19:5-6)[1]

How unimaginably high and precious are His plans for His people! But mankind, blinded by our prideful human nature, has always seemed prone to resist His laws. Incredibly, we miss the message that they represent God's best and highest good for us. We want to be free from them, so we call them repressive. As if fighting the law of gravity, we fling off these protective laws and find ourselves slaves of every sort of destructive force.

God the Lawgiver has moved all through history with a broken Father-heart. Over and over His prophets of doom and judgment stop in the midst of their strong tirades against evil to cry out with heartfelt grief and tears, "Oh Israel, if only you would listen to My voice and return to Me!"[2]

He is no tyrannical, capricious God who creates laws to make His subjects squirm in order to satisfy His own selfish whims. Ours is a redemptive God. All He does is for His own glory. And everything that brings glory to Him also redeems us and fills us fully with what He designed us to be.

The law of the LORD is perfect, restoring the soul. (Psalm 19:7)

O how I love Your law!
It is my meditation all the day. (119:97)

For further glimpses of God the Lawgiver, read: Psalm 37:31; 40:8; 119 (this entire psalm is filled with references to God's Law, which is sometimes called His word, commandments, precepts, way, testimony, ordinances, judgments or promises); Isaiah 51:4-7; James 1:23-25; 4:12.

Let God's LAW remind us that

Love

Always

Wins!

Judge

When I select an appointed time,
It is I who judge with equity.
The earth and all who dwell in it melt;
It is I who have firmly set its pillars.
I said to the boastful, "Do not boast,"

And to the wicked, "Do not lift up the horn; . . .
Do not speak with insolent pride."
For not from the east, nor from the west,
Nor from the desert comes exaltation;
But God is the Judge;
He puts down one and exalts another. (Psalm 75:2-7)

Judge One who enforces the laws created by the law-giver.

Learning the borders of God's laws involves our minds. Recognizing their beauty and benefit is a matter of the heart. Keeping them engages us in a lifelong struggle against our sinful human natures.

Strive as we may, not a one of us, no matter how godly or devout, can possibly live in such perfect obedience to the Law that we never need to stand before the Judge. When we stand there, looking into His eyes, what do we see? The Lawgiver Himself who knows the fullest intent of His own laws and all the minutest details of our lives that have crossed over the line into disobedience? Our Creator who sees the deepest intents of our hearts and knows fully why we transgressed His commandments? Our Confidant and Just Deliverer, who can judge all wrongs against us with perfect accuracy and mete out a justice that none can question? The Judge of all the earth is all of these things. We can be sure that He will always do what is right.

We may not see the judgment. The wrongs we suffer may seem to go unpunished. The little ways we break God's laws, the hidden motives of our hearts, may seem to be overlooked. But His eye misses nothing. His wisdom, justice and mercy will conspire to address all the issues. He will set all things straight, either in this life or the next.

> God has but to show himself, and the good cause wins
> the day. He comes, he sees, he conquers![3]

In Revelation 5, all heaven awaits the arrival of the supreme Judge, the Lion of the Tribe of Judah, who alone is worthy to open the seals of the book and unleash God's judgment upon the earth. When He steps forward, He comes in the form of a "Lamb . . . as if slain" (5:6).

Never before has the universe seen the like!

> The God who wrote the laws
> and has the power to obliterate all who break them
> stands before a waiting world
> with a broken heart open for us all to see,
> gaping wounds in His hands and feet,
> tears bathing His fevered cheeks,
> thorns crowning His royal head,
> blood matting His hair
> and trickling over His emaciated brow.
> This is the Judge of all the earth
> before whom we present our guilty plea
> and from whom we beg for mercy.

For further glimpses of God the Judge, read: Genesis 18:25; Psalm 7:11; 35:24; 58:11; 94:2; 110:5-7; Jeremiah 11:20; Hebrews 10:30; Revelation 19:11; 20:11-15.

> *The Lord . . . is patient toward you, not wishing for any to perish but for all to come to repentance.* (2 Peter 3:9)

To Ponder

Consider the vast, choreographed purposes for the intricate net-work of God's laws of nature and morality. _____

_____

_____

_____

Pray

Dear All-Wise Lawgiver and Just Judge, _____

_____

_____

_____

Consuming fire

The glory of the LORD rested on Mount Sinai. . . . And to the eyes of the sons of Israel the appearance of the glory of the LORD was like a consuming fire on the mountain top.

(Exodus 24:16-17)

Remember the day you stood before the LORD your God at Horeb . . . and the mountain burned with fire to the very heart of the heavens: darkness, cloud and thick gloom.

(Deuteronomy 4:10-11)

God's probing Spirit that shows us the extent of His holiness and the true extent to which we have broken His laws.

onsuming fire set a wall around Mount Sinai when God placed the Law in Moses' hands. In clear, visible form, God let us know that He is apart from us, other than us, holy and far above us all. His expectations of us will always challenge our natural inclinations and our comfort zones. His holiness and His glory will always terrify us, hampered as we are by these sinful natures.

His consuming fire also burns away the impurities of our lives, delivering us step by step and bit by bit from the sin that separates us from His presence.

Who can endure the day of His coming? And who can stand when He appears? For He is like a refiner's fire and like fuller's soap. He will sit as a smelter and purifier of silver, and He will purify the sons of Levi and refine them like gold and silver, so that they may present to the LORD offerings in righteousness. (Malachi 3:2-3)

The hotter the fire, the purer the gold.[1]

Those who disregard the laws of God and go on their own way have reason to fear His just judgment—"*the fury of a fire which before long will devour the enemies of the truth*" (Hebrews 10:27, Wey.). Those who weep over their sins and repent of them have recourse in the mercy of God.

For further glimpses of God the Consuming Fire, read: Exodus 24:12-18; Deuteronomy 4:9-24; Psalm 97:1-6; Isaiah 30:27, 30; 33:14-16.

Grant me never to lose sight of
    the exceeding sinfulness of sin,
    the exceeding righteousness of salvation,
    the exceeding glory of Christ,
    the exceeding beauty of holiness,
    the exceeding wonder of grace.[2]

Examiner

*I, the LORD, search the heart,
I test the mind.* (Jeremiah 17:10)

One who helps us to see our deepest motivations and the secret places of our spirits and shows us who we really are in the light of God's moral laws.

*G*od's consuming fire can be devastating. If we were to read through the Old Testament not knowing that the New was coming, we should likely see very little more than the fire and pain. But, to the eye trained or desperate to see it, hope does break through the clouds and smoke in shafts of brilliant light, promising something better to come.

God must examine us and reveal the darkness in our own selves before we are ready for the rays of hope, the message of redemption. Jesus' disciples had to see the clouds within themselves to be ready for the light to come from the cross.

The night before He offered Himself up as a sacrifice for our sins, He ate with His disciples. The Judge with the broken heart, He spoke heavy words none of them ever dreamt they would hear: *"In solemn truth I tell you that one of you will betray me"* (Matthew 26:21, Wey.).

A chorus of gasps around the candlelit room was followed quickly by an outburst of identical questions: *"Lord, is it I?"*

These men had walked with Him long enough and disappointed Him often enough that they were learning to mistrust what was in their own hearts. Spontaneously they opened up their fragile inner beings and asked Him to examine them. Their request echoed the words of the familiar psalm they all knew so well:

> *Search me, O God, and know my heart;*
> *Try me and know my anxious thoughts;*
> *And see if there be any hurtful way in me,*
> *And lead me in the everlasting way.* (Psalm 139:23-24)

Then Jesus passed the broken bread and the ritual cup to them before they went out together into the night with all its unprecedented events. Years later, when the Apostle Paul instructed the church at Corinth in the sacrament of bread and cup that would remind them of that holy night, he added, *"But a man must examine him-*

self, and in so doing he is to eat of the bread and drink of the cup" (1 Corinthians 11:28).

When examining ourselves, we must rely on Him to enlighten us, to show us our areas of weakness and failure. How subtle a danger lies in introspective, self-directed searching of lists of sins to show us the nature of our unrighteousness. Such probing of our own depths may obscure the real hidden motives for many of our actions, thoughts and words. Or it may never lead us up and beyond our sin to a real deliverance. Rather, the end of much self-focused meditation on sin is oppressive guilt and depression.

Inviting God Himself to search our hearts for us opens wondrous doors to wholeness. We begin by looking at His character, giving ourselves to meditation on the great wideness and beauty of who He is. As we beg Him to search us out, we are startled, dazzled by the glorious rays of His holiness. Then, quietly, almost imperceptibly at first, a clear, piercing light begins to shine on our own imperfect selves. God never throws a list of sins at our trembling hearts or points a condemning finger at our bowed heads. Rather, one by one, He gives us a consciousness of those things that are out of line with His godly expectations—the things He longs to change.

In a new and irresistible way, His Spirit draws us upward to Him and leads us to worship Him in the beauty of His holiness. With eyes still focused on Him, a confession of our sinfulness tumbles out of broken hearts and we experience a healing and revival of our spirits.

No examination but His examination can redeem us from ourselves.

For further glimpses of the Examining God, read: Psalm 7:9-11; 26:2; Proverbs 17:3; 1 Thessalonians 2:4.

> *"This is the covenant which I will make with the house of Israel after those days," declares the LORD, "I will put My law within them and on their heart I will write it; and I will be their God, and they shall be My people."* (Jeremiah 31:33)

To Ponder

Think much on the nature of His holiness and ask Him to show you whatever it is He wants you to see as a result. _____

_____

_____

_____

Pray

Dear Examining God, Consuming Fire, _____

_____

_____

_____

Merciful/Compassionate

The LORD is gracious and merciful;
Slow to anger and great in lovingkindness.
The LORD is good to all,
And His mercies are over all His works. (Psalm 145:8-9)

Mercy/Compassion

A feeling of pity for and desire to help a person in need, especially one who does not deserve it.

The prospect of standing before the Judge at the gate of heaven can be terrifying. However, this Judge is like none other in the universe: He is absolutely holy in character and demanding as our Lawgiver, but He is also a God of infinite mercy.

> His grandeur hinders not his clemency; though his throne be high, his bowels are tender.[1]

In one breath, this compassionate God *"is a consuming fire, a jealous God"* (Deuteronomy 4:24), demanding the unadulterated love of His people. He promises to send judgment if they break covenant with Him. But in the next breath, He assures them that when they repent and seek after Him with their whole hearts, He will take them back.

> *For the LORD your God is a compassionate God; He will not fail you nor destroy you nor forget the covenant with your fathers which He swore to them.* (Deuteronomy 4:31)

God is compassionate with His creatures, whom He loves.

Therefore the LORD longs to be gracious to you,
And therefore He waits on high to have compassion on you.
For the LORD is a God of justice;
How blessed are all those who long for Him. . . .
He will surely be gracious to you at the sound of your cry.

(Isaiah 30:18-19)

Jesus was compassion incarnate as He walked the dusty roads of Galilee, Judea and Samaria. He was ever looking out for the needs of the people that thronged about Him. More than once we read that He saw the multitudes and felt compassion on them as sheep without a shepherd. As if directed by impulse, He reached out to them with that compassion. He healed the sick; He fed the hungry. He taught His disciples to pray for them and to minister to them with messages of the good news that He had come to be their Savior (see Matthew 9:36-38; 14:14; 15:32-39).

In that wonderful parable of the prodigal son, Jesus showed us the lengths to which His heart will go in search of His lost sons and daughters. The faithful father of the wayward son waited daily in anticipation of the boy's return until at last he lifted up his eyes and saw him coming over the horizon. A godly compassion drove him out to meet the prodigal, embrace him and transform him from a tattered swineherd into a royal son (Luke 15:11-32).

Who is a God like You, who pardons iniquity
And passes over the rebellious act of the remnant of
*   His possession?*
He does not retain His anger forever,
Because He delights in unchanging love.
He will again have compassion on us;
He will tread our iniquities under foot.
Yes, You will cast all their sins
Into the depths of the sea. (Micah 7:18-19)

For further glimpses of the Compassionate/Merciful God, read: (in some versions, the word *mercy* is translated *loving-kindness*) Psalm 86:5; 103:1-18; 116:5; 119:77; Jeremiah 31:20; Lamentations 3:32; Hosea 11; Matthew 5:7; Romans 9:15; Colossians 3:12-14.

> *It is of the LORD's mercies that we are not consumed, because his compassions fail not. They are new every morning: great is thy faithfulness.* (Lamentations 3:22-23, KJV)

> *Mercy triumphs over judgment.* (James 2:13)

Gracious

> *God, being rich in mercy, because of His great love with which He loved us, even when we were dead in our transgressions, made us alive together with Christ (by grace you have been saved).* (Ephesians 2:4-5)

Grace God's lavish favor poured out on His human creatures whose sin and rebellion cause them to deserve His judgment.

God's grace represents the greatest passion of His heart to do us good and give us His heavenly joy. He yearns over us with a deeply inscribed longing that grows from the innermost core of who He is.

God's highest glory consists in His securing our deepest happiness. What a God is this![2]

His deep motivations of tenderness and passion to bless us go beyond the fondest emotions we humans are capable of. Parenthood brings us as close as we can ever come, but even this analogy falls short—far short.

> Grace is the pleasure of God to magnify the worth of God by giving sinners the right and power to delight in God without obscuring the glory of God.[3]

We begin to catch a glimpse of grace from our side only when we come to fathom the depths of our sin and the offense that our rebelliousness and prideful self-efforts offer the holiness of God. Then His grace grows ever deeper, wider and more profound in our eyes.

> Grace being what it is, is always drawn by need.[4]

The more we meditate on the extent to which His grace has gone to make us right with Him as holy and transcendent Lawgiver, the flatter we fall on our faces before Him. Those old, familiar words, often sung as a popular folk song, take on new meaning in light of deeper meditation on the mercy and grace of God:

> Amazing grace, how sweet the sound
>   That saved a wretch like me!
> I once was lost, but now am found—-
>   Was blind, but now I see.[5]

Grace!
Totally incomprehensible!
Wonder beyond all wonders!
Everlasting source of rapturous joy!
Reaching earthward
Into blind alleyways of our defiled darkness,
Radiant beams of heaven's dazzling glory
Transform our hopeless iciness
Into inexplicable warmth!

For further glimpses of the God of Grace, read: Exodus 33:12-19; 34:6; Nehemiah 9:31; Psalm 116:5; 145:8-9; Isaiah

30:18-21; Jeremiah 31:20; John 1:16; 2 Corinthians 12:9; Ephesians 2:8-9; James 4:6; 2 Peter 3:18.

> Grace is a stubborn, lovely flower that picks the harshest deserts in which to bloom.[6]

To Ponder

How deep and how wide must grace flow in order to cover all the need we bring to God? _____

_____

_____

_____

Pray

Dear Gracious God, _____

_____

_____

_____

forgiving/Pardoning

The LORD, the LORD God, compassionate and gracious, slow to anger, and abounding in lovingkindness and truth; who keeps lovingkindness for thousands, who forgives iniquity, transgression and sin. (Exodus 34:6-7)

forgive
To release an offending debtor from guilt.

Pardon
To free a convicted offender from punishment.

The God of infinite mercy quivers with anticipation
At His judgment bar,
Eager to absolve the guilty defendant of all:
Iniquity—the filth of a contaminated nature
Transgression—actions that trample the Law underfoot
Sin—every lingering inclination
that violates His Glorious Holiness.

Seek the LORD while He may be found;
Call upon Him while He is near.
Let the wicked forsake his way
And the unrighteous man his thoughts;
And let him return to the LORD,
And He will have compassion on him,

And to our God,
For He will abundantly pardon.
"For My thoughts are not your thoughts,
Nor are your ways My ways," declares the LORD.

(Isaiah 55:6-8)

Our wicked deeds need forgiveness and pardon. But there is more to it than that. Our basic moral nature is sinful. We do not share the Lord's thoughts or His ways. Our motivations, our thought patterns are all defiled by the sinful nature we inherited from Adam and Eve. Nothing in us can ever measure up to His standards of righteousness.

Oh, the awful, nagging pain
That wrenches my soul when I see the ugliness of my sin!
Arrogant rebellions,
Self-serving acts of cowardice,
Flagrant misrepresentations of truth
All mix together with the deeper, subtler offenses:
Thoughtless words or deeds,
Visions of personal grandeur,
Flesh-motivated busyness,
Faithless fears and worries.
Abundant sin calls for abundant pardon.
Show me, great pardoning God,
How abundant is my need!

I want to remember that I am a sinner because it keeps
before me my constant debt to the Forgiver.[1]

For further glimpses of a Forgiving God, read: Numbers 14:19; Nehemiah 9:17; Psalm 32; 86:5; 130:3-4; Micah 7:18; Matthew 26:28; Acts 10:43; Colossians 2:13.

O God of mercy, grace and glory,
You stand far more ready to forgive

Than I to be forgiven.
Bless the LORD, O my soul!

Cleansing

Be gracious to me, O God, according to Your lovingkindness. . . .
Wash me thoroughly from my iniquity
And cleanse me from my sin.

Purify me with hyssop, and I shall be clean;
Wash me, and I shall be whiter than snow.

Create in me a clean heart, O God,
And renew a steadfast spirit within me.

(Psalm 51:1-2, 7, 10)

Cleanse

To rid of all impurity and to make clean and pure.

When David prayed this prayer, he was guilty of the terrible sins of lust, adultery and murder. To believe that God would forgive such awfulness stretches our confidence even in His forgiveness. Surely these sins would leave a perpetual blot on David's character that could never be cleansed! How could such a sinner ever come to a holy God expecting to be made clean?

Our humanity draws the borders of justice in ways that would effectively shut out grace. In our sinfulness and self-centeredness, we do not know how to set a guilty person free. Because God is both holy and compassionate, His grace will always push the borders of

197

justice beyond our comprehension. David had walked with God long enough and closely enough that, once he recognized and confessed his sin, he had no doubt God would both forgive and cleanse. He knew the key:

> *The sacrifices of God are a broken spirit;*
> *A broken and a contrite heart, O God, You will not despise.*
>
> (51:17)

Over and over, throughout Scripture, God promises a forgiveness that reconciles us with Him. We can be right with Him, and know He will not hold our sin against us any longer. But He will always go farther. What He forgives, He totally removes and casts into the depths of an undrainable sea.

> *As far as the east is from the west,*
> *So far has He removed our transgressions from us.*
> *Just as a father has compassion on his children,*
> *So the LORD has compassion on those who fear Him.*
> *For He Himself knows our frame;*
> *He is mindful that we are but dust.* (103:12-14)

While we may have to live the rest of our lives with certain earthly consequences for our sins, so far as our fellowship with God is concerned, He is ready to hold us once again close to His heart and show us fresh glimpses of His glory. In fact, the joy we experience when we have been contaminated by evil and then cleansed is one of the deepest joys possible.

> *How blessed is he whose transgression is forgiven,*
> *Whose sin is covered!* (32:1)

Forgiveness and cleansing strengthen our trust in God by showing us how desperately we need Him. They grant us access into the presence of the God who demands that we come with *"clean hands and a pure heart"* (24:4). They can also give us increased credibility with unbelieving sinners who may feel they have failed too greatly to come to God, helping us to show unbelievers that no matter how great the sin, the Lord will forgive those who confess their sins with a contrite and penitent heart.

If we confess our sins, he is faithful and just to forgive us our sins, and to cleanse us from all unrighteousness.

(1 John 1:9, KJV)

For further glimpses of a Cleansing God, read: Psalm 32:1-5; 51:1-17; Isaiah 1:16-18; Jeremiah 33:8; Ezekiel 36:25; 37:23; Ephesians 5:26-27; Revelation 7:14; 22:14.

You offer us forgiveness, Lord Jesus,
Not because You love us
with grandfatherlike sentimental indulgence.
Nay, God of uncompromising holiness,
but rather because You paid sin's horrendous price
You are free to gather us up
in Your nail-scarred hands
and present us
in white robes
before the eternal Father's throne.
Amen! Alleluia!

To Ponder

What makes the heart of God yearn to forgive our sins? _____

_____

_____

_____

_____

Pray

Dear Forgiving and Cleansing God, _____

_____

_____

_____

friend

Greater love has no one than this, that one lay down his life for his friends. You are My friends if you do what I command you. No longer do I call you slaves, for the slave does not know what his master is doing; but I have called you friends, for all things that I have heard from My Father I have made known to you.

(John 15:13-15)

friend   A person we love, enjoy, care about and trust.

We long for a few people who understand us, who genuinely care for us, people to whom we can trust our hearts and with whom we can form deep emotional bonds. In short, we want at least a few souls on this planet to whom we really matter.[1]

God made us this way—to need each other, enjoy each other, enrich each other, stick by each other, help each other through life's tough places. Through the process of these friendships He shows us Himself. The Godhead is a friendship—Father, Son and Holy Spirit communing together, working together for their mutual glory in the universe and beyond, throughout the cosmos.

God created human beings, in His image, to be His friends—re-cipients of the wealth of His loving-kindness and loyal devotees, sharing His passion and purpose to extol His glory within the con-fines of the universe that borders our lives.

> I am gripped by a thought I can scarcely grasp. . . . It seems so utterly unbelievable. Yet it is eternally true. . . . God, the Creator and Ruler of the universe, chose me to be His child and to be His *friend*.[2]

Great condescending God, my Friend,
You love at all times,
You stand by me in adversity,
You stick closer than a brother,
You talk to me face-to-face and heart-to-heart,
And when You afflict me with wounds
You design them to bring me new strength.
You are my beloved,
You befriend sinners and criminals,
You laid down Your life
Once for all
For the mean and lowly likes of me.
What a Friend indeed!

For further glimpses of God our Friend, read: Exodus 33:11; 2 Chronicles 20:7; Proverbs 17:17: 18:24; Song of Solomon 5:16; Isaiah 41:8; Matthew 11:19; John 11:11; 15:13-15.

Companion

> *Lo, I am with you always, even to the end of the age.*

(Matthew 28:20)

Companion

A person who stays with you, does things with you, shares your life and goals.

When all of life grows dark and cold
   and we feel encroaching spear-point pressure
from the enemies of God's Spirit on every side,
   we hear His voice and pause to let it seep
into the rubbed-raw edges of our souls:
   "I will be with you;
I will not forsake you.
   Be strong and courageous."
Uplifted by fresh vigor,
   we feel the gloom turn into light,
calm peace replace the fright,
   an overflowing of delight.

The nearness of my God is . . . good. (Psalm 73:28)

God created us to walk in pairs, in groups, in families. And no matter what the twisting, obscuring and cluttering of the way that lies before us, we need never walk it alone. Even when all human companionship is gone, we are not alone! God has committed Himself to be our constant, faithful, intimate Companion. We can safely follow in the steps of a long line of men and women who have known the thrill and the wonder, the miracle and the glory of His companionship.

- Enoch and Noah walked with God.

- Moses talked with God face-to-face, as with a friend.

- Caleb and Joshua trusted God to be with them as they prepared to enter the hostile land of Canaan at His command.

- David played his harp and flute to God in the sheep pasture and grew to know Him as his Shepherd/Friend.

- Elijah sought out God in the wilderness and met Him in the small stillness of a cave following the rain and thunder.

- Mary of Magdalene followed her Lord all the way to the garden tomb, where He broke upon her grieving loneliness with His resurrected presence.

- Paul walked with God on all the roads of Rome, sailed with Him over unfriendly seas, sat with Him chained to guards in a Roman prison.

- John, banished to exile on the Isle of Patmos, saw unparalleled visions of the King of kings and Lord of lords, the eternal Lamb of God.

Nothing seems to bring more pleasure to the heart of the eternal God than to walk with us in a sweet companionship where He can meet our needs and draw us ever closer and deeper into the mysteries of His grace and glory.

For further glimpses of God our Companion, read: Genesis 5:22-24; 6:9; Exodus 33:14-16; Leviticus 26:11-12; Deuteronomy 31:6-8; Joshua 1:5-9; Psalm 23:1-4; Isaiah 41:10; 43:2-5; John 14:23.

Walk Companion

Be with me when the way lies clear
Or when the shadows tempt to fear,
When in the light the trail I trace
Or when I cannot see Your face.

When fearful in a foreign land
or when I feel You squeeze my hand
There is no map, no unknown place,
for every walk is through Your grace.[3]

Loyal (God of Loving-kindness)[4]

Give thanks to the LORD, for He is good,
For His {loyal love} is everlasting.
Give thanks to the God of gods,
For His {loyal love} is everlasting.
Give thanks to the Lord of lords,
For His {loyal love} is everlasting.

Give thanks to the God of heaven,
For His {loyal love} is everlasting. (Psalm 136:1-3, 26)

Loyal Love God's love for us based on (1) His covenant to love us forever and (2) His passionate longing to do us good.

The love that makes God our Friend and our Companion is rooted in His eternal, unchanging and absolutely faithful character. Never can it grow lukewarm or be diluted or destroyed. We can always count on it to be as strong today as it was the day we were born! He will never love us less than He did the day He bore our sins in His nail-torn body on the cross.

Have you ever found Psalm 136 tedious to read with all its repetition? Does the recurring phrase "for His {loyal love} is everlasting" seem to interrupt the flow of the mini-narratives the psalmist is trying to communicate?

Look again.

The real flow is not the narratives, but the passionate poetic litany of perpetual, irrepressible praise to a loyal God. The psalmist's mind is absolutely staggered by the wonder that a holy God could love His imperfect, earthbound creatures enough to create for us a stable world, deliver us from oppression and provide for all our needs!

Rearrange the psalm on the page, and think of it this way: The recurring line is a bold message, in the center of the page, written in golden calligraphic letters with endless interweaving flourishes:

His {loyal love} is everlasting!

All the other lines are penned from a palette full of brilliant colors, like radiating rays, on an elegant matting that sets off the message, giving it richness and depth. In its never-tiring, single-minded theme it reminds us that nothing—absolutely nothing—can bring cohesion and purpose to our lives like God's loyal love. Everything can be seen through the eyes of faith to have purpose because we can trust that His love is forever loyal.

> *I have loved you with an everlasting love;*
> *Therefore I have drawn you with {loyal love.}*

(Jeremiah 31:3)

Our God is too wise and too powerful to leave us in the lurch, too loyal to forsake us. His loyal love is the prompting impetus, the fountainhead, the deep bubbling spring of His commitment to us and all that is best for us.

"Many waters cannot quench love" (Song of Solomon 8:7). Nor can the eons, nor even our own willful scorn of that love. He lavishes it upon us and we grow strong as we remind ourselves of it day by day and hour by hour.

For further glimpses of a Loyal God, read: Exodus 34:6-7; Deuteronomy 10:15; Psalm 59:10, 16-17; 86:15; 144:1-2; Jeremiah 31:3-5, 10-14; Micah 7:18.

> Loved with everlasting love,
>   Led by grace that love to know;
> Spirit, breathing from above,

Thou hast taught me it is so!
Oh, this full and perfect peace!
Oh, this transport all divine!
In a love which cannot cease,
I am His and He is mine.[5]

To Ponder

Thank God for every way you can think of in which He has shown
His friendship and loyal love to you. _____

_____

_____

_____

Pray

Dear God, my Loyal Friend and Companion, _____

_____

_____

_____

Omnipotent

Jesus . . . came near and said to them, "All power in Heaven and over the earth has been given to me. Go therefore and make disciples of all the nations; baptize them into the name of the Father, and of the Son, and of the Holy Spirit; and teach them to obey every command which I have given you. And remember, I am with you always, day by day, until the Close of the Age."

(Matthew 28:18-20, Wey.)

Omnipotent

Having absolute ability and strength for all things combined with the authority to do them.

Our personal, intimate God is also the power above all other powers in the universe and the universes beyond. No other power can begin to challenge, threaten or frighten God. None can annul His power or the authority on which it is based. He alone is God and will always be God. He is the ultimate absolute of every attribute that He embodies, which means that He sets the standards and the limits for all things, including power! His all-inclusive, all-pervasive power can never know defeat of any kind, from any source or combination of sources.

Now the salvation, and the power, and the kingdom of our God and the authority of His Christ have come.

(Revelation 12:10)

When we have stood beside a Niagara or Victoria Falls and gazed and listened and felt the trembling of their thunder and foam and marveled at a power beyond our comprehension; when we have felt or seen the destructive force of a hurricane, an earthquake, a flooding river or an enormous landslide gaining momentum; when we have crouched, fear-stricken, on the edge of a landscape lit up and sliced by a hundred bolts of forked lightning; when we have witnessed a herd of elephants rampaging across an African savanna or the fury of a lion loosed on its antelope prey; when we have watched a cancerous child made whole or a heart-transplant patient breathing new life; all this is less than the slightest wiggle of God's weakest little finger lifted in some microscopic corner of this infinitesimally tiny cosmic speck we call earth!

> *Yours, O LORD, is the greatness and the power and the glory and the victory and the majesty, indeed everything that is in the heavens and the earth; Yours is the dominion, O LORD, and You exalt Yourself as head over all.* (1 Chronicles 29:11)

What wonder! What inexpressible amazement! What exhilarating joy to contemplate, in the depths of my spirit, that:

- All things are created and sustained "by the word of His power" (Hebrews 1:3).
- "No purpose of [His] can be thwarted" (Job 42:2).
- His "hand is not so short that it cannot save; nor is His ear so dull that it cannot hear" (Isaiah 59:1).
- The virgin birth of Jesus Christ was the handiwork of the "power of the Most High" (Luke 1:35).
- The Gospel of Christ "is the power of God for salvation" (Romans 1:16).
- Today the Son, our Savior, sits "AT THE RIGHT HAND OF POWER" (Mark 14:62).

- His "power is perfected in [my] weakness" (2 Corinthians 12:9).
- We can know "the surpassing greatness of His power toward us who believe" (Ephesians 1:19).
- One day our Redeemer will come "IN CLOUDS with great power and glory" (Mark 13:26).

All hail the power of Jesus' name!
Let angels prostrate fall. . . .
Bring forth the royal diadem,
And crown Him Lord of all.[1]

For further glimpses of an Omnipotent God, read: Genesis 18:14; Exodus 15:6; Numbers 11:23; Job 42:2; Isaiah 50:2; Jeremiah 32:17-19; Philippians 3:21; Revelation 12:10.

Arm

You have a strong arm;
Your hand is mighty, Your right hand is exalted.

(Psalm 89:13)

Arm Metaphor for force, help, might, power and strength.

The God with the strong and holy arm is powerful enough to be victorious over every force of evil that threatens us, or His cause, in any way. With this arm, He undergirds us, cradles us, holds us and sustains us in all hostile places. He judges and rules from the heavenlies by the show of that arm of both strength and irresistible authority.

Wonder of wonders, it was in the process of hanging on a cross, His physical arms pinned and rendered powerless, that He revealed the strength of His mighty spiritual arm (see Isaiah 53:1). No mere man would have willingly submitted himself to the cruel indignities and apparent defeat of the cross. Such suffering, which He could have escaped had He but called on His Father to send His legions of rescuing angels, was evidence of a superhuman strength. It showed, as nothing else could have, that His arm is powerful to save and His heart eager to redeem.

For further glimpses of the powerful Arm of God, read: Exodus 6:6; Psalm 44:3; 98:1; Isaiah 40:10; 51:5; 53:1.

Like a shepherd He will tend His flock,
In His arm He will gather the lambs
And carry them in His bosom;
He will gently lead the nursing ewes. (Isaiah 40:11)

Strengthener

Ascribe strength to God;
His majesty is over Israel
And His strength is in the skies.
O God, You are awesome from Your sanctuary.
The God of Israel Himself gives strength
and power to the people.
Blessed be God! (Psalm 68:34-35)

Strengthener

One who makes us strong and able to handle life's challenges.

ow often we feel our hearts failing! How keenly we sense our weakness! How we tremble before our enemies! How we moan because we cannot lift so much as one finger in our own deliverance!

Let us come then and lift our impotent hands Godward. Rejoice! For He offers us an adequacy of strength that takes our breath away. His strength is:

- Inexhaustible, without limit, without boundaries, without end. All limits to His power are imposed by our unwillingness to yield to His wisdom, timing and control.

  God is the strength of my heart and my portion forever.

  (Psalm 73:26)

- Invisible, filling and empowering us in all those deeply hidden springs of life and energy and wisdom.

  How blessed is the man whose strength is in You,
  In whose heart are the highways to Zion! . . .
  They go from strength to strength. (Psalm 84:5, 7)

- Infallible: God will *never* let us down, disappoint us or turn against us. When we do not experience the strength we think we need, or when it doesn't come in the manner in which we expect it, then we can know we have simply not understood His purposes or yielded to them.

  My grace is sufficient for you, for power is perfected in weakness. (2 Corinthians 12:9)

- Invincible, above and beyond all others, subjecting all others to itself and its working.

The LORD is the strength of my life; of whom shall I be afraid? (Psalm 27:1, KJV)

- Indwelling: He fills and empowers us from within. What a miracle of grace that He would take up residence in our beings and pour His divine strength through our weakness!

Be strong in the Lord and in the strength of His might.

(Ephesians 6:10)

- Immutable: It cannot change or be dissipated or lessened or retracted from us. God only withdraws His power and strength when we rebel against Him, when we refuse to follow His guidelines for obtaining it or when we trust in our own strength instead of His.

Since the creation of the world . . . His eternal power and divine nature, have been clearly seen. (Romans 1:20)

For further glimpses of a Strengthening God, read: Psalm 18:32; 29:11; 31:2, 4; 43:2; 59:16-17; 68:28, 34-35; Isaiah 40:31.

To Ponder

Try to imagine a challenge to God's power that He could not meet. How does the thought that nothing can challenge God's power encourage your heart to face the challenges of your day?

_____

_____

_____

_____

Pray

Dear God of Power and Strength, _____

_____

_____

_____

Life

All things came into being through Him, and apart from Him nothing came into being. . . . In Him was life, and the life was the Light of men. (John 1:3-4)

Gift of God that connects our spirits with His, enabling us to have fellowship with Him and grow more and more like Him.

ife is the most precious of all gifts. It is priceless!
God Himself is our life. He is the goal, the origin, the focus, the center and the spring of all life, at every level, in every area, in all its dimensions. He gives us purpose and reason to live and enjoy life through the days. When all our efforts seem to be thwarted or unappreciated; when we cannot see anything good to come from our visions; when we are so confused by a dozen choices—all looking bad—that we want to hide in a deep cave and pull the ground in over us; when our health is broken, our fortune is smashed, our possessions are taken from us, our dearest friends have forsaken or betrayed us; when everything simply feels like too much work for too little reward: *God is our sole source of purpose and life!*

God's Life is

Absolute righteousness—
blameless, holy standard for all moral purity;
It towers over us like a mighty mountain,
strong, impregnable,
rewarding those who scale its crags
with vigor and incredible, awe-inspiring vistas.

God's Life is

Absolute loving-kindness—
Fatherly, motivating tenderness and compassion;
Utterly faithful,
it reaches to the heavens,
leads us all the way upward,
into the presence of Christ Jesus Himself.

God's Life is

Absolute judgment—
wisdom, justice and fairness in eternal balance
to match His glory;
It lies like an ocean,
vast and deep beneath our souls
where we cannot live and breathe,
but from whence we draw up fruits
that nurture every kind of life.
God is a fountain of Life,
a protective wing,
an abundant overflow of good things,

,a river of delights
that never can run dry.

(A picture of life from Psalm 36:5-9)

For further glimpses of God our Life, read: Psalm 16:11; Ezekiel 47:1-12; John 3:36; Romans 6:23; Galatians 2:20; Colossians 3:1-4; 1 John 1:1-2.

He who has the Son has the life; he who does not have the Son of God does not have the life. (1 John 5:12)

Immortal

Our Saviour, Christ Jesus . . . has put an end to death and has brought Life and Immortality to light through the Good News. (2 Timothy 1:10, Wey.)

Imperishable, not subject to death.

God was not born, nor can He die. As a man, Christ's life could never be snatched or wrested from Him by another. He had to voluntarily submit Himself to the laws of physical death.

I lay down My life so that I may take it again. No one has taken it away from Me, but I lay it down on My own initiative. I have authority to lay it down, and I have authority to take it up again. (John 10:17-18)

When Jesus, the God-man, laid down His life for us, it was temporary. Because He was essentially immortal, death could not hold His body as it does every other human body. Thanks to His involvement with us on our turf, we have a glorious reassurance:

> *DEATH IS SWALLOWED UP in victory!*

(1 Corinthians 15:54)

God is the sole source of interminable, indestructible life. He created us to receive life as His gift for all eternity. Then sin entered the picture and the process grew grim. While our souls shall always be immortal, our bodies must now die. And after this physical death, we face the awful prospect of an eternal living death—immortal souls forever cut off from the presence of the living God.

Only Jesus' victory over sin's deadly influence has qualified Him to revive us with His special quality of life that can know absolutely no decay or crumbling toward disintegration. His victory has taken the power away from the hands of the would-be destroyer of our immortal souls.

> *O DEATH, WHERE IS YOUR VICTORY? O DEATH, WHERE*
> *IS YOUR STING? The sting of death is sin. . . . But thanks be*
> *to God, who gives us the victory through our Lord Jesus Christ.*

(1 Corinthians 15:55-57)

Redeemed souls, we hold the dearly purchased gift of life in hearts that burst with spontaneous praise, declaring that to "the immortal and invisible King of the Ages, who alone is God, be honour and glory to the Ages of the Ages! Amen" (1 Timothy 1:17, Wey.).

Sustainer

> *Listen to Me, O house of Jacob . . .*
> *You who have been borne by Me from birth*
> *And have been carried from the womb;*
> *Even to your old age I will be the same,*
> *And even to your graying years I will bear you!*

I have done it, and I will carry you;
And I will bear you and I will deliver you. (Isaiah 46:3-4)

Sustain To hold up, maintain and keep alive.

God didn't create His world and then wind it up like some great clock maker, leaving it to run on its own until it finally winds down and stops. God is not only Creator/Artist/ Life-Giver, but tender Father/Life-Sustainer. He loves each work His fingers sculpt with such an involved passion that He commits all His resources to maintaining them. If He withheld them for a fraction of a second, the whole of our delicately balanced universe would disintegrate.

Every moment of every day
He continues to breathe life into all of His creation.
He preserves the rhythms
In their never-ending, revolving reflection of a faithful God—
Seasons, pregnancies, growth cycles,
A host of laws of harvest and cause-and-effect,
Circling us round in compassionate embrace,
Sustaining with magnificence
His most precious gift of Life.

What He does for our bodies, He does also for our souls:

- Birthing us by blood at Calvary;
- Nourishing us on the milk and the meat of His living Word;
- Protecting, guiding, strengthening, cleansing, teaching, delighting;
- Indwelling us with the divine life;

- Holding us close to His bosom where we learn the rhythms of His living heartbeat.

The Lord is the sustainer of my soul. (Psalm 54:4)

The LORD sustains all who fall
And raises up all who are bowed down. (145:14)

Sustain me with raisin cakes,
Refresh me with apples,
Because I am lovesick. (Song of Solomon 2:5)

For further glimpses of the Preserver/Sustainer, read: Nehemiah 1:5; Psalm 16:1; 31:23; 37:17, 24; 40:11; 55:22; Proverbs 2:8; 1 Thessalonians 5:23.

Sustainer

Not until
the heart of the Living God should cease to beat
and His eyelids flutter shut
will His hands drop to His side
empty, impotent and cold.
Knowing that day shall never come,
we can, we must,
cast ourselves at His feet in utter confidence.
Our God sustains!

To Ponder

How is all of life influenced by the character of the God who gives it to us? _____

_____

_____

_____

_____

Pray

Dear Immortal God, Giver and Sustainer of Life, _____

_____

_____

_____

Controller

For the love of Christ controls us, having concluded this, that one died for all, therefore all died; and He died for all, so that they who live might no longer live for themselves, but for Him who died and rose again on their behalf.

(2 Corinthians 5:14-15)

Controller

One who has ultimate power and dominion over another.

The God who created us, sustains us day by day, purchased us at the cost of His Son's last drop of blood and has given us new life, has every right to control every part of our lives. Only He is wise enough to know what is best for us and only He is strong enough to protect us from the subtle wiles of evil that surround and tempt us.

Heavenly Father, gracious Protector

You hold the reins,

Not I.

You have no obligation

to explain Your ways to me

about the tiniest of matters!

Ah! Lord!

When You strip me bare

of all those things I cherish more than You and Your glory,
teach me to cast myself
upon Your mercy
and accept the garments of Glory
You yearn to throw over my nakedness.

Once we have given our hearts to Him and joined His family, our God never ceases to prod and carve us into His image. Our right attitudes toward His will and His ways can prevent untold disappointments and the need for His corrective intervention along the way.

Even in the most basic of all spiritual pursuits, which is to seek after Him with our whole hearts, we stand in need of His controlling assistance.

Teach me to seek You, Lord,
Show me where and how. . . .
You have invited us to come, please now help us.[1]

For further glimpses of God the Controller, read: 1 Chronicles 29:9-20; Job 25:2; Psalm 8:6; 103:22; Ephesians 1:20-22; Colossians 1:13-20; 1 Peter 5:11.

So that in all things God may be glorified through Jesus Christ, to whom belongs the glory and dominion forever and ever. Amen. (1 Peter 4:11)

Ruler

Behold, the Lord GOD will come with might,
With His arm ruling for Him.
Behold, His reward is with Him
And His recompense before Him. (Isaiah 40:10)

Ruler

First in command, who governs with official authority.

- Our Creator, God made the rules by which all things and beings in the universe can coexist in harmony.

- Our Judge, He shows His power to defeat those who refuse to submit to His holy and rightful lordship.

- Our Father, He motivates us with love, setting boundaries that protect us from self-destruction.

- Our Shepherd, He rescues us from danger, provides for us, leads us, gathers us to His heart in the cold and desolate darkness of the night.

- Our King, He reigns in majesty and exercises ultimate control over all people and events of history.

"Let the peace of Christ rule in your hearts,"
    calming, dispelling fear and worry, gloom and despair.
"Let the word of Christ richly dwell within you,"
    enlightening your mind with His insights,
    deepening your passion for His joy,
    binding you to one another in His body.
Let the glory of the name of Christ rule your every
        "word {and} deed,"
    overflowing your being with thanksgiving
    to God the Father of us all.

(From Colossians 3:15-17)

For further glimpses of God our Ruler, read: Psalm 2:8-9; 59:13; Ezekiel 20:33; Micah 5:2; Zechariah 6:13; Romans 15:12; Ephesians 1:20-23.

Sovereign

He who is the blessed and only Sovereign, the King of kings and Lord of lords, who alone possesses immortality and dwells in unapproachable light, whom no man has seen or can see. To Him be honor and eternal dominion! Amen.

(1 Timothy 6:15-16)

Sovereign Potentate, mighty ruler or officer of greatest authority, controlling and ruling above and over all lesser authorities.

God is the final, supreme authority in our lives. We can choose to argue with Him, attempt to set ourselves above Him or fancy that we are qualified to stand alongside Him, and in this life, for a time, we may appear to have success. But when we stand before Him in the next life we shall know that He has the last word. He alone is sovereign!

Lord, I in my sinful state cannot fully view your reign—I would be consumed, destroyed by your glory. You are sovereign and I dare not bristle at this—for I am not invited to share your reign. You rule in my heart and though I cannot always pierce the clouds that surround your glory, I must rest in knowing that you are sovereign.

I am vain to think I can understand you.

I am wretched to fret and fume.

I am foolish to tell you what to do.

Human arrogance denigrates your reign, for I cannot see through the clouds and darkness that stand between my sin and your glory. Oh, my God, how dare I try?[2]

For further glimpses of the Sovereign God, read: Psalm 97; 103:19; Ephesians 4:6; Colossians 1:17.

"The Psalm of Omnipotent Sovereignty"[3]

The LORD reigns, He is clothed with majesty;
The LORD has clothed and girded Himself with strength;
Indeed, the world is firmly established, it will not be moved.
Your throne is established from of old;
You are from everlasting.
The floods have lifted up, O LORD,
The floods have lifted up their voice,
The floods lift up their pounding waves.
More than the sounds of many waters,
Than the mighty breakers of the sea,
The LORD on high is mighty.
Your testimonies are fully confirmed;
Holiness befits Your house,
O LORD, forevermore. (Psalm 93)

Crowned

But we do see Him who was made for a little while lower than the angels, namely, Jesus, because of the suffering of death crowned with glory and honor, so that by the grace of God He might taste death for everyone. (Hebrews 2:9)

Crowned

Wearing the symbol of supreme, sovereign, ruling power and authority.

From eternity past, Jesus was the Crown Prince of heaven. At the time appointed by His Father, Christ came to earth, leaving His crown behind. Here He walked the streets as a common rabbi-servant. His followers offered Him allegiance, but with reservations. The crowns they placed on His head were made of straw and blew away with the winds of opposition.

In His final hours on earth, He assumed a crown of shame. King of sinners for a moment in time, He took the judgment deserved by all the sinners of all the ages and wore a torturous crown of thorns. Forty-three days later, He returned to heaven's throne for His grand coronation. The crown He has worn ever since is the eternal crown of the King of kings. He will wear it throughout the endless eons of eternity.

> The head that once was crowned with thorns,
>> Is crowned with glory now;
> A royal diadem adorns
>> The Mighty Victor's brow.[4]

For further glimpses of God as the Crowned One, read: Psalm 8:5; Matthew 27:29; Mark 15:17; John 19:2, 5; Philippians 2:5-11; Hebrews 2:5-9; Revelation 14:14; 19:12.

To Ponder

What qualifies God to reign as our ultimate Sovereign? _____

_____

_____

_____

_____

Pray

Dear Sovereign God, _____

_____

_____

_____

Love

Dear friends, let us love one another; for love has its origin in God. . . . God is love. God's love for us has been manifested in that He has sent His only Son into the world so that we may have Life through Him. This is love indeed—we did not love God, but He loved us and sent His Son to be an atoning sacrifice for our sins. (1 John 4:7-10, Wey.)

Selfless, passionate acts that seek the benefit, well-being and pleasure of another.

The love of God for sinners is a preposterous thing. . . . That the Creator of the cosmos, holy Adonai, omnipotent El Shaddai, the great I AM, who has always been and forever will be, deigns to love me, is unimaginable, almost unspeakable.[1]

All love that is true love indeed has its sole source and origin in God. In His many words to mankind and in His ways with us all, we learn that true love is:

- "Better than life" (Psalm 63:3)
- Wholehearted (Matthew 22:36-40)
- Sacrificial (John 15:13)
- Patient and kind (1 Corinthians 13:4)

- Unselfish (1 Corinthians 13:5-6)
- Unfailing (1 Corinthians 13:8)
- Produced by the Spirit of God (Galatians 5:22)
- Forgiving (Ephesians 4:32)
- "Covers a multitude of sins" (1 Peter 4:8)

> All human beings have experienced some degree and quality of love. But . . . only one act of pure love, unsullied by any taint of ulterior motive, has ever been performed in the history of the world, namely the self-giving of God in Christ on the cross for undeserving sinners. That is why, if we are looking for a definition of love, we should look not in a dictionary, but at Calvary.[2]

> Stand and gaze into the high anguish of Calvary if you seek to see love at its maximum.[3]

All love that is true love and not some sentimental, self-serving, comfort-preserving substitute springs from the sacrificial, broken heart of God. However, the ability of all human beings to experience love in any form, be it ever so limited, will always be a reflection of God's image in us—pale, uncertain, misguided and inconstant though it may be. Even the anemic substitutes echo—though at a distance—the genuine. And echoing in godless hearts, they pave the way to see and one day receive the real treasure He so longs to give to all who breathe the breath of life on earth.

Dear Lord,
Let me not be satisfied with
pale, distant reflections,
wispy human-spawned imitations of the real thing.
Rather,

Overwhelm me with the rich, full depths of
Your unfathomable love—
pulsing through my veins
pouring itself out on all around me
drawing others—
steadily, gently, persistently, wisely—
Godward.

For further glimpses of the God of Love, read: Deuteronomy 4:37; Ezra 3:11; Psalm 86:5; Proverbs 3:12; Jeremiah 31:2-3; John 3:16; Romans 5:8; Ephesians 5:25-27; 1 Thessalonians 1:4; 1 John 4:16, 19.

Beloved Bridegroom

His mouth is full of sweetness.
And he is wholly desirable.
This is my beloved and this is my friend. . . .
I am my beloved's and my beloved is mine.

(Song of Solomon 5:16; 6:3)

Bridegroom Metaphor of God as lover of our souls, committed to cherishing and caring for us forever.

With the incomparable skill of the poet *par excellence,* God has painted for us one of the most beautiful word pictures of the special love between a man and a woman in all of English literature. But the Song of Solomon is more than a love letter: It is a soul-ravishing metaphor for the love of Jesus Christ and His bride for one another.

Lacking adequate words to describe the wonders she experiences, the bride refers repeatedly to her bridegroom as "my beloved." Through a series of lavish metaphorical terms and dramatic scenes gleaned from early Jewish culture, the poet presents the incredible beauty of a love relationship between a "darling" bride and her "beloved" bridegroom.

As both Beloved and Lover, the heavenly Bridegroom loves His bride with a pure and undying love. He sacrifices for her, cleanses and purifies her, nourishes her, cherishes her. He pursues her for Himself and clings only to her. God continually courts His people no matter how far they wander away from Him. And when we have indulged our souls in the depths of wantonness and spiritual adultery, He woos us still, always awaiting our return with open arms and the love of a fresh new Bridegroom.

> Oh, Lover of my soul,
> Wrap me up, Your ransomed Bride,
> in protective embrace,
> wooing my heart,
> entrapping it in the secure forever-fastness
> of Your love that will not let me go.
> Lure me with Your belovedness
> from all lesser loves
> to Your side—
> hollowed out at Calvary—
> Daily fan the
> flame of my first love
> for You!
> My Beloved Bridegroom!

For further glimpses of the Beloved Bridegroom, read: Song of Solomon 1-8; Isaiah 62:1-5; John 3:28-30; Ephesians 5:25-32.

> O LOVER TO THE UTTERMOST,
> May I read the meltings of thy heart to me
> in the manger of thy birth,
> in the garden of thy agony,
> in the cross of thy suffering,

in the tomb of thy resurrection,
in the heaven of thy intercession.
May I never dally with the world and its allurements,
but walk by thy side,
listen to thy voice,
be clothed with thy graces,
and adorned with thy righteousness.[4]

Caring

Therefore humble yourselves under the mighty hand of God, that He may exalt you in due time, casting all your care upon Him, for He cares for you. (1 Peter 5:6-7, NKJV)

To have an interest in and a compassionate concern for someone who matters deeply.

I humble myself before You, Lord . . .

All I have, I have because of You, Lord. All gifts, talents and skills are possible because of You.

. . . under Your mighty hand . . .

where I am protected, loved, nurtured, fed and guided.

. . . that You might exalt me in due time . . .

Even time is under Your control, God. Even there I have nothing to fret about, for Your plan for me will come together at the right time.

. . . casting all my care upon You . . .

Even when my concerns are for other people, there is nothing I can tell You that You don't already know. I cast all that weighs so heavily upon me at Your feet and leave it there.

. . . for You care for me.

In this is absolute rest. The bottom line is that You love me and all else pales by comparison.[5]

You can throw the whole weight of your anxieties upon him, for you are his personal concern. (1 Peter 5:7, Phillips)

For further glimpses of the God Who Cares, read: Psalm 55:22; 142:4-7; Matthew 6:25-32; Mark 4:36-41.

To Ponder

Can you begin to measure the height or depth or length or breadth of God's love? Just let it boggle your mind and awe your heart into worship. _____

_____

_____

_____

Pray

Dear Beloved Bridegroom, God of Love and Caring, _____

_____

_____

_____

_____

The Amen

The Amen, the faithful and true Witness, the Beginning of the creation of God. (Revelation 3:14)

One who gives our lives value and shouts over us with delight, "So be it!"

In Revelation 3:14 Christ is, in His often strange and paradoxical way, revealing Himself as "the Amen" to an unfaithful Church. Jesus

> has said "Amen" to every truth of the Scripture, but the church [at Laodicea] has failed to follow in His footsteps. She has the truth, for she has Himself, and He is the Way, the Truth and the Life . . . ; but she has not said "Amen."[1]

The Laodicean church was so hypocritical, so lukewarm and nauseatingly unholy that the Lord's natural reaction was to vomit her out of His mouth. Instead, however, He opened His arms and invited her into His embrace. He had purchased the Church with His life's blood, shouting aloud, "Amen! I have loved you with an everlasting love," but they turned away from Him, their everlasting Lover. They said "Nay" to all His pleadings and went their own way in search of value and self-esteem. With a bleeding heart, He reprimands them:

> *You say, I am rich, and have wealth stored up, and I stand in*
> *need of nothing; and you do not know that if there is a*
> *wretched creature, it is you—pitiable, poor, blind, naked. . . .*
> *All whom I hold dear, I reprove and chastise; therefore be in*
> *earnest and repent.* (Revelation 3:17, 19, Wey.)

The world had convinced the Laodiceans that God is the great "spoilsport" who delights in making unreasonable demands, then condemning all who fail. But Jesus Christ stands before them as a positive, affirming and encouraging God. He had created them with a wisdom too great to make a mistake and a passion too strong to do them harm.

He longs to hear them say, "Amen, so be it, we repent of our waywardness and accept Your will and purposes." How eager He is to indulge all the passion of His heart toward them and breathe His eternal, rapturous "Amen" over every part of their being!

"I am now standing at the door and am knocking" (Revelation 3:20, Wey.). The picture is clear. He stands on the outside, seeking entrance into the intimacy of the lives of these people. *"If any one listens to My voice and opens the door, I will go in to be with him and will feast with him, and he shall feast with Me"* (3:20, Wey.).

What a hauntingly beautiful invitation to enter into the profoundest of all mysteries—prayer!

> To pray is to let Jesus come into our hearts. . . . It is Je-
> sus who moves us to pray. He knocks. Thereby He
> makes known His desire to come in to us . . . to move us
> by prayer to open the door and accept the gift which He
> has already appointed for us.[2]

Prayer, then, is a partnership between God, the Amen, and His people. It does not begin with our need. It is birthed in His passion for His own glory to be released into our lives so we might fulfill the eternal purpose for which He created us.

Over and over, throughout the Scriptures, He pleads with us to:

- "Come to Me" (Matthew 11:28).
- "Seek Me that you may live" (Amos 5:4).
- "Call to Me" (Jeremiah 33:3).
- "Pray without ceasing" (1 Thessalonians 5:17).

For further glimpses of the Amen who invites us to pray, read: Psalm 41:13; 50:14-15; Isaiah 55:6; Jeremiah 29:11-13; Romans 16:27; 2 Corinthians 1:20; Revelation 22:20-21.

Prayer is the
gentle knock of
God's great Amen
Seeking after men and women in darkness
to be removers of the hinges,
wide-throwers of the gates
who, with abandon, usher in
His Majesty
The King of Glory! (based on Psalm 24:7-10)

Prayer-Answering God

Call to Me and I will answer you, and I will tell you great and mighty things, which you do not know. (Jeremiah 33:3)

A God who solicits our prayers then listens intently when we offer them and answers each one in His time.

How often we limit our concept of answered prayer to the fixing of obviously broken things—physical illnesses, rebellious children, lost jobs, unsaved souls and the like!

These are all good and important things to pray about and, just like a human father, God delights when His children come to Him with our pieces in disarray and cry out, "Daddy, please fix!" But with dismaying frequency we return over and over with the same broken pieces that never seem to enjoy His mending touch. Often, the pieces grow more shattered, until we all but despair.

> Did God not answer [my] prayer? Indeed He did, and proceeded at once to fulfill it. But He Himself reserved the right to decide when and how the answer was to be given. And in His own time the answer came. We, however, did not experience it as an answer. . . . We had planned for a very definite answer of our own; and when we did not receive the answer we had planned for, we thought we would receive no answer at all.[3]

Jeremiah 33:3 gives a clue to what is going on here. God promises, "*I will answer you, and I will tell you . . . things . . . you do not know.*" Can we not trust Him to answer in the way and time He knows are best? To take care first and foremost that He receive glory through the answer that He brings? To turn this whole experience of prayer itself into an opportunity to learn something precious about Him—something we did not know before?

Ah, then perhaps prayer is not about meeting needs so that we, His creatures, may be comfortable in life. Prayer is, after all, God's thing. Could it not be, first of all, a way to bring His creatures into line with His heavenly agenda? It is all about His passion to release His glory in human lives around the world.

So, when we pray, we need to bow before His awesome holiness, confess our own neediness, wait in His presence and let Him fill us with His glorious fullness. Then, when we are still and emptied of our shrill demands that He do what we ask when we ask it, we are ready to pour out the pitiful contents of our trembling hearts. We can give it all up to Him and freely grant Him the con-

trol He must have if He is to answer—and to teach us more about
Himself.

> Gracious Lord,
>> Grant me more and more
>>> to prize the privilege of prayer,
>>> to come to thee as a sin-soiled sinner,
>>> to find pardon in thee,
>>> to converse with thee,
>>> to know thee in prayer as
>>>> the path in which my feet tread,
>>>> the latch upon the door of my lips,
>>>> the light that shines through my eyes,
>>>> the music of my ears,
>>>> the marrow of my understanding,
>>>> the strength of my will,
>>>> the power of my affection,
>>>> the sweetness of my memory.[4]

For further glimpses of the Prayer-Answering God, read: 1 Kings
8:30-50; Psalm 18:6; 39:12; 55:1-2; 65:2, 5; 66:16-20; Matthew
7:7-11; Luke 18:1-14; John 14:13-14; 16:23-24; 1 John 4:14-15.

To Ponder

What does it mean for God to answer our prayers? _____
_____
_____

Pray

Dear Prayer-Answering God, _____

_____

_____

_____

Mediator

For there is one God, and one mediator also between God and men, the man Christ Jesus, who gave Himself as a ransom for all. . . . Therefore I want the men in every place to pray, lifting up holy hands, without wrath and dissension.

(1 Timothy 2:5-6, 8)

Mediator A reconciler who goes between two enemies and makes peace.

Oh High and Holy and Transcendent God,
    to whom we go in prayer,
  You are unapproachable.
  You are absolutely pure and spotless.
  Your motives are without the slightest taint of
    impropriety.
  Your wisdom is beyond reproach or correction or
    error.
  Your character sets the ultimate standards for all
    morality.
  Your demands are absolute, rigorous, unachievable.

    Before You, and all in our own merits,
  we will always stand in our naked depravity,
  condemned, banished from Your presence!
    BUT JESUS

Divinely appointed
Mediator,
God, yet man,
High Priest and sacrifice for sin,
The sinless One
You bear our depravity
and bridge the eternal gap between
Your holiness and our sinfulness,
Your high exaltedness and our lowly insignificance.
"No man comes unto the Father but by Me."
In Jesus Christ we are
accepted, enriched, beautified,
crowned, chosen and adopted.
"If you shall ask the Father for anything,
He will give it to you
in My name."

For further glimpses of God the Mediator, read: Job 9:2-33; Hebrews 8:6; 9:15; 12:24-29.

> *Since we have a great high priest who has passed through the heavens, Jesus the Son of God, let us hold fast our confession. . . . Therefore let us draw near with confidence to the throne of grace, so that we may receive mercy and find grace to help in time of need.*
>
> (Hebrews 4:14, 16)

Intercessor

> *Christ Jesus is He who died, yes, rather who was raised, who is at the right hand of God, who also intercedes for us.*
>
> (Romans 8:34)

Intercessor One who prays "a prayer of meeting, of bringing two or more parties together for reconciliation, for healing, for mutual enjoyment."[1]

Prayer is God's domain, His chosen way to reign on earth today. As such, "intercessory prayer originates in the heart of God the Father," the Amen.[2] He invites us to participate with Him in it and answers when we pray.

As God Incarnate, Jesus' heart beat for reconciliation. "As man, He spent His life and died His death building bridges to connect us with the Father who created us for Himself."[3] He modeled prayer for us. His whole earthly life was like one continuous breath of the Spirit, calling down God's favor and will on mankind. He taught His disciples to pray by instructing them, giving them a sample form for prayer, praying with them and for them.

As the resurrected Christ, enthroned with the Father in the heavenlies, He prays continuously for us, with us and in us. Our Mediator, He makes it possible for us to partner with Him in this divine enterprise. He who never forgets what it was like to be touched with every pain, doubt, weakness and coldness of our hearts eagerly invites us to *"draw near with confidence to the throne of grace"* (Hebrews 4:16).

> When we intercede, we reflect His image. We listen to two heart-cries. We stand firmly in the shoes of the person in need—feel his hurt, carry his burden, try to understand the attitudes that alienate him from God. But we also get to know the God who wants to bring him healing.[4]

We are God's sacred temple—His holy place of worship, communion and tenderness. Christ knocks gently on our heart's door and we open up to Him and pour out all the burdens He has laid upon us. Oh, in what weak and inadequate form we present them, even at our best! He takes each relinquished request and bears it to the Father's throne above. He transforms it with the divine will and purpose until it glows with His eternal glory. In the days and weeks that follow, He delights to bring His answers. He watches the angels of heaven rejoice in the wonder of His sovereign majesty. Then, wonder of wonders, He sees the brightening of the glow in our hearts where praying for others' needs has shoved the door a little wider and let in a widened ray of His glory. Hallelujahs explode in massive profusion in all the courts of heaven and in our earthly temples below.

For further glimpses of God the Intercessor, read: Luke 11:1-13; Romans 8:26-39; Hebrews 7:25; 9:24.

> Oh Father, mentor me daily in Your presence,
> teach me the wonders of prayer,
> not just uttering all the right words
> (not even at all the right times and for all the right reasons),
> in hidden depths of my naked spirit,
> teach me the mysteries of intercession—
> heaven-breathed and partnered prayer!

To Ponder

How does God want to quiet your soul more deeply so He can lead you into this adventure of shared intercession? _____

_____

_____

_____

Pray

Dear Heavenly Mediator and Prayer Partner, _____

_____

_____

_____

Unchangeable

For I, the LORD, do not change; therefore you, O sons of Jacob, are not consumed. (Malachi 3:6)

Unchangeable Incapable of change.

Everything touched by time is in a state of perpetual flux and alteration. All things on earth change but change itself. Human beings shift and grow and move and alter, just as the world around us does. Across this shifting, convulsing horizon of unpredictability, God stands like an unweathered monolith on a high mountain, absolutely unchanging and unchangeable.

Our perceptions of Him may change as we change and grow, His ways appearing to change with the circumstances of our lives and the maturity level of our hearts. In our smallness and restricted vision, we simply cannot see what He is doing. In our perception it seems as though God is changing, but in reality it is simply our understanding and view of Him that changes.

Unbrushed by the winds of time, His character and purposes are eternal, constant, unaltering. The fresh approaches with which He surprises us are but startling glimpses of some newly revealed aspect of His incomprehensibly complex character.

O Lord my God,
a million mysteries surround You
like early morning clouds,

veiling the distant mountain peaks.
One irrefutable assurance
quickens my soul
with bright anticipation:
You are always there—
even behind the clouds
that shift and drift and dissipate,
or sometimes cast shadows
that turn a golden dawn sky to smoky gray.
You do not change.
You do not shift or drift.
Your deep affections,
Your compassionate heart yearnings over Your people—
these never dissipate!
Hallelujah! What a God You are!

Of old You founded the earth,
And the heavens are the work of Your hands.
Even they will perish, but You endure. . . .
You are the same,
And Your years will not come to an end. (Psalm 102:25-27)

The design of the penman is to confirm the church in the
truth of the divine promises; that though the foundations
of the world should be ripped up, and the heavens clatter
together, and the whole fabric of them be unpinned and
fall to pieces, the firmest parts of it dissolved; yet the
church should continue in its stability, because it stands
not upon the changeableness of creatures, but is built
upon the immutable rock of the truth of God, which is as
little subject to change, as His essence.[1]

For further glimpses of the Unchangeable God, read: Psalm 93; 119:89-96; Isaiah 46:4-5, 10; Micah 7:18; Hebrews 6:17; 13:8; James 1:17.

> Change and decay in all around I see;
> > O Thou who changest not,
> Abide with me.[2]

Unforgetting

> *But Zion said, "The LORD has forsaken me,*
> *And the Lord has forgotten me."*
> *Can a woman forget her nursing child*
> *And have no compassion on the son of her womb?*
> *Even these may forget, but I will not forget you.*
> *Behold, I have inscribed you on the palms of My hands;*
> *Your walls are continually before Me.* (Isaiah 49:14-16)

Committed never to put us out of mind, but to remember us with affection and to attend to all that concerns us.

Our unchangeable God does not forget His children! We are too precious to Him, for He is absolutely faithful and loyal to us. The more we read His Word and walk in close relationship with Him, the more we believe and sense that this is true. However, no matter how well we know Him, we all have times of severe pain when we are tempted to suspect that He has forgotten us because He has not answered our prayer by healing our hurt. At such moments we must refuse to live by our feelings and instead put our faith in His Word alone. All through

Scripture we see that He is too faithful, too dependable, too infallible, too loyal in His love and compassion to forget us.

He will never forget our needs and our pains. He has experienced them all Himself and remembers them well (see Hebrews 2:14-18; 4:14-16). He will never forget to give us strength when His great wisdom may ordain a delay to the answer and relief we anticipate. Nor will He forget to teach us something beautiful about Himself through every experience. He will not forget to deliver us when the time is right.

> *Sing praises to the LORD, who dwells in Zion;*
> *Declare among the peoples His deeds.*
> *For He . . . remembers them;*
> *He does not forget the cry of the afflicted.* (Psalm 9:11-12)

One thing alone He is faithful to forget: He forgets every sin confessed and forgiven and does not hold them over us!

For further glimpses of an Unforgetting God, read: Psalm 77:8-9; 78:39; 98:3; 103:11-14; 105:42; Isaiah 43:25; 44:21; Jeremiah 31:34; Hebrews 6:10.

> *Are not five sparrows sold for a penny? and yet not one of them is a thing forgotten in God's sight. But the very hairs on your heads are all counted. Away with fear: you are more precious than a multitude of sparrows.*
>
> (Luke 12:6-7, Wey.)

Rock

> *The LORD is my rock and my fortress and my deliverer,*
> *My God, my rock, in whom I take refuge;*
> *My shield and the horn of my salvation, my stronghold. . . .*
> *For who is God, but the LORD?*
> *And who is a rock, except our God? . . .*

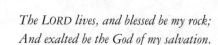

> *The LORD lives, and blessed be my rock;*
> *And exalted be the God of my salvation.*

> (Psalm 18:2-3, 31, 46)

Rock

Firm, unshifting stone for a solid foundation and a sure refuge.

"I am; therefore I do! And you can trust Me forever!" Great God of powerful words and actions, all He ever does or says is rooted firmly in His eternal, secure and changeless character.

> Immutable, immovable, impregnable, sublime resort . . . wherein I may dwell in safety, not merely running to Thee for temporary shelter, but abiding in Thee for eternal salvation.[3]

Because our world is unstable and unworthy of our trust, we desperately need this divine Rock on which to build our lives. He will always be for us:

- an anchor in a raging storm;
- a foundation to give permanence and structure to all we do;
- a hiding place in a harsh and desolate desert or in the midst of a ferocious battlefield;
- a solid place for our feet to stand in the midst of shifting sands, quaking earth and unpredictable mudslides.

Who can forget Jesus' graphic word picture from the Sermon on the Mount?

> *Everyone who hears these words of Mine and acts on them, may be compared to a wise man who built his house on the rock. And the rain fell, and the floods came, and the winds blew and slammed against that house; and yet it did not fall, for it had been founded on the rock. Everyone who hears these words of*

Mine and does not act on them, will be like a foolish man who built his house on the sand. The rain fell, and the floods came, and the winds blew and slammed against that house; and it fell—and great was its fall. (Matthew 7:24-27)

For further glimpses of God our Rock, read: Deuteronomy 32:4, 15, 18; Psalm 31:1-5; 61:2; 71:3; 89:26; Isaiah 26:4; 44:8.

To Ponder

How does God's constant changelessness provide a firm rock for your faith? _____

_____

_____

_____

Pray

Dear Unchangeable, Unforgetting and Rock-solid God, _____

_____

_____

_____

_____

Chief Cornerstone

Behold, I am laying in Zion a stone, a tested stone,
A costly cornerstone for the foundation, firmly placed.

(Isaiah 28:16)

Jesus Christ the Nazarene, whom you crucified, whom God
raised from the dead. . . . He is the STONE WHICH WAS
REJECTED by you, THE BUILDERS, but WHICH BECAME
THE CHIEF CORNER stone. And there is salvation in no one
else. (Acts 4:10-12)

"Principal stone around which construction in antiquity was achieved . . . the focal point of a building, the thing on which it most depends for structural integrity."[1]

O Jesus, blessed Rock,
both Capstone and Cornerstone!
Firmly rooted, unmovable, secure,
Your gracious excellence creates a level foundation
for the strong, imposing Temple
whence radiates God's eternal glory.
In You alone
walls from far separated right angles
join and bond and

> rise heavenward
> One structure for Your holy dwelling place,
> Stumbling block to those who will not see,
> Sanctuary to all who believe.
> Marvel of a watching universe!

By the great Architect he had been laid of old in Zion,
the chief foundation of the great spiritual edifice to be
reared out of the ruins of the Fall.[2]

Oh, tragedy! When Jesus came as God's holy Messiah,
He was rejected by the very ones He came to save! True
to their depraved human nature, millions of men and
women have tripped over the unassuming simplicity and lowliness of Jesus, failing to recognize Him for what He is. Millions of
others have been offended because He insists that all who come to
God must come only by the way of His cross.

No building can have more than one cornerstone, and the crucified Jesus is that one and only key piece of the foundation for God's
spiritual house on earth. Only He could pay the price of sacrifice demanded by our crooked and rebellious natures. Only He qualified to
level the ground to found a Church. Only He could draw all the factions together into a perfectly plumbed corner adequate to hold up a
building for eternity. Only He can both define the boundaries and
dimensions of our lives and bear their heavy weight.

*You belong now to the household of God. Firmly beneath you is the
foundation, God's messengers and prophets, the actual foundation-
stone being Jesus Christ himself. In him each separate piece of building, properly fitting into its neighbour, grows together into a temple
consecrated to God.* (Ephesians 2:19-21, Phillips)

For further glimpses of Jesus Christ, the Chief Cornerstone, read:
Psalm 118:22-23; Isaiah 8:14; Matthew 21:42-44; Mark 12:10-11;
Luke 20:17-18; Romans 9:33; 1 Peter 2:4-8.

foundation

For no man can lay a foundation other than the one which is laid, which is Jesus Christ. (1 Corinthians 3:11)

Underlying rocklike layer of a building that establishes and gives it stability and determines its dimensions and orientation to its environment.

God is the only totally trustworthy foundation we will ever know. His character and His rule are firmly, unalterably and eternally established, both in heaven and on earth.

Ascribe to the LORD glory and strength. . . .
Worship the LORD in holy attire;
Tremble before Him, all the earth.
Say among the nations, "The LORD reigns;
Indeed, the world is firmly established, it will not be moved;
He will judge the peoples with equity."
Let the heavens be glad, and let the earth rejoice;
Let the sea roar, and all it contains;
Let the field exult, and all that is in it.
Then all the trees of the forest will sing for joy
Before the LORD, for He is coming,
For He is coming to judge the earth.
He will judge the world in righteousness
And the peoples in His faithfulness. (Psalm 96:7, 9-13)

This God—changeless trinity of Father, Son and Holy Spirit—is the absolute deepest and most basic bedrock, the ultimate source of my:

- faith;
- knowledge of truth;
- value system and guidelines for living;
- hopes and dreams;
- sense of worth and purpose.

Everything I learn about living the life that wins for eternity is built on the foundation of His holy character. This building on the foundation of God means so much more than giving lip service to Him, attending church on Sundays and observing long lists of religious rules. It goes beyond studying the Bible to learn all it has to tell me or becoming a proficient and active minister to the needs of others.

If God is my foundation, I will strive more and more to obey not the lettered details of His laws—every jot and tittle—but to be conformed from the inside out to the spirit of those laws—the full, deep intent of each commandment.

Building on His foundation causes me to care more about His glory in my life than about my comforts and being treated fairly. On His foundation, I have a passion to be transformed from within through a life of consistent walking with Him. I desire to love Him with the deepest, highest, most intense passion my heart is capable of and to seek to know Him more intimately with each passing day. My goal is to aid in the construction of the building by allowing Him to pour out His love for others in abundance through me.

To build on this foundation is to be able always to trust that it is safe, sure, never failing or shifting. It will never crack in an earthquake or sink into the soil of the earth beneath. This foundation will never let me down or collapse beneath my weight or crumble with stress or be blown away by winds of adversity.

For further glimpses of God our Foundation, read: Psalm 87:1; 96:10; 2 Timothy 2:19; Hebrews 11:8-10.

> How firm a foundation, ye saints of the Lord,
> Is laid for your faith in His excellent Word!
> What more can He say than to you He hath said,
> To you who for refuge to Jesus have fled?
>
> The soul that on Jesus hath leaned for repose,
> I will not, I will not desert to his foes;
> That soul, though all hell should endeavor to shake,
> I'll never, no never, no never forsake![3]

To Ponder

How does the character of God provide a firm foundation for your faith? _____

_____

_____

_____

Pray

Dear God, my strong Foundation, _____

_____

_____

_____

Infinite

Great is our Lord and abundant in strength;
His understanding is infinite. (Psalm 147:5)

Infinite "Having no boundaries or limits. Immeasurably . . . large."[1]

We probe the nature of God's character and His ways, and our tape measures run out long before we even have the end in sight. All the parchment rolls on earth would be too small to contain the zeros needed to create a number big enough to record His measure.

The pages of Scripture are filled with word pictures, each showing us a different aspect of His immense character. They are an accommodation to the limits of our minds to grasp and our hearts to love. But gather them all together and read them every day you live, and you will still have only hints of the scope of His expansive greatness.

Our God is measureless! When we've climbed to the highest mountain of knowledge and wisdom that we can perceive, hoping to approach His level, we discover yet more mountains. Always we have farther to go, more to learn. And never will we know where the limits lie.

He knows what angels know, what man knows, and in-finitely more; He knows Himself, His own operations, all His creatures, the notions and thoughts of them; He is understanding above understanding, mind above mind, the mind of minds, the light of lights.[2]

Oh, Mind-boggling God!
You have no boundaries
but set them all—
Orbits in the heavens,
Shorelines for the seas,
Currents of air for soaring birds,
Surging waterways for creatures of the deep,
Day and night,
Spring and summer, fall and winter,
Threescore years and ten,
Limits of body, mind and spirit
for the creatures in Your image.
Your boundless ways
create deep stirrings
that bend the knee
and bathe the cheek with tears
in awe of Your infinity!

For further glimpses of an Infinite God, read : 1 Kings 8:27; Job 9:10-12; 11:7-11; 26:14; Psalm 40:5; 139:17-18; Romans 8:37-39; Philippians 4:7.

Infinite

Nor height nor breadth nor length is separation,
For holiness construes its own dimensions.[3]

Very Great

Bless the LORD, O my soul!
O LORD my God, You are very great;
You are clothed with splendor and majesty. (Psalm 104:1)

Absolutely great, greater than anything we have seen either in reality or in our wildest imagination.

With God, we can never use too many "verys." He is worthy of them all and then some. In the 104th Psalm alone, He is:

- great in *Creation*;

- great in *control* of all things created;

- great in *design and provision* for all creatures;

- great in *sovereignty* over all creation;

- great in *satisfaction* of all His creatures;

- great in *praiseworthiness* and *honor;*

- great in *judgment* and *wisdom.*

Let God be magnified. (Psalm 70:4)

Even if we add all the "verys" it takes to show Him as the absolute greatest of all powers and authorities and persons we can never exaggerate when we talk about our God's greatness. The biggest we can conceive or speak will always be an understatement, capable of giving off only occasional elusive flashes of His great glory!

O Great and Mighty God,
Very Great One above all others,
You are the God of history,
God of today,
God of all that lies beyond—
God of eternity and Ages of the ages—
Measureless, Infinite God
Beyond the borders of the absolutes
I stretch my mind to fathom!
Lost in the glorious wonder
I bow my total being
Trembling, worshiping, reveling at the feet of
My Transcendent God!

For further glimpses of the Very Great God, read: Deuteronomy 3:24; 5:24; 7:21; 32:3; Psalm 48:1; 96:4; 111:2; 145:1-7; Isaiah 12:6; Jeremiah 10:6; 32:17-19.

> Faith gives the soul a view of the great God. It teacheth the soul to set His almightiness against sin's magnitude, and His infinitude against sin's multitude.[4]

Transcendent

Out of the north comes golden splendor;
Around God is awesome majesty.
The Almighty—we cannot find Him;
He is exalted in power. (Job 37:22-23)

Beyond all we are and think, out of reach, in another league.

*O*ur God defies simple explanations or answers! We cannot summarize or wrap Him up in a Theology 101 course. Even if we could master all the facts, His transcendent otherness would urge us ever upward into unsearchable reaches and onward into unplumbed depths. He surpasses the most intelligent of us all in every conceivable way—in wisdom and knowledge, in power, faithfulness, integrity and love. . . .

> However nuanced and profound it may be, every theology finally fails in describing God with total adequacy, and no one, not even New Testament stalwarts of faith such as Paul, Mary or James, has *fully* experienced God.[5]

God is

A vast Grand Canyon,
A glorious panorama at my feet.
I stand on the rim,
Toes nudging the crumbling sands,
And gaze out across His horizon-to-horizon canyonness.
Is there an end?
I strain and exult and ponder.
Each morning I return
to tread my pathway farther down and farther on.
To sing the wonder of its endlessness . . .
Some days, from out the depths, a voice
coaxes me so near the gaping edge
I feel the sands give way
beneath my feet to
send me spiraling through space,
past multi-colored canyon walls.
Exhilarated, breathless
wrapped in holy shiverings
I plunge

until I feel broad wings beneath my body.
We swoop and soar,
we penetrate to golden depths
I never dreamed the Canyon held.
At length, He lifts and carries me along the rim,
then lets me gently down once more
on solid ground.
He flies away, gigantic wings creaking through
the smoldering dusk.
I shade my eyes before the setting sun
and strain again to see
the borders that define my new position
on the canyon's rim.
Horizon calls to horizon,
All shimmering purple, gold and rose.
Glorious wonder!
My Grand Canyon God fills the landscape still
with grandeur enough
to lure me on and feed my ravenous soul
for ages of ages,
and world without out end!

For further glimpses of a Transcendent God, read: 1 Chronicles 29:10-14; 2 Chronicles 2:5-6; Job 11:7; 1 Corinthians 2:10-16; 13:12.

When the mystery is gone, so is the church—at least the vitality of the church. . . . We must put the inscrutable wind and fire back in our communion.[6]

To Ponder

Push your mind to think the largest thoughts possible about the
character qualities of God that defy you to define them. _____

_____

_____

_____

_____

Pray

Dear Transcendent God, _____

_____

_____

_____

Shepherd

The LORD is my shepherd,
I shall not want. (Psalm 23:1)

I have gone astray like a lost sheep; seek Your servant.

(119:176)

Shepherd One who dedicates his life to pasturing and caring for a flock of sheep.

If God had wanted to pat us on the back and make us feel good about ourselves, He never would have called us sheep. While these woolly animals have a unique charm that evokes warm, fuzzy feelings in our imaginations, the reality is that they are amazingly helpless and not too bright. Easily distracted by many things, they wander off and then cannot find their way home again. A lost sheep will remain lost until someone rescues it. Further, when a sheep is "cast" (turned onto his back) he is totally incapable of rolling over or righting himself. Unless his shepherd comes to his aid, he will remain on his back, legs extended straight toward the heavens, and eventually die of starvation in that position. No other animal is so utterly dependent on or loyal to its caretaker. The more a sheep stays close to the shepherd, the more readily it recognizes his voice and seeks to remain under his protection.

Weak and helpless sheeplike creatures that we humans are, we desperately need a strong, wise, capable and compassionate Shepherd. Our souls lie in constant danger of starvation, mortal wounding and being misled either by false shepherds or by our own naïve and often rebellious hearts.

Little wonder then that Psalm 23, the shepherd psalm, speaks such deep comfort to us all.

The LORD is my shepherd,

He has a personal concern for me as an individual. I will never get lost in the press of His milling flock.

I shall not want.

He nourishes me with all the good things my spirit could ever crave.

He makes me lie down in green pastures;

No quick gobble at a fast food bar set up in the midst of the chaos of my life; the Lord's repast combines a nourishing rest with abundance that leads to glorious satisfaction.

He leads me beside quiet waters.

He knows I cannot drink from an agitated stream.

His water for the spirit will always run placidly, cool and inviting at my feet.

He restores my soul;

All that I am within—my wandering mind, my fickle emotions, my obstreperous will—suffers continual contamination and bludgeoning.

How my soul needs His constant restoration to wholeness!

He guides me in the paths of righteousness

His ways—those paths He created for my feet to walk upon—will always be best for me. And bring me pleasure that fills up all my deep-down empty places.

For His name's sake.

Through the unglamorous mundanity of this one foolish lamb's daily protected life, the world will see what a great, good Shepherd God is!

Even though I walk through the valley of the shadow of death, I fear no evil,

Death and its tormenting shadows hold no fear to the lamb accustomed to acknowledging his own weakness and snuggling close to the Shepherd for protection.

for You are with me;

In His strong, capable and compassionate presence I need never fear the evil that howls about me in the wind and in the hunger cries of wild animals.

Your rod and Your staff, they comfort me.

The rod of correction keeps me from straying and the staff rescues me from the tight crevasses where my careless abandon and heedlessness have trapped me.

You prepare a table before me in the presence of my enemies;

No matter what the struggle and opposition that assail me, His peace controls my inner depths and nourishes my soul with heavenly food.

You have anointed my head with oil;

His soothing balm can cool the wildest heat, ease the sharpest pain, heal the deepest wound.

My cup overflows.

No joy can compare with the abundance He lavishes on me.

Surely goodness and lovingkindness will follow me all the days of my life, And I will dwell in the house of the LORD forever.

Eternal perspectives cheer my every waking hour
and assure me that He will always be my Shepherd.

Shepherd me, Father, over all the rough and perplexing ways of
life. It is my nature to wander, to stumble, to lie on my back and flail
in the air until, exhausted, thirsty and malnourished, I die. How desperately I need Your shepherding.

> Cuddle me when I tremble.
> Guide me when I cannot find the way.
> Chasten me with Your rod when I disobey.
> Prod and correct all my erroneous wanderings.
> Ever and always, gently lead me home.

For further glimpses of God as our Shepherd, read: Psalm 28:9;
80:1; Jeremiah 31:10; John 10:1-18; Hebrews 13:20-21; Revelation 7:15-17.

Humans are such pliable creatures. Immersed in the
push-and-shove of daily living, we are in danger of being squeezed into a misshapen caricature of what God
intended us to become.[1]

The Shepherd who guards and protects us day by day is in the
process of remolding us into the perfection of His true image.

Provider

> My God—so great is His wealth of glory in Christ Jesus—
> will fully supply every need of yours. And to our God and Father be the glory throughout the Ages of the Ages! Amen!
>
> (Philippians 4:19-20, Wey.)

Provider One who meets the tangible needs of another.

God created us from a heart bursting with unfathomable love. This same God lives with a never-satisfied passion to provide for all our needs. In the birthing days of earth, He made the choice not to say, "I love you," in words of human language. Rather, He said it with actions that played out the eternal drama of His relationship with His beloved creatures. Imagine how His vast resources of creativity burst forth with unbridled joy as:

- He flung the universes into endless space and created the enormous Rocky Mountains, then carpeted their high places with a royal tapestry of miniature blossoming jewels—snow buttercups, Alpine avens, clover-leaved roses. . . . Who could name them all?

- He created an infinite array of fragrances both aromatic and putrid, sights in colors and shapes, tastes both sweet and sour, grainy and prickly textures, purring sounds and clinking, movements that sway and jerk. . . . Then He made us with noses to smell, eyes to see, tongues to taste, skin to feel, ears to hear and bodies to respond to movements.

- He created us emotional beings to experience a full spectrum of moods—from jovial to serene to angry to anxious to somber to secure. . . .

- He made us capable of being surprised, delighted by His own inexhaustible sense of humor—a rainbow of promise, a talking donkey, manna on the ground, lights and pitchers and trumpets to win a war. . . .

Art is

God chuckling at
Gaping mouths
Open laughter

Quickened heartbeats
And bended knees.

Nothing delights our Shepherd God more than providing for our needs and giving us the desires of our hearts. In the beginning, He sent a daily mist to nurture the plants in the ground. Later He provided a wife for Cain, an ark for a devastating flood, a cloud by day and a pillar of fire by night, fixed seasons that have never failed. The list goes on and on. Scripture is packed with examples of His provision and so are our lives.

Most important of all, He provides for the deep, throbbing needs of our hearts. He comforts us in our anguish, calms our fears, enlightens our befuddled minds and, with incredible patience, teaches us His ways. He created us with souls that will always remain empty until we allow Him to fill them. Then, as we open the floodgates and give Him entrance, He reveals the magnitude of His character in ever-increasing dimensions.

When we read His promises in Scripture, we are tugged into the edges of His full, rich passion to provide for us the things we still have no idea we need.

"I will fill the soul of the priests with abundance,
And My people will be satisfied with My goodness,"
declares the LORD. (Jeremiah 31:14)

Our minds can never fancy a need or want that our God cannot supply!

For further glimpses of a Provident God, read: Genesis 16:1-13; 22:1-13; Exodus 16-17; Ruth 1-4; 1 Kings 17; Nehemiah 9:15; Psalm 68:10; 145:14-16; Daniel 6; Jonah 1-4; Matthew 6:25-34; John 6.

To Ponder

Ask God to show you the immense depths of His love that keeps Him attending to and providing for each of His wayward sheep.

_____

_____

_____

_____

Pray

Dear Loving and Provident Shepherd, _____

_____

_____

_____

Passover

> Now the LORD said to Moses and Aaron in the land of
> Egypt . . . on the tenth of this month they are each one to
> take a lamb for themselves . . . an unblemished male a year
> old. . . . The whole assembly of the congregation of Israel is
> to kill it at twilight. Moreover, they shall take some of the
> blood and put it on the two doorposts and on the lintel of the
> houses in which they eat it. They shall eat the flesh. . . . It is
> the LORD's Passover. . . . The blood shall be a sign for you
> on the houses where you live; and when I see the blood I will
> pass over you, and no plague will befall you to destroy you
> when I strike the land of Egypt.
>
> (Exodus 12:1, 3, 5-8, 11, 13)

Passover Time when God delivered Israel from bondage
in Egypt, following a time of severe plagues on
the Pharaoh and his land.

From that fateful day in Eden when Adam and Eve sinned
and tried to hide from God, mankind has been subject to
an eternal law. Human sin could be atoned for only by a
blood sacrifice, the price demanded by a holy God. Since no human was without guilt of his own, sacrificial victims must always
be animals—amoral creatures incapable of sin. When God instructed His people to bring sacrifices, He told them to bring an

animal without blemish of any kind—a picture of the guiltless perfection needed to pay for sin.

Oh the beauty of that great drama of redemption in the book of Exodus! All the pieces are in place:

- An enslaved people in need of deliverance and a relationship with their God;
- A pure and blameless lamb, killed, then eaten;
- The sprinkling of pure blood as an act of faith in the mercies of a God who longed to deliver His people;
- The death angel and the protection of the blood of the Lamb.

The system was temporary. No animal sacrifice could ever actually *remove* the sin—it could only *cover* the sin. God planned from the ages of eternity past to one day send a human who would be sinless and innocent to pay the final price and take away all the sins that, until that time, could only be covered by animal blood.

Jesus became our Passover! He told His disciples the disturbing news of His impending betrayal at a Passover feast. "Take, eat! This is My body broken for you. . . . Drink this cup! My blood shed for you" (see 1 Corinthians 11:24-25).

Christ our Passover also has been sacrificed.

(1 Corinthians 5:7)

For further glimpses of Christ our Passover, read: Exodus 12:1-51; Mark 14:12-25.

Lamb of God

The next day {John} saw Jesus coming to him and said, "Behold, the Lamb of God who takes away the sin of the world!"

(John 1:29)

Lamb of God

Jesus as God's final offering to take away the world's sin.

Jesus! Pure and spotless and undefilable Son of the holy, holy, holy God!

Jesus! Rightful possessor of all authority both in heaven and on earth!

Jesus! Only created being ever worthy to stand guiltless before God's dazzling holiness!

Jesus! Only being in all the cosmos qualified to bear the sin of a world dying of wounds inflicted by its own miserable failure and rejection of God!

According to God's legal system, a guilty sinner must bring an unblemished lamb to a priest in an appointed place of atonement. The priest would then offer up the animal to cover over the offender's sin.

When the fullness of His timing came, God, the offended One, sent His spotless Son, His eternal High Priest, to complete the work of sacrificial redemption. Voluntarily, God's chosen Lamb offered up Himself in payment for the accumulation of sins committed and sinful natures inherited by an entire race of men, women and children.

The paradox of it all is heightened when we realize that the offenders, those who should have been offering up the lamb in penitence, instigated the awful slaughtering of Jesus, the Innocent One. But they did it in an unrepentant state. It was not an offering, but one more expression of their contaminated sin natures. Little did they realize when they crucified the troublesome Jesus of Nazareth that they were fulfilling God's purposes by slaying His sacrificial Lamb for the sins of the whole world.

O Holy Lamb of God,

Show me again, every time I bow at Your sacred altar,
the effulgence of Your glory
expressed in a total self-giving compassion.
Captivate my heart with sheer wonder
in contemplation of the mystery:
You, the hopelessly offended God,
wrung with passion for my restoration,
made the ultimate sacrifice
to accomplish for me
what I could never do for myself,
even if I offered up
every unblemished lamb on earth
as a blood sacrifice for my dreadful, awful,
condemning sin.
Let me meditate on the fullness of the wonder
and fall prostrate in a silence
forever resonant with Your GLORY!

For further glimpses of the Lamb of God, read: Isaiah 53; Acts 8:26-35; 1 Peter 1:13-21; Revelation 5:6; 7:9-17; 12:10-11; 19:7-9; 22:1-3.

When a prophet wishes to paint a picture of heightened helplessness and innocence, he chooses the lamb that is led to the slaughter without uttering a sound (Isaiah 53:7).[1]

Sacrifice

I am the good shepherd; the good shepherd lays down His life for the sheep. . . . For this reason the Father loves Me, because I lay down My life so that I may take it again. No one has taken it away from Me, but I lay it down on My own initiative. I have authority to lay it down, and I have authority to take it up again. (John 10:11, 17-18)

Sacrifice

Slaying of an innocent being who absorbs the judgment deserved by the guilty in order to free him from destruction.

All the innocent animals offered in the Old Testament were unwilling victims. God's chosen Lamb to bear the sins of the world was a willing sacrificial offering. Not only did He not deserve to die, He could have escaped death by the simple word of His mouth. Heaven stood ready with ten thousand angels to deliver Him. But He was our Good Shepherd! He came to be our sacrifice and He would not back down, even when the temptation pressed upon Him.

Sacrifice becomes real sacrifice only when we have a choice and decide to offer ourselves up for the well-being of another. Jesus taught us the meaning of these words and wrote the message with His blood.

He who offered Himself to become the sacrificial Lamb
was raised to new life by the Father,
that He might be the Good Shepherd of His sheep.
No one understands us more profoundly than He,
or feels with us more deeply
or sympathizes better with our weaknesses
and those dreaded onslaughts of temptation.
As Lamb-become-Shepherd
He qualifies like no other
to be the Door into the fold

where we are sheltered.
Jesus stands ever at the gateway,
hands and feet forever pierced,
banishing every imposter
so none can harm the sheep
or steal a place in the flock
engraved upon His heart.

For further glimpses of Jesus as our Sacrifice for sin, read: John 15:13; Romans 5:6-8; Ephesians 5:1-2; Hebrews 9:11-28; 10; 1 John 3:16.

To Ponder

Why was Jesus, the divine and royal Son of the eternal God, willing to lay down His life as a sacrificial lamb for the sins of a world that would largely reject Him throughout the ages of time? _____

_____

_____

_____

Pray

Dear Sacrificial Passover Lamb of God, _____

_____

_____

_____

High Priest

It was necessary that in all respects He should be made to resemble His brothers, so that He might become a compassionate and faithful High Priest in things relating to God, in order to atone for the sins of the people. (Hebrews 2:17, Wey.)

Inasmuch, then, as we have in Jesus, the Son of God, a great High Priest who has passed into Heaven itself, let us hold firmly to our profession of faith. For we have not a High Priest who is unable to feel for us in our weaknesses, but one who was tempted in every respect just as we are tempted, and yet did not sin. Therefore let us come boldly to the throne of grace, that we may receive mercy and find grace to help us in our times of need.

(4:14-16, Wey.)

High Priest Representative of God to man and man to God. He offers sacrifices and enters legal pleas to an offended God on behalf of His flock of worshipers.

Earthly high priests were men. They knew the joys and sorrows, pains, frustrations and failures of their fellowmen. Like all the people they represented before a holy God, they were sinners. Only Jesus Christ, our heavenly High Priest, ever perfectly fulfilled all the requirements of this office. None but He was ever absolutely:

- *Compassionate and faithful.* He cares about His office as our redeemer.

- *Great.* He ministers not from earth but from heaven.

- *Eternal.* He never had a beginning, will never have an end, is timeless in nature and endurance.

- *Holy, guileless, undefiled.* Though He came as one of us, He is totally other than us, belonging to that separate and glorious holiness of the godhead.

- *Tempted, yet without sin.* He is free to offer us grace enough to restore us to right standing with a holy God.

- *Experienced in the ultimate extent of suffering.* We can never say He doesn't know what it is to bleed.

- *Authoritative.* He was appointed, not by men on earth, but by God the Father Himself. All that God is stands behind all that Jesus is and says and does!

Old Testament priests were ministers of a covenant of law based on adhering to a list of works. In the New Testament, a new covenant of faith was both created and administered by Jesus Christ. With crude nails and drops of sacred blood, He has inscribed this covenant on our hearts and promised to transform our thoughts and motives and lives.

Great High Priest,
God of Glory, Prince of Peace,
remind me hourly of
the depth of my need for Your priesthood,
how much I owe to You as my great High Priest,
the breadth and import of Your priestly work

representing me, interceding for me
before God's exalted Throne!

For further glimpses of Jesus as our High Priest, read: Hebrews
2-10.

Jesus "became the road by which the prodigal could return home, for 'no one comes to the Father but through
Me' (John 14:6). . . . His whole life was . . . his great
high priestly prayer."[1]

Atonement

*When we were enemies, we were reconciled to God by the death
of his Son. . . . But we also joy in God through our Lord Jesus
Christ, by whom we have now received the atonement.*

(Romans 5:10-11, KJV)

"At onement." Paying the price to break down
barriers of sin between a holy God and sinful
mankind, bringing us together into a state of
harmony.

The most incredible story ever told can be summarized in
one sentence: An absolutely holy God loves His rebellious
human creatures so much that He made a way, at unthinkable personal cost, to reconcile us to Himself. This is atonement, the central theme of God's Word, the Bible. In the myriad
pictures hanging on the walls of the galleries of Holy Scripture, we
see this theme worked out, repeatedly, using a multitude of images and scenes, colors, faces and actions.

In no picture does the theme come clearer than that scene on the cross, where the eternal Lamb of God hangs in excruciating pain with His enemies sneering beneath His mangled feet. Above the hushed silence imposed by the supernatural curtain of night enveloping them all at midday, His words echo out across the shuddering landscape: "Father, forgive them; for they know not what they do" (Luke 23:34, KJV).

Never has a crime of such proportions been committed—neither before this moment nor since. Never has justice been so flagrantly brought to shambles. Never has the night been so dark, so soul-invading.

Nor have human words exploded with so much heavenly mystery and power. This sort of forgiveness could come only as "the crowning accomplishment of love."[2] It surpassed the glory of thousands of Days of Atonement. In one afternoon on a hill of execution, God satisfied the stringent demands of an unachievable legal covenant and set all mankind free to choose for and experience harmony with Himself.

> Christ's atoning work is so complex and our minds are
> so small. We cannot take it all in.[3]

> Oh, the love that drew salvation's plan!
> Oh, the grace that brought it down to man!
> Oh, the mighty gulf that God did span
> At Calvary![4]

For further glimpses of Jesus, our Atonement, read: Leviticus 1; 16; Mark 10:45; Romans 3:21-26; Galatians 2:20; Colossians 1:20; 1 Peter 2:21-25; Revelation 5:6, 12; 7:14.

> *Although You were angry with me,* [With just cause, God
> was angry with me. I deserve nothing better.]
> *Your anger is turned away,* [You heaped it all, instead,

upon Your sacrificial Lamb.]
And You comfort me. (Isaiah 12:1-2)

To Ponder

What do we learn about forgiveness from Jesus' words on the cross, "Father, forgive them; for they know not what they do" (Luke 23:34, KJV)? _____

_____

_____

_____

Pray

Dear Atoning High Priest, _____

_____

_____

_____

"In my Father's house there are many resting-places. . . . I am going to make ready a place for you. . . . I will return and take you to be with me, that where I am you also may be. And where I am going, you all know the way."

"Master," said Thomas, "we do not know where you are going. In what sense do we know the way?"

"I am the Way," replied Jesus, "and the Truth and the Life. No one comes to the Father except through me."

(John 14:2-6, Wey.)

The Way

We have confidence to enter the holy place by the blood of Jesus, by a new and living way which He inaugurated for us through the veil, that is, His flesh. (Hebrews 10:19-20)

Pathway, way of life, road that leads to a destination.

The most important journey we'll ever take begins with a doorway—the cross of Jesus who said, "I am the door" (John 10:7). The pathway it follows is an intimate walk with this same Jesus who said, "I am the way" (14:6). The destination it leads to is a rare quality of life modeled only once in history—by Jesus.

Jesus is the one and only way that will lead us to the Father of glory. His way is a high way, a way of impeccable holiness. *"The unclean will not travel on it. . . . And fools will not wander on it. . . . But the redeemed will walk there"* (Isaiah 35:8-9). When we come to the Door, all of us are both unclean and fools at heart. The act of entering in through the Door begins a miraculous transformation. It frees Jesus Christ to redeem us, make us clean and fit to learn wisdom and holiness from walking in the Way with Him.

The Way of Jesus Christ is flooded with penetrating light. Every sin, no matter how tiny, is clearly visible here. Jesus, the Way, welcomes our penitent hearts and cleanses us of each sin as we move on. *"If we walk in the Light as He Himself is in the Light, we have fellowship with one another, and the blood of Jesus His Son cleanses us from all sin"* (1 John 1:7).

Wonder above all wonders, this way is also a way of joy and gladness of the God kind.

> *And the ransomed of the LORD will return*
> *And come with joyful shouting to Zion,*
> *With everlasting joy upon their heads.*
> *They will find gladness and joy,*
> *And sorrow and sighing will flee away.* (Isaiah 35:10)

What an incredible walk! How abundantly He sustains us for each step! With a holy and heart-stopping fullness He teaches and instructs and deepens us! Ah, what dazzling glory! Redolent with heaven's hues and sounds and scents and filled with healing balm sufficient for every broken piece of our lives!

> O Master, let me walk with Thee
> In paths of lowly service free.
> Teach me Thy secret; help me bear
> The strain of toil, the fret of care.

In hope that sends a shining ray
Far down the future's broadening way,
In peace that only Thou canst give,
With Thee, O Master, let me live.[1]

For further glimpses of Jesus as the Way, read: Acts 9:2; 19:9, 23; 22:4; 24:14, 22; Colossians 2:6.

The Truth

And the Word came in the flesh, and lived for a time in our midst, so that we saw His glory—the glory as of the Father's only Son, sent from His presence. He was full of grace and truth. (John 1:14, Wey.)

Truth

"Honesty, reality, a revelation of things as they really are."[2]

Jesus, as the God-man, defined the boundaries of our pathway by living the truth about God in blood and flesh and skin. Everything He said and did and every attitude He expressed was absolutely true. No shadow of a lie or deviousness ever issued from His person or His lips. Through His unique human life, He illustrated all the truth the Scriptures had ever taught about God.

Grace and truth came through Jesus Christ. No human eye has ever seen God: the only Son, who is in the Father's bosom—He has made Him known. (John 1:17-18, Wey.)

As we walk with Him along the way of holiness, He also reveals to us both the beauty and the ugliness of the truth about ourselves. And always He offers us the unbelievable opportunity to put them both at His disposal so He can transform us into show-places of His glory.

Amazing! His truth always comes to us mingled with grace. In fact, God's truth would be incomplete—and hopelessly condemning—without grace. At Calvary, grace and truth met in one supreme moment of God's involvement with His beloved mankind. For three long days and nights a wondering world stood stunned at the apparent failure of both truth and grace. But in that Easter garden they burst forth and shone on a waiting world. They have been doing their healing work ever since.

God, the merciful doctor of broken spirits and lives, is a truthful doctor. He doesn't gloss over the truth and apply a bandage on our sin that says, "This man is good," and send him on his way smiling. Rather, the Great Physician tells us the truth, that *"the soul who sins will die"* (Ezekiel 18:4). Then with tender voice and compassionate eyes, He implores us to trust Him to treat our sin with His healing blood. Only this godly truth can set us free from all sorts of deadly maladies.

> *Search me, O God,*
> *Make me to know all You know to be true about me.*
> *Try me and show me all my anxious, untrusting thoughts,*
> *Reveal to me in vivid colors*
> *Every evil thing in me that wounds Your gentle Father heart,*
> *And correct my steps to bring me again into Your everlasting*
> *way.* (Psalm 139:23-24, author paraphrase)

For further glimpses of God the Truth, read: Psalm 25:10; 61:7; 85:10; 115:1; 119:160; Isaiah 65:16; Matthew 22:16; John 8:32; 17:17; 18:37.

The Life

In Him was life, and the life was the Light of men. (John 1:4)

The goal of our journey: oneness with God, as the opposite of death, which is separation from God.

A religion that does not come through Jesus, the Door, rarely offers the human spirit life. Such religions deny that there is only one way to God or any absolute truth about anything. They envision their goal as some vague sort of cosmic light, with rays broad enough to encompass all forms of belief.

Jesus came to show us that without life, all light will be sterile, rigid, cold and meaningless. To a dead person, nothing has a shred of value. No matter how bright the light, it can never warm lifeless limbs or stimulate a non-functioning brain. We must have life if we are to see the light and enjoy any of God's gifts.

Light-focused religions have no lasting hope to offer beyond death. Jesus, the Life, conquered death and offers us all a whole new quality of life. He opens wide His arms and calls us to enter through His door, walk in His way, believe His truth and be invigorated with His life.

Once on the way with Him, we expect to be blessed by God, to experience moral and spiritual victory, power, holiness and healing for our many ills and battle wounds. How eager He is to give us all these things! But they are not His ultimate goal for our journey. The real destination God has placed at the end of His pathway is for us to know the Father more intimately, to see His glory more brightly and to enjoy more and more of Jesus Christ, our Life.

The chief end of man is to glorify God by enjoying Him forever.[3]

Dear God,
You stand squarely at the end of my journey,
The origin and goal of my life,
The focus, center and spring of my life
At every level,
In every area,
In all its dimensions—
My joy, my peace, my wisdom, my purpose and my success—
YOU AND YOU ALONE ARE MY LIFE!

For to me, to live is Christ and to die is to have more of Him.
(Philippians 1:21, paraphrased by Bryan Jessup in a sermon)

For further glimpses of God as our Life, read: Psalm 16:11; 36:9; John 3:36; 6:35-36; 7:37-39; 11:25; Romans 4:17; 6:23; Galatians 2:20; Colossians 3:1-4; 1 John 1:1-2; 5:11-12.

To Ponder

In what ways did Jesus' life and truth and teachings point us to God?

_____

_____

_____

_____

Pray

Dear Father, whose Son is my Way, my Truth, my Life, _____

_____

_____

_____

Water of Life

Jesus stood and cried out, saying, "If anyone is thirsty, {let him keep coming} to Me and {let him keep drinking}. He who believes in Me, as the Scripture said, 'From his innermost being will flow rivers of living water.'" (John 7:37-38)

That which satisfies our deepest spiritual thirst, our yearning to be one with God.

e are thirsty creatures. In the deepest recesses of our hearts, every man, woman and child on earth has an emotional/spiritual craving of ravenous proportions. The world in which we live offers us a multitude of drinking fountains and begs us to come slake our thirst. We sip and drink and guzzle at them all, but no matter how desperately we seek for the one fountain which will at last satisfy, we come up empty, still panting, mouths dry and hope diminishing. The things we buy, the relationships we nurture, the religions we follow, the ambitions we pursue, the noble and creative purposes we give ourselves to—all are temporary. They provide us, at best, with momentary satisfaction. The finest fountains earth can produce leave us craving in more desperation than when we first began.

To us in our thirst, God cries out,

Ho! Every one who thirsts, come to the waters. . . .
Incline your ear and come to Me.
Listen, that you may live. (Isaiah 55:1, 3)

The water He offers us is a perpetual fountain, springing from His inexhaustible character, from everything that makes Him God. He bubbles forth a never-ending stream of sweet water. Gushing, spurting, flowing, spraying, cascading—in a glorious array of actions all suited to our individual and circumstantial needs, He dispenses His life to our dusty, feverish, thirsting souls.

To know wherein lies the one true source of Living Water and reject it in favor of so many fake substitutes constitutes the greatest folly of all time. And it breaks His heart.

"Be appalled, O heavens . . .
And shudder, be very desolate," declares the LORD.
"For My people have committed two evils:
They have forsaken Me,
The fountain of living waters,
To hew for themselves cisterns,
Broken cisterns,
That can hold no water." (Jeremiah 2:12-13)

In amazement, we can stand with the prophet Ezekiel in chapter 47 of his book and look upon a remarkable vision of water and life and fruitfulness.

An angel takes the prophet to the temple where he sees water flowing from under the threshold. In Revelation 22:1, where John paints a similar picture, he calls it *"a river of the water of life, clear as crystal, coming from the throne of God and of the Lamb".*

In Ezekiel's vision, he follows his angelic guide and wades into the water, which first laps about his ankles, then reaches to his knees, his loins and finally buoys him up. Then he is returned to the bank of the full-flowing river where he sees the effect of this outpouring from God's throne.

"These waters go out toward . . . the sea, {the angel tells him,} and the waters of the sea become fresh. It will come about that every living creature which swarms in every place where the river goes, will live. . . . Everything will live where the river goes." (Ezekiel 47:8-9)

We listen to the words and let our hearts exult at the very thought. Along the banks of the river grow

. . . all kinds of trees for food. Their leaves will not wither and their fruit will not fail. They will bear every month because their water flows from the sanctuary, and their fruit will be for food and their leaves for healing. (47:12)

Sacred water of life
Surging from the royal throne above all thrones
Swirl about our ankles
Bend our stiffened knees
Buoy us up in rapids of the Spirit
Invigorate and resuscitate
With spark of vigor
That issues forth in
Abundance of food for our famished souls
And green leaves dripping balm
For the healing of our deadly ills.

For further glimpses of the Living Water, read: Psalm 36:8; 42:1-2; 63:1; 143:6; Isaiah 12; 41:17; John 4:1-14; Revelation 7:17; 21:6; 22:17.

The well is deep and I require
A draught of the Water of Life;
And none can meet my soul's desire
For a draught of the Water of Life;
Till One draws near who the cry will heed,
Helper of men in their time of need,

And I, believing, find indeed
That Christ is the Water of Life.[1]

Thirsty

After this, Jesus, knowing that everything was now brought to an end, said—that the Scripture might be fulfilled, "I am thirsty." There was a jar of wine standing there. With this wine they filled a sponge, put it on the end of a stalk of hyssop, and lifted it to His mouth. As soon as Jesus had taken the wine, He said, "It is finished." And then, bowing His head, He yielded up His spirit. (John 19:28-30, Wey.)

Thirsty A condition in which one craves water.

Wonder of wonders, the Christ who so often called thirsty souls to come and be satisfied submitted Himself to experience the very depths of thirst in all its dimensions. As Jesus hung on the cross, He suffered unimaginable physical pain and anguish. He had been without food or water for many long and grueling hours. During that time, He had undergone unspeakable abuse and anguish—sweating blood in Gethsemane, enduring mocking and anger, beatings and that most cruel of all tortures—crucifixion. Little wonder, then, that His body thirsted.

But the thirst of the only begotten Son of God went far deeper than physical deprivation. Weighted down as He was with the sins of the whole world, for all of time, both behind Him and yet to come, He suffered the ultimate emotional, spiritual and mental anguish. His own beloved Father had forsaken Him and left Him hanging there to complete the awful job alone.

In that blackest of all black moments of human history, Jesus, the Living Water, knew a deep, heart-wrenching spiritual thirst such as no human heart can ever fully appreciate. Cut off from an intimacy with His Father that He'd always known and still deserved, He thirsted after Him with every fiber of His being. For what must have felt like an eternity of time, He knew the thirst of the human heart for God. His emptiness, His pain, His passionate yearning were magnified and intensified beyond our wildest imagination.

We may know what it is to hunger and thirst after God, but Jesus was the only man who ever knew a complete filling with the God we all yearn after (see Colossians 1:19; 2:9). He Himself was God, sinless in action, word and motivations. He hadn't the slightest imperfection in His being that could take away any of the fullness of His deity and leave Him empty. But the dreadfulness of the depraved sinful nature He bore for us was complete. The contrast between His fullness and our assumed emptiness left Him with a desolation and a thirst far deeper than that which any human being will ever know.

This was the Man who earlier had offered the quenching of spiritual thirst to the crowds gathered in the temple for the Feast of Tabernacles. An essential part of qualifying Himself to make good on this offer was His identification with our thirst. Once He had finished the work of the cross and been raised from the grave, He was able to grant to all who heed His invitation living water for spiritual thirst.

In the process of His suffering, He showed us what to do with our spiritual thirst. Our depraved human nature leads us far too often to seek satisfaction in all the wrong places. Our thirst goes on gnawing away at us. But because Jesus endured those long hours of emptiness, we can keep coming to Him and keep drinking of the water He purchased for us with His blood.

For further glimpses of a Thirsty God, read: Matthew 25:35-45.

To Ponder

In what ways do you crave an increased intimacy with God?

_____

_____

_____

_____

Pray

Dear God who experienced my thirst, _____

_____

_____

_____

Satisfaction

O satisfy us in the morning with Your lovingkindness,
That we may sing for joy and be glad all our days.

(Psalm 90:14)

The thing which fills all our cravings and ful-
fills all our longings.

God is our Creator. With absolute wisdom and skill, He
made all things on this planet to fit together in ecological
and spiritual harmony. And He created us with the capacity to grow and learn and rejoice in it. He has gifted us abundantly with physical provisions, friends, talents, aptitudes and
insights. Then, in His infinite wisdom, He planted within us cravings for all the gifts He has provided. Every human being ever to
come from the hand of the Creator is a veritable masterpiece of
complex workmanship and interrelated parts.

Stunning!

Awe-inspiring!

But great and fitting though these things may be, they do not
satisfy us completely. When we have lived our lives to the fullest
and enjoyed all earth's magnanimous blessings, we feel less than
satisfied. Staring in wonder at hands still empty, we raise them
heavenward and cry out, "What am I missing?"

The answer is simple, yet difficult to see. Deep in the heart of each individual, God has formed a hollow space. In that space we hunger and thirst and crave and yearn to be filled with something beyond the obvious surface pleasures and provisions, yet we know not what that may be. This empty core is often called a "God-shaped vacuum." Only He can fill the space. When we ignore Him, all the good and nurturing things that life can offer are a mere substitute for the real thing, a senseless rabbit trail that leads us farther and farther away from the satisfaction we seek.

If God isn't enough, nothing will ever satisfy.[1]

Our Creator God designed us to be filled in our innermost beings with Himself, so we can reflect His image in the world where He has placed us. When we are satisfied with God, we do not crave for anything other or beyond or in addition to Him. Oh yes, we enjoy every kind of blessing He pours out on us. However, we recognize and treat them only as gifts from His hand. We do not allow them to take His place in our affections.

For true deep-down satisfaction, we move past His provisions and gifts to meditate on Him, listen to His voice, seek Him first. The satisfaction that He offers us through His person fills our empty spaces.

> With the abundance of Thy house
> We shall be satisfied.
> From rivers of unfailing joy
> Our thirst shall be supplied.[2]

The river of this truly satisfying water flows on and on, never ceasing. By its very nature, our deepest thirst is like physical thirst. Once we have assimilated the few sips or gulps we could take in at one time, they only make us ravenous for more and more of His transcendent, inexhaustible person and glory. As we come and drink, we are filled up at a progressively deeper level. As in a healthy body, so in the growing spirit, there will always be a renewal of thirst. And in Him we will always find more to seek, more to thirst for, more to be satisfied with.

Enough! Sufficient!
Lord God, You are my Satisfaction:
My joy, my sustenance,
my guidance, wisdom, strength.
If you are all of this to me
—and so much more—
why do I so rarely
allow my soul to be
God-contented?

Nothing we do grieves the heart of our Creator Father so much as when we spend our lives rushing about, frantically stuffing ourselves with things that cannot satisfy the hunger He placed in us. He has one deep yearning for us—that we come to Him to be filled up in the way He made us to be complete. He wants to both nourish us and fill us with delight.

> *I would feed you with the finest of the wheat,*
> *And with honey from the rock I would satisfy you.*

> (Psalm 81:16)

God is most glorified in us when we are most satisfied in Him.[3]

For further glimpses of the Satisfying God, read: Psalm 17:14-15; 63; 81:10; 103:5; 107:9; 145:16; Isaiah 41:17-20; 58:11; Joel 2:19, 26.

Inheritance/Portion

> *The LORD is the portion of my inheritance and my cup;*
> *You support my lot.*
> *The lines have fallen to me in pleasant places;*
> *Indeed, my heritage is beautiful to me.* (Psalm 16:5-6)

Inheritance

"The gift of a good father to his children."[4]

God is our Father. With sacrificial tenderness and passionate abandon, He cares intimately about every one of our needs. He considers nothing insignificant or too much labor, as long as it will bring us maturity, joy and fulfillment. Fatherlike, He plans and provides for our present and our future, an allotment of eternal proportions and endurance.

Many earthly fathers are quick to lavish material gifts on their children to entertain and make them comfortable, but the fathers themselves are often absent. They seem never to understand or be able to meet the deep emotional and psychological needs of their children for their presence and an open sharing of who they are. Our heavenly Father is not such an absentee parent. He never holds Himself aloof. His greatest joy lies in giving all He is to us and He yearns for us to ask and to receive. He wants above all else to be our most treasured gift, our priceless inheritance.

We shall never knock at His door and find Him away on "important business." Nothing is more important to Him than our confidence and our fellowship. When we call on Him, even when He seems not to answer immediately, He speaks peace to our hearts and we know we have not connected with some impersonal answering machine. We shall never turn to Him on our journey and find an empty space where He has promised always to be.

The terms of our inheritance are settled in the courts of heaven. They cannot be altered or reassigned or rescinded. It is His greatest privilege to give Himself to us, His beloved creatures. Further, He calls us His priests and urges us not to depend on the material and physical wealth of this life, but to claim Him for our inheritance. Under the Mosaic covenant, the Hebrew priests knew this principle well. While the people were given an inheritance of land, each in the section assigned to his tribe, the priests had no landed holdings. They were scattered throughout the tribes, where they ministered to the spiritual needs of all. Each tribe provided them a place to live. They were fed by the offerings God commanded His people to bring.

> *The LORD is their inheritance, as He promised them.*
>
> (Deuteronomy 18:2)

> *I am their inheritance . . . I am their possession.*
>
> (Ezekiel 44:28)

Under the new covenant sealed with the blood of Jesus, we are His priests. He gives us His very self for an *"inheritance which is imperishable and undefiled and will not fade away, reserved in heaven for you"* (1 Peter 1:4).

The soul captivated by the wonders of this unique and incomparable inheritance cries with glorious spontaneity:

> *You are my refuge,*
> *My portion in the land of the living.* (Psalm 142:5)

> It is something to have Jehovah for our refuge . . . it is everything to have Him for our portion.[5]

In keeping with that ever-recurring pattern of interrelationship between God and His children, not only is He our inheritance, but we are also His inheritance as well. How can it be that we could bless and nourish His heart? That He could call us His beloved ones, His treasured inheritance?

> *Blessed is the nation whose God is the LORD,*
> *The people whom He has chosen for His own inheritance.*
>
> (Psalm 33:12)

> *But you are A CHOSEN RACE, A royal PRIESTHOOD, A HOLY NATION, A PEOPLE FOR God's OWN POSSESSION.*
>
> (1 Peter 2:9)

> Riches I heed not, nor man's empty praise,
> Thou mine Inheritance, now and always;
> Thou and Thou only, first in my heart,
> High King of heaven, my Treasure Thou art.[6]

For further glimpses of God as our Inheritance and mankind as God's inheritance, read: Numbers 18:20; Deuteronomy 18:1-8; 32:9; 1 Kings 8:51; Psalm 28:9; 33:12; 74:2; Isaiah 19:25; Jeremiah 51:19; Ephesians 1:18.

To Ponder

In what ways can only God satisfy the deepest recesses of the human heart and mind? _____

_____

_____

_____

Pray

Dear God, my Portion and Inheritance who alone satisfies, ____

_____

_____

_____

_____

Silent

He was oppressed and He was afflicted,
Yet He did not open His mouth;
Like a lamb that is led to slaughter,
And like a sheep that is silent before its shearers,
So He did not open His mouth. (Isaiah 53:7)

Silent Not expressing one's heart, showing one's face
or revealing one's plans.

At the very moment when the guiltless, inoffensive Son of
God had the opportunity to defend Himself with the
truth and win His freedom, He did not speak. When
questioned by the high priest, "Jesus kept silent" (Matthew 26:63).

Pilate asked Him, "Where are You from?"

But "Jesus gave him no answer" (John 19:9).

He chose to remain silent, to let the false accusations take their
course, and in silent solitude to bear the full weight of all the injustice of a world's sin. Even as He hung suspended on the cross, suffering untold agonies of body, soul and spirit, when His accusers
railed on Him and taunted Him, He hung in silence. He could
have hurled back words to His tormentors: "This is temporary. I
will have the final word, and then your day will come!"

But no. His thoughts were all redemptive—and so were His few
words. He saved His breath for words to bring comfort and healing,

words to admit the depths of His apparent defeat. The prattle of self-defense had no place in God's plan for His Son, whose life had been characterized by a silence rarely understood by His fellowmen.

How silently He was born in the obscurity of a stable to a simple peasant woman! The voices of angels and the music of heaven broke the silence of that first night in Bethlehem, but it was only heard by a handful of shepherds on a chilly hillside. He grew to manhood in an obscure occupation—carving wood and shaping it into useful articles for the simplest of daily pursuits. He began His ministry in the quiet Judean hills, with only John the Baptist and a handful of onlookers as witnesses when the dove descended upon Him and His Father announced, *"This is My beloved Son, in whom I am well-pleased"* (Matthew 3:17).

Then before He touched a twisted limb or a simple lunch or spoke peace to a raging, stormy sea, He spent forty days alone in the silence of the wilderness. The desert place echoed only with the sounds of sighing winds, blowing sands and the tempter's shrill voice. There was much He could have said to Satan, but He chose few words with which to put him in his place:

- "MAN SHALL NOT LIVE ON BREAD ALONE, BUT ON EVERY WORD THAT PROCEEDS OUT OF THE MOUTH OF GOD" (Matthew 4:4).

- "YOU SHALL NOT PUT THE LORD YOUR GOD TO THE TEST" (4:7).

- "YOU SHALL WORSHIP THE LORD YOUR GOD, AND SERVE HIM ONLY" (4:10).

For the three years that He roamed the streets and byways of the land we now call holy, He taught of God and heavenly paradigms. He shouted only against hypocrisy in religious places. His words were measured, His compassion poured out in abundance. And often He withheld the answers the people sought because He knew the purposes of His Father—things no man or woman or child could grasp, however clearly He might speak.

Before He allowed evil men to take Him from His dear ones, He warned them it would happen and promised them He would rise again. When events happened as He had told them, they did not remember, and stood weeping in the shadows, feeling alone, isolated, suffocated by three endless days of silence. When He appeared to them once more and showed them the nail prints and spear hole, it all came back, bursting through their agonizing silence.

Later, the Holy Spirit came to indwell them and reminded them of the full range of Scriptures that revealed a silent God at work on the human scene. "Be still, and know that I am God" (Psalm 46:10, KJV). In the silence of allowing ourselves simply to know and trust, we are nourished and strengthened for the dark times and tough blows.

God's silent moments are like the empty spaces in a violin—sacred chambers that create the resonance needed to give quality to the sounds our lives produce. They are His gift to us, harried souls in a dissonant world. When we train our spirits to "[wait] in silence for God only" (Psalm 62:1), we luxuriate in the quietness next to His heart. Our woundedness is healed. We join His vast orchestral symphony where each instrument harmonizes to create the beautiful music He composed for us long before He made mud and shaped us into living beings. This is the music that fills the spheres of heaven and earth with His glory! Without silence—His silence—the symphony would never be.

I believe in the sun,
Even when it's not shining.
I believe in love,
Even when not feeling it.

I believe in God
Even when He is silent.[1]

For further glimpses of a Silent God, read: Genesis 39-40; 1 Kings 19; Job 1:20-22; 2:7-10; 42:1-6; Psalm 13; 37:1-9; 42-43; 83:1; 109:1; Isaiah 30:15.

The Lamb was a silent warrior, as silent in His victory as in His redemptive death. . . . Jesus as the Lamb never speaks a word in the entire book of Revelation.[2]

Hidden One

Behold, these are the fringes of His ways;
And how faint a word we hear of Him!
But His mighty thunder, who can understand? (Job 26:14)

One veiled from full view, always shrouded in a mystery we can never fully comprehend.

Three million Hebrews stood in the shadow of Mount Sinai awaiting a word from God. They had washed their garments and pledged themselves to obey whatever covenant God would create for them. He had already told them He would speak to them from a thick cloud. When He came, there was much more. Fire blazed like a furnace, smoke rose in a column on the horizon, the mountain quaked violently and the sound of a trumpet grew louder and louder. The first message was a peal of thunder and then a warning that the people were not to approach the mountaintop (Exodus 19:21-23).

303

Then God called Moses up higher and hid him away for forty days. All Israel was left at the foot of the terrifying mountain, wondering. Who was this mysterious God who hid behind clouds and shouted in thunder and made the earth to tremble beneath them? What message did He have for them that only Moses could receive from His hand? Would Moses return or would he be swallowed up in the hidden terror?

When Moses did return, his face shone with a glory so bright he had to wear a veil so they could look on him. The words he brought from their God were chiseled into stone—absolute commands, the unalterable structure for all morality among them. And the purpose for all this? It sounded profound, exalted, but still mysterious:

> *You shall be My own possession among all the peoples, for all the earth is Mine; and you shall be to Me a kingdom of priests and a holy nation.* (Exodus 19:5-6)

It became a pattern of worship in Israel. Only Moses and Aaron, the high priest, could ever enter into the presence of God. He was shrouded in clouds to protect His people from the intensity of His holiness.

> *Clouds and thick darkness surround Him.* (Psalm 97:2)

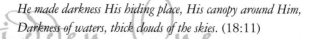

> *He made darkness His hiding place, His canopy around Him, Darkness of waters, thick clouds of the skies.* (18:11)

> Wisdom veils her face and adores the mercy which conceals the divine purpose; folly rushes in and perishes, blinded first, and by and by consumed by the blaze of glory.[3]

At last the day came when God pulled back the veil and showed the whole world a glimpse of His hidden glory. In the person of Jesus Christ, He walked our earth, revealed His perfect plan for human life, then went to the cross to pay for our sin. While He hung there dying, He reached down and tore the thick veil of the temple in two, from top to bottom. He opened up for all men and women who will come to Him a way into the sanctuary of His presence.

"Come to Me," He calls to us today. " . . . Learn from Me" (Matthew 11:28-29).

Little by little, as we walk with Him and come to Him, we see more and more of the Hidden One. But we shall never see all of Him on this side of heaven. There will always be mysteries beyond the ability of our human minds to conceive.

> I am Thine, O Lord, I have heard Thy voice,
> And it told Thy love to me;
> But I long to rise in the arms of faith
> And be closer drawn to Thee.
>
> Draw me nearer, nearer, blessed Lord,
> To the cross where Thou hast died;
> Draw me nearer, nearer, nearer blessed Lord,
> To Thy precious, bleeding side.[4]

For further glimpses of the Hidden One, read: Exodus 33:18-23; 40:34-35; Deuteronomy 29:29; Job 13:24; Psalm 44:24; Isaiah 8:17; 57:17; Habakkuk 3:4; Romans 11:33-34; 2 Corinthians 4:3-4; 1 Timothy 6:16; Revelation 2:17.

To Ponder

What did the life of Jesus show about the value of silence? _____

_____

_____

_____

Pray

Dear Silent, Hidden One, _____

_____

_____

_____

Dwelling Place

Lord, You have been our dwelling place in all generations.

(Psalm 90:1)

A home, a place of refuge where values are learned and honored and love is assured.

Deep in the human heart, God has built a yearning after the ideal home. A yearning for a comfort zone, a point of reference, refreshment, acceptance, nurture, discipline, warmth, safety and companionship. A place where deep roots—philosophies, habits, values, attitudes—grow. A place where character is sculpted with loving care. A base from which we can go out and make a difference in our world, then return for acceptance, instruction and rest.

God meets all the criteria He has given us the longing to find. Our one and only secure, nurturing dwelling place, He is our tender and capable heavenly Father. He protects us, trains us, disciplines us, gives us rest and challenges us, stretching our capacities. Best of all, when living with Him we can always rest assured of finding an eternal supply of absolutely unconditional love. There is nothing we can do to cause Him to love us less than He has from eternity.

The eternal God is a dwelling place,
And underneath are the everlasting arms. (Deuteronomy 33:27)

The door of this dwelling place stands ever open to us. In fact, the Lord and Father of this household goes with us wherever He sends us. Home in Him is never more than a heart's cry away from any place on earth we may be.

He who communes with God is always at home.[1]

If we would dwell with Him, we must trust in Him, take our stand for Him, follow Him, meditate on Him.

Dwell in the land and {feed securely on His} faithfulness.

(Psalm 37:3)

God offers us the best accommodations for our spirits. But are we enjoying them? The choice is ours to make.

Where do I allow my mind
to habitually wander?
Do I feast on fears and doubts and terrors?
Am I always preoccupied with plans and schedules?
Do I take refuge for my own weaknesses
by always criticizing others?
Do I brood on disappointments?
Abuses? Failures?
Feelings of inadequacy and purposelessness?
How often am I a self-controlling runaway?

Hear my cry, O God;
Give heed to my prayer.
From the end of the earth I call to You when my heart is faint;
Lead me to the rock that is higher than I.
For You have been a refuge for me,
A tower of strength against the enemy.
Let me dwell in Your tent forever;
Let me take refuge in the shelter of Your wings.

(Psalm 61:1-4)

For further glimpses of God our Dwelling Place, read: Deuteronomy 33:26-29; Psalm 43:3; 71:3; 84:1-4; 90:1; 91:1, 9-10; John 15:1-10.

Sanctuary

And {I} will set My sanctuary in their midst forever. My dwelling place also will be with them; and I will be their God, and they will be My people. (Ezekiel 37:26-27)

Sanctuary A consecrated meeting place, refuge and protection in the midst of peril.

God's tabernacle in the wilderness was a sanctuary for sinners. It housed a basin for cleansing, a candlestick for light, a table for bread and an incense altar for prayer. And in its innermost sanctuary stood the holiest item of all—the ark of the covenant. Its lid was the mercy seat, overspread with the wings of golden cherubim. It was at the mercy seat that once a year the high priest sprinkled blood to make atonement for the sins of the people. And here the glory of God came down to accept the offerings, to communicate with Moses, to make clear the demands of God's holiness.

When Jesus came to earth, we are told He "became flesh, and [tabernacled] among us" (John 1:14). A tabernacle is a rough tent sanctuary that looked ordinary on the outside, but held the treasures of heaven within. Jesus came as a meeting place between God and all of mankind. He became a basin for our cleansing, a candlestick to give us light, a table spread with heavenly bread, an altar of incense where we can offer our prayers in His name. Most of all, He became our mercy seat, where He spilled out His own blood to make atonement for our sin. And when the offering had been made, the glory descended and He assumed a heavenly tabernacle, a temple.

> *We saw His glory, glory as of the only begotten from the Father, full of grace and truth. . . . For the Law was given through Moses; grace and truth were realized through Jesus Christ.* (John 1:14, 17)

Moses built the wilderness sanctuary with the instructions God gave him on Mount Sinai. He was the channel of a law chiseled in stone, designed to make us accountable and bring us to brokenness when we could not keep the law to perfection.

When Jesus came, a heavenly tabernacle in flesh and blood, He showed us the dazzling glory of moral perfection. He spread His arms wide and invited us to, "Come to Me," then spread them again, the Lamb of God offered up for our sin. In that stunningly remarkable process, He finished the work Moses had begun. He gathered together both truth as revealed in the law and grace that only He could show. This is glory at its brightest in all the moral universe! Incredible, humbling and oh-so-full of tender mercy to us whose very nature is programmed to sin. Unlike His law, God's grace is not chiseled in stone. Instead, He inscribes it deeply on broken, fleshy hearts gathered into His eternal sanctuary for healing.

Dear God of Truth and Grace
Make every chamber of my life—
be it the dark and muffled hollows of my silent grief
or the sun-splashed salons of my sparkling celebration—
A sanctuary
purified by Your grace
hushed by Your presence
radiant with Your GLORY!

For further glimpses of God our Sanctuary, read: Psalm 27:5-6; 73:16-17; Isaiah 8:13-14; Ezekiel 11:16.

Temple

> *Then I saw a new heaven and a new earth. . . . And I saw the holy city, new Jerusalem, coming down out of heaven from God, made ready as a bride adorned for her husband. . . . I saw no temple in it, for the Lord God the Almighty and the Lamb are its temple.* (Revelation 21:1-2, 22)

Temple The home and symbol of God's presence among mankind.

The tabernacle was a tent, a temporary sanctuary for a wandering people. Jesus, in His earthly body, was God, sojourning among men for a time, providing healing and shelter in that tent. The temple, on the other hand, was a building, a permanent place for pilgrims, a perpetual symbol of the eternal presence of God. Jesus, enthroned in heaven, will forever be that temple.

In the days of the glory of Solomon's temple, that magnificent, gold-covered structure "was not only the worship center of Hebrew culture, but also the art gallery, concert plaza and poetry library."[2] In that temple, everything that was beautiful and wholesome and of spiritual value combined as one glorious reminder of the ever-present, ever-communicating, ever-redemptive Jehovah God.

Jesus was and is and always will be, for His people, that kind of temple sanctuary. His presence is everything—nothing else matters but His presence, His redemption, His healing.

God's holy Book of Scripture begins with the simple line: "*In the beginning God created*" (Genesis 1:1).

It concludes with line upon line, emphasizing it again and again, using a host of His glorious names, reminding us of the nearness of His presence:

> *I am coming quickly, and My reward is with Me. . . . I am the Alpha and the Omega, the first and the last, the beginning and the end. . . . I am the root and the descendant of David, the bright morning star. . . . "Yes, I am coming quickly."* Amen. Come, Lord Jesus. The grace of the Lord Jesus be with all. Amen. (Revelation 22:12-13, 16, 20-21)

For further glimpses of God our Temple, read: Psalm 65:4; Ezekiel 47:1-12 with Revelation 22:1-2.

To Ponder

How can we dwell in God as our home, sanctuary or temple?

_____

_____

_____

_____

Pray

Dear God, my Dwelling Place, my Sanctuary, Tabernacle and Temple, _____

_____

_____

_____

Majestic

Who is like You among the gods, O LORD?
Who is like You, majestic in holiness,
Awesome in praises, working wonders? (Exodus 15:11)

Majestic Glorious, worthy, lordly, characterized by grandeur and honor.

In our natural human state, we cannot appreciate God's majesty. Our sinful natures blind us and keep us earthbound. All God's glorious plans and designs lack luster in our eyes. Instead, His laws hover over us like so many cold engravings chiseled into tablets of stone on a dry-as-dust mountain.

Once we feel the trembling of the thunder, however, and catch a glimpse of the majesty of the flaming presence of the King of Glory, our viewpoint changes. Bright, flashing darts of His majesty arrest our wayward hearts and draw us toward the King. As our eyes grow more and more accustomed to the brilliance, we see that *"out of the north comes golden splendor; around God is awesome majesty"* (Job 37:22).

God's glorious majesty
arrests my trivialized attention,
boggles my mind,
lights a celestial fire in my soul,
turns my tongue to stammering

then, silence . . .
Hovering, His majesty hangs above me
caught in a web of mystery
and whispering pure, sweet strains
of absolute holiness
into the hungry ears of my spirit.

From hearts too smitten by the wonder of it all to restrain our full exuberance, we cry out,

O LORD, our Lord,
How majestic is Your name in all the earth,
Who have displayed Your splendor above the heavens!

(Psalm 8:1)

You are resplendent,
More majestic than the mountains of prey. (76:4)

For further glimpses of the Majestic God, read: 1 Chronicles 29:11; Psalm 93:1; 96:6; Isaiah 33:21; Micah 5:4; Hebrews 1:3; 8:1; 2 Peter 1:16-17; Jude 25.

I will extol You, my God, O King,
And I will bless Your name forever and ever. . . .
On the glorious splendor of Your majesty
And on Your wonderful works, I will meditate.

(Psalm 145:1, 5)

Splendor

Splendor and majesty are before Him,
Strength and joy are in His place.
Ascribe to the LORD, O families of the peoples,
Ascribe to the LORD glory and strength.
Ascribe to the LORD the glory due His name;

Bring an offering, and come before Him;
Worship the LORD in holy array.
Tremble before Him, all the earth. (1 Chronicles 16:27-30)

Splendor

Imposing form and appearance, excellence, majesty and honor.

The list of words used in the Old Testament to translate the Hebrew word *splendor,* in these verses, shines like a jewel filled with many fine and soul-stirring nuances of meaning. With holy awe, I hold each one of these defining words to the light of His glory. I let my heart meditate long on its rich fullness and captivating beauty. I praise Him for each new glimpse of truth my meditation brings to light.

- *Grandeur* (an imposing form and appearance)
- *Beauty, comeliness*
- *Excellency*
- *Majesty*
- *Glory*
- *Honor*

Nothing in all of heaven above or earth beneath can compare with the radiating splendor of our God. Thanks to His immeasurable grace, He rewards our most diligent and ceaseless search after Him with visions of grandeur and an overpowering display of that most transcendent of all good things—the holy glory of Almighty God.

But grace does not stop here. It goes on to infuse our lives with glimmers and reflections of the splendor. The glow that fills and radiates out from us will always be borrowed from the perfect and never-exhaustible source—the God of Glory Himself.

For God, who said, "Light shall shine out of darkness," is the One who has shone in our hearts to give the Light of the knowledge of the glory of God in the face of Christ. But we have this treasure in earthen vessels, so that the surpassing greatness of the power will be of God and not from ourselves.

(2 Corinthians 4:6-7)

Ah, good friends, the charm of the earthen vessel abides in the sterling treasure it enshrines. Think! The Father at whose will, on creation's morn, light blazed out of darkness, doth use our humble, human hearts to exhibit His cap-sheaf splendor—the light of the knowledge of His glory in the face of our Beloved. These hearts of ours are very lowly at best, but how altogether beautiful when the Borrowed Glow gets upon them![1]

For further glimpses of the God of Splendor, read: Psalm 8:1; 34:5; 45:3; 76:4; 111:3; 148:13; Habakkuk 3:3-4; Matthew 17:1-8.

His goodness shines with brightest rays
When we delight in all His ways.
His glory overflows its rim
When we are satisfied with him.
His radiance will fill the earth
When people revel in his worth.
The beauty of God's holy fire
Burns brightest in the heart's desire.

(from *Desiring God* by John Piper)[2]

To Ponder

Open up your heart to be overwhelmed by the majesty and splendor of God. _____

_____

_____

_____

Pray

Dear God of Majesty and Splendor, _____

_____

_____

_____

Awesome

*Our God, the great, the mighty, and the awesome God, who
keeps covenant and lovingkindness.* (Nehemiah 9:32)

Awesome. A quality which stirs in us "an emotion of mingled reverence, dread and wonder inspired by
something majestic or sublime."[1]

The word *awesome* has grown tarnished in recent years since
being added to the faddish jargon of teenagers. However,
despite the mundanity of its current usage, the word *awesome* still applies to the spell cast by overpowering persons and phe-
nomena.

We experience this awe every time we stand in the presence of
anything that holds an air of mystery—something begging to be dis-
covered, but always just beyond our reach. We feel this mixture of
wonder and awe at the foot of a towering mountain or thunderous
waterfall or on the brink of the Grand Canyon or when we hold a
newborn baby or snorkel through a school of bright orange fish in a
blue Caribbean bay.

At a deeper level, in worship, we take time to allow our hearts to
be captivated by the wonder and awesomeness of a God who withholds far more mysteries about His character than all the mountains,
waterfalls, canyons, newborns and tropical fish ever created by His

mighty hand. Everything about the King of Glory in His majesty and splendor will always defy both our understanding and our imagination.

When we give ourselves to the stunning demands of meditating on the royal splendor of this King of Glory, we enter into worship in its highest and deepest dimensions. Such worship excites a most remarkable response from the depth of our beings. It leads us to exclaim repeatedly at the wonders of His awe. But it can also bring to a dead stop the flow of all words. David was experiencing such awed quietness when he said:

My soul waits in silence for God only. (Psalm 62:1)

This kind of delighted silence in the presence of God is a rare and precious jewel! How we need it in our clamorous world, where technology offers prospects of incredible answers that, in turn, produce terrifying questions we can never answer! God is still creating us with hollowed-out quiet spaces in our souls shaped just right to enable us to reflect on our awesome God and be nurtured by the glory of the King.

> Awesome King of Glory
> God of wonder
> Towering above me
> Stooping to love me
> Freeing the gates
> From the hinges that bind.
> Oh!
> God of transcendence
> Stagger my feebleness
> Into dumbfoundedness:
> Who is a God like You?

For further glimpses of an Awesome God, read: Deuteronomy 7:21; Nehemiah 1:5.

The King of Glory

The earth is the LORD's, and all it contains,
The world, and those who dwell in it.
For He has founded it upon the seas
And established it upon the rivers. (Psalm 24:1-2)

Ruler over all things in the places where God's glory shines.

ll things are God's and God's alone. He has created them for Himself and His expansive glory. He is the King of the natural universe—origin, guardian and sovereign revealer of all the mysteries it holds.

Who may ascend into the hill of the LORD?
And who may stand in His holy place?
He who has clean hands and a pure heart,
Who has not lifted up his soul to falsehood
And has not sworn deceitfully.
He shall receive a blessing from the LORD
And righteousness from the God of his salvation.

(Psalm 24:3-5)

Our lives are ordered by God's righteous laws of sowing and reaping. He alone determines how we may come to stand before Him in the throne room of His majesty's glory. For He is and always will be King of the moral universe. He holds it together by the breath of His decrees.

Our human nature tells us it is enough to keep our hands clean by doing and saying only right things. We think that surely then God will be pleased to accept us. His glory, however, goes another step, insisting that we maintain not only clean hands, but also pure hearts in order to be allowed into the dazzling glory of His presence.

> *Lift up your heads, O gates,*
> *And be lifted up, O ancient doors,*
> *That the King of glory may come in!*
> *Who is the King of glory?*
> *The LORD strong and mighty,*
> *The LORD mighty in battle.*
> *Lift up your heads, O gates,*
> *And lift them up, O ancient doors,*
> *That the King of glory may come in!*
> *Who is this King of glory?*
> *The LORD of hosts,*
> *He is the King of glory.* (Psalm 24:7-10)

All the multitude of works God has performed throughout history build toward one glorious climactic goal—to throw open wide the gates and usher in the King of Glory, clothed in robes of righteousness and holy majesty, sweeping up His people into the absolutely perfect glory of His Kingship!

Our hands are never clean enough, nor our hearts pure enough to enable us to open the gates into His holiness. He alone can throw them open. His love operating through grace makes it happen.

> Lord, the door is locked and Thou hast the key; I have been trying what I can do, but the wards are so rusty that I cannot possibly turn the key. . . . Lord, throw the door off the hinges . . . so that thou wilt but come in and dwell here. Come, O mighty God, break through doors of iron, and bars of brass, and make way for thyself by thy love and power. Come, Lord, and make thyself welcome; all that I have is at thy service; O fit my soul to entertain thee![2]

All Your works shall give thanks to You, O LORD . . .
They shall speak of the glory of Your kingdom . . .
To make known to the sons of men . . .
The glory of the majesty of Your kingdom.

(Psalm 145:10-12)

For further glimpses of the King of Glory, read: Psalm 145; Isaiah 60:1-3, 15-22.

Worship is a way of reflecting back to God the radiance of His worth.[3]

To Ponder

Open your heart up to the King of Glory. Ask Him, in your own words, to show you where to look for that glory in your daily life.

_____

_____

_____

Pray

Dear Awesome, Splendid and Majestic King of Glory, _____

_____

_____

_____

Still More Glory

For fifty-two weeks now you have been experiencing a deepening revelation of the glory of God. You have encountered Him in many facets of His fathomless character. At this point, you may be asking yourself, "What's next?"

There are a number of options. You may want to go back and reread the meditations, looking for something more, something deeper the next time through. Or, you may begin your own primary research, digging out gems in Scripture that were not covered here.

Regardless of what you do in a regular quiet encounter time, you now have the necessary tools to help you turn your little chunks of daily, unscheduled time into gems of reflective thought. Your mind is already filled with names, titles and attributes of God, a base from which you can launch yourself into further exploration of God's multifaceted character.

An exciting adventure lies ahead. You can now use your newly acquired knowledge and intimacy with God to fill the frequent moments of waiting in your life—at the grocery store, at traffic lights, in a quiet place of natural beauty, out walking in your neighborhood or at the beginning of a session of prayer either alone or with a group. Wherever life gives you blanks, fill them with thoughts of God.

The following are some suggested ways of filling those moments of waiting:

- Shut out the distractions of the world around you and open your heart up to God. Ask Him, "Lord, show me Your glory!"

- Write down whatever name, title and/or attribute He brings to your mind.

- Meditate on it, along with one or more Scriptures that present it. Roll it around in your mind much like you would roll a golden ball of hard candy in your mouth. Savor it with every power of your spiritual senses.

- Speak the word aloud, slowly, letting it fall on your ears and heart like strains of freshly harmonized music. Repeat it again and again, giving yourself completely to the thoughts it inspires and the glimpses of the superior greatness of His glory it engenders in your awestruck heart and mind.

- Bow your head and/or fall on your knees and give yourself to the worship of the God who has so lavishly revealed Himself to you. Thank Him for what He has done. Praise Him for who He is. Worship Him as an act of personal surrender to the God of the universe and King of Glory!

Praise the LORD!
Praise God in His sanctuary;
Praise Him in His mighty expanse.
Praise Him for His mighty deeds;
Praise Him according to His excellent greatness.
Praise Him with trumpet sound;
Praise Him with harp and lyre.
Praise Him with timbrel and dancing;
Praise Him with stringed instruments and pipe.
Praise Him with loud cymbals;
Praise Him with resounding cymbals.
Let everything that has breath praise the LORD.
Praise the LORD! (Psalm 150:1-6)

Endnotes

Introduction

1. See Exodus 32-34 for the scriptural account of this story. Cf. also Exodus 24.
2. Timothy Jones, *Prayer's Apprentice: A Year with the Great Spiritual Mentors* (Nashville, TN: Word Publishing, 2001), p. 68.

Week One

1. Henry Maskill in Charles Haddon Spurgeon, *The Treasury of David* (McLean, VA: MacDonald Publishing Company, n.d.), 1, 1:310.
2. Ibid., 1:302.

Week Two

1. Leland Ryken, James C. Wilhoit, Tremper Longman III, *Dictionary of Biblical Imagery* (Downer's Grove, IL: InterVarsity Press, 1998), p. 445.
2. Stephen Charnock, *The Existence and Attributes of God* (Grand Rapids, MI: Baker Book House, reprinted 1979), 1:298.
3. John Piper, *The Pleasures of God* (Portland, OR: Multnomah Press, 1991), p. 98.

Week Three

1. John Piper, *Desiring God* (Sisters, OR: Multnomah Press, 1996), p. 45.
2. Ken Gire, *Windows of the Soul* (Grand Rapids, MI: Zondervan, 1996), p. 55.
3. Paul Schullery, *Echoes from the Summit* (San Diego, CA: Harcourt Brace, 1996), p. 3.

4. Brennan Manning, *The Ragamuffin Gospel* (Sisters, OR: Multnomah Press, 1990), p. 108.

Week Four

1. Piper, *Desiring God*, p. 44.
2. Ethel Herr, "Handiwork," *Chosen Families of the Bible* (Chicago, IL: Moody Press, 1981), p. 122.

Week Six

1. *American Heritage Dictionary of the English Language* (Boston, MA: Houghton Mifflin Company, 1973), p. 567.
2. Charnock, *The Existence and Attributes of God*, 2:210-2.
3. Piper, *Pleasures of God,* p. 189.
4. John Newton, "Amazing Grace," *Hymns of the Christian Life* (Camp Hill, PA: Christian Publications, 1978), 197.

Week Seven

1. This word appears as *beauty* in most translations. But in the margin of the NAS Bible, the alternative reading is *delightfulness.*
2. Roy and Revel Hession, *We Would See Jesus* (Ft. Washington, PA: Christian Literature Crusade, 1997), p. 33.
3. Tricia McCary Rhodes, *Taking Up Your Cross* (Minneapolis, MN: Bethany House Publishers, 2000), pp. 198-9.

Week Eight

1. S. Conway, *The Pulpit Commentary* (Grand Rapids, MI: Eerdmans, reprinted 1977), 11:230.
2. Isaac Watts, "When I Survey the Wondrous Cross," *Hymns of the Christian Life*, 82.
3. Traditional spiritual, "There Is a Balm in Gilead," *Hymns for the Family of God* (Nashville, TN: Paragon Associates, 1976), 48.

Week Nine

1. Ryken, Wilhoit and Longman, *The Dictionary of Biblical Imagery* (Downers Grove, IL: InterVarsity Press, 1998), p. 389.
2. Charnock, *The Existence and Attributes of God*, 2:110.

Week Ten

1. Richard Ellsworth Day, *The Borrowed Glow* (Grand Rapids, MI: Zondervan Publishing House, 1937), p. 23.
2. K. Bockmuel, *New Dictionary of Theology* (Downers Grove, IL: InterVarsity Press, 1988), p. 615.

Week Eleven

1. Roderick T. Leupp, *Knowing the Name of God* (Downers Grove, IL: InterVarsity Press, 1996), p. 14.
2. William Cowper, "Light Shining Out of Darkness," *The New Oxford Book of Christian Verse* (New York: Oxford University Press, 1988), p. 199.

Week Twelve

1. Jan Johnson, *Living a Purpose Full Life* (Colorado Springs, CO: Waterbrook Press, 1999), p. 7.
2. Day, *The Borrowed Glow*, p. 321.
3. The Hebrew word *manna* means "what is it?" Information taken from "Hebrew Chaldee Dictionary" in *Strong's Exhaustive Concordance of the Bible* (New York: Abingdon-Cokesbury, 1890), p. 67.
4. Day, *The Borrowed Glow*, p. 321.

Week Fourteen

1. Thomas Ken in Spurgeon, *Treasury of David,* 1, 2:18.

Week Fifteen

1. George Herbert, "The Storm" in *George Herbert Selected Poems* (London: Everyman, J.M. Dent, 1996), p. 55.
2. Ibid., 1, 2:5.

Week Sixteen

1. Key words repeated many times in Isaiah 43-46.
2. Piper, *Pleasures of God*, p. 162.

Week Eighteen

1. Jones, *Prayer's Apprentice*, p. 33.
2. Per author's personal conversation with Tricia Rhodes.
3. Hession, *We Would See Jesus*, p. 129.

Week Nineteen

1. Floyd McClung, *The Father Heart of God* (Eugene, OR: Harvest House Publishers, 1985), p. 52.
2. P.D. James, "The Baroness in the Crime Lab," *Books and Culture,* Mar./Apr. 1998, 15.

Week Twenty

1. William Cowper in Spurgeon, *Treasury of David,* 1, 1:131.

Week Twenty-One

1. Spurgeon, *Treasury of David*, 3, 1:317.
2. Roderick T. Leupp, *Knowing the Name of God* (Downers Grove, IL: InterVarsity Press, 1996), p. 47.
3. Spurgeon, *Treasury of David,* 3, 1:70.
4. Samuel T. Francis, "Oh, the Deep, Deep Love of Jesus," *Hymns of the Christian Life,* 177.

5. F.B. Meyer, *My Daily Prayer* (London: Fleming H. Revell, 1913), January 23.

6. G. Rawlinson in *The Pulpit Commentary: Isaiah* (Grand Rapids, MI: Eerdmans, reprinted 1977), 2:70.

Week Twenty-Two

1. Psalm 46:1, margin, *New American Standard Bible* (La Habra, CA: Collins World, 1975).

2. Jones, *Prayer's Apprentice*, p. 33.

Week Twenty-Three

1. Edith G. Cherry, "We Rest on Thee," *Hymns of the Christian Life*, 371.

Week Twenty-four

1. Roy and Revel Hession, *We Would See Jesus* (Ft. Washington, PA: Christian Literature Crusade, 1997), pp. 124-5. Used by permission.

2. Calvin Miller, *The Finale*, now part of The Singer Trilogy (Downers Grove, IL: InterVarsity Press, 1979), p. 21. Used by permission.

3. Calvin Miller, *Into the Depths with God* (Minneapolis, MN: Bethany House Publishers, 2000), p. 40.

Week Twenty-five

1. Ryken, Wilhoit and Longman, *The Dictionary of Biblical Imagery*, p. 451.

2. Spurgeon, *Treasury of David,* 3, 2:246.

3. Lorna Anderson, "Nugget," reprinted from *Songs of the Soul* (Grand Rapids, MI: The Church Herald, 1977), p. 9. Copyright © by The Church Herald, Inc. Used by permission.

4. Manning, *Ragamuffin Gospel*, p. 109.

Week Twenty-Six

1. Taken from a sermon by Paul Steele, former pastor of The Valley Church, Cupertino, CA.
2. C. Vernon Grounds, *Zondervan Pictorial Encyclopedia of the Bible* (Grand Rapids, MI: Zondervan Publishing House, 1976), 1:500.

Week Twenty-Seven

1. Richard Francis Weymouth, *The New Testament in Modern Speech* (Boston, MA: Pilgrim Press, 1909), p. 532.
2. Marjorie Myers, "Towels," *alive now!*, March/April 1983, p. 54. Used by permission of author.

Week Twenty-Eight

1. James Glentworth Butler, *Butler's Bible Work Gospels* (New York: Funk and Wagnulls Publisher, 1889), p. 490.
2. Hession, *We Would See Jesus*, pp. 133-4.
3. Butler, *Butler's Bible Work*, p. 490.
4. Meyer, *My Daily Prayer*, February 5.
5. H.R. Reynolds in *The Pulpit Commentary: The Gospel of St. John* (Grand Rapids, MI: Eerdmans, 1977), 2:277.
6. John R.W. Stott, *The Cross of Christ* (Downer's Grove, IL: InterVarsity Press, 1986), p. 317. Used by permission.
7. Ibid., p. 41.
8. Ralph W. Seager, *Wheatfields and Vineyards* (Chappaqua, NY: Christian Herald House, 1975), p. 12. Used by permission of author.
9. Stephen D. and Jacalyn Eyre, *Abiding in Christ's Love* (Downer's Grove, IL: InterVarsity Press, 1994), p. 46.
10. Kathleen Norris, *Amazing Grace: A Vocabulary of Faith* (New York: Riverhead Books, 1998), p. 41.

11. Andrew Murray, *Abide in Christ* (Fort Washington, PA: Christian Literature Crusade, 1974), p. 43.

Week Twenty-Nine

1. Compare His similar words about His Church in First Peter 2:9-10.
2. E.g., Deuteronomy 30:1-3; Jeremiah 3:22; Hosea 12:6; 14:1; Malachi 3:7. Ezekiel 16 is a powerful passage that pictures this passion of God for His rebellious people. It can break your heart to read it.
3. Spurgeon, *Treasury of David,* 2, 2:142.

Week Thirty

1. Taken from a sermon by John Worley, former pastor of The Valley Church, Cupertino, CA.
2. Arthur Bennet, compiler, *The Valley of Vision* (Carlisle, PA: Banner of Truth Trust, 1975), p. 76.

Week Thirty-One

1. Charnock, *The Existence and Attributes of God,* 2:359.
2. Hession, *We Would See Jesus,* p. 33.
3. Piper, *Pleasures of God,* p. 19.
4. Hession, *We Would See Jesus,* p. 41.
5. John Newton, "Amazing Grace," *Hymns of the Christian Life,* 197.
6. Calvin Miller, *My Son, My Savior* (Colorado Springs, CO: Chariot Victor Publishing, 1997), p. 8.

Week Thirty-Two

1. Jones, *Prayer's Apprentice,* p. 37.

Week Thirty-Three

1. Pamela Reeve, *Relationships: What It Takes to Be a Friend* (Sisters, OR: Multnomah Books, 1997), pp. 9-10.
2. *Ibid.*, p. 88.
3. Written at a time when Alice (my mother) realized she had Alzheimers, this was her prayer for the continuing companionship of the God she had walked with all her life. It was a prayer He answered through the dark years that followed.
4. The word often translated *loving-kindness* in Scripture could also be translated *loyal love*. Information taken from a sermon by Paul Steele.
5. George W. Robinson, "I Am His, and He Is Mine," *Hymns of the Christian Life*, 199.

Week Thirty-four

1. Edward Perronet, "All Hail the Power of Jesus' Name," *Hymns of the Christian Life*, 114-6.

Week Thirty-Six

1. Prayer of Anselm, from *Proslogion,* rendered by Timothy Jones in *Prayer's Apprentice*, p. 91.
2. Tricia McCary Rhodes, *Taking Up Your Cross* (Minneapolis, MN: Bethany House, a division of Baker Book House Company, 2000), p. 135. Used by permission.
3. Spurgeon, *Treasury of David,* 2, 2:134.
4. T. Kelley in *The Church Hymnal* (Boston, MA: Partish Choir, 1879), 372.

Week Thirty-Seven

1. Rhodes, *Taking Up Your Cross*, p. 189.
2. Stott, *The Cross of Christ*, p. 212. Used by permission.

3. Day, *The Borrowed Glow*, p. 149.

4. Arthur Bennet, ed., *The Valley of Vision* (Edinburgh: Banner of Truth, 2001), p. 18. Used by permission.

5. From an unpublished work by Marsha L. Gubser.

Week Thirty-Eight

1. T.C. Horton and Charles E. Hurlburt, *The Wonderful Names of Our Wonderful Lord* (Uhrichsville, OH: Barbour Books, 1996), p. 174.

2. O. Hallesby, *Prayer* (Minneapolis, MN: Augsburg Publishing House, 1959), p. 51. Reprinted by permission from *Prayer* by O. Hallesby, copyright © 1959 Augsburg Publishing House. Used by permission of Augsburg Fortress.

3. Ibid., p. 51.

4. Arthur Bennet, ed., *The Valley of Vision* (Edinburgh: Banner of Truth, 2001), p. 149. Used by permission.

Week Thirty-Nine

1. Sister Margaret Magdalen, *Jesus, Man of Prayer* (Downer's Grove, IL: InterVarsity Press, 1987), p. 107.

2. Ethel Herr, "Intercession: A Holy Partnership," *Discipleship Journal,* Issue 90, 1995, p. 96.

3. Ibid.

4. Ibid.

Week Forty

1. Charnock, *The Existence and Attributes of God*, 1:10-11.

2. Henry Lyte, "Abide with Me," *Hymns for the Family of God*, 500.

3. Spurgeon, *Treasury of David*, 1, 2:58.

Week forty-One

1. Ryken, Wilhoit and Longman, *Dictionary of Biblical Imagery*, p. 166.
2. William Hanna in Butler, *Butler's Bible Work*, p. 420.
3. "K" in John Rippon, Selection 1787, "How Firm a Foundation," *Hymns for the Family of God*, 32.

Week forty-Two

1. *American Heritage Dictionary*, p. 673.
2. Charnock, *The Existence and Attributes of God*, p. 409.
3. Chad Walsh, *The Psalm of Christ* (Philadelphia, PA: Westminster Press, 1963), p. 26.
4. William Gurnall in Spurgeon, *Treasury of David*, 1, 2:49.
5. Leupp, *Knowing the Name of God*, p. 23.
6. Miller, *Into the Depths with God*, p. 121.

Week forty-Three

1. Spencer Marsh, *Beginnings: A Portrayal of the Creation* (Portland, OR: Multnomah Press, 1981), p. 70.

Week forty-four

1. Ryken, Wilhoit and Longman, *Dictionary of Biblical Imagery*, p. 484.

Week forty-five

1. Magdalen, *Jesus, Man of Prayer*, p. 162.
2. Andrew Elphinstone in Magdalen, *Jesus, Man of Prayer*, p. 137.
3. L.L. Morris in Bockmuel, *New Dictionary of Theology*, p. 56.
4. William R. Newell, "At Calvary," *Hymns of the Christian Life*, 479.

Week forty-Six

1. Washington Gladden, "O Master, Let Me Walk with Thee," *Hymns for the Family of God*, 442.
2. Hession, *We Would See Jesus*, p. 48.
3. Piper, *Desiring God,* p. 15.

Week forty-Seven

1. Roy and Revel Hession, *We Would See Jesus* (Ft. Washington, PA: Christian Literature Crusade, 1997), p. 127. Used by permission.

Week forty-Eight

1. Rhodes, *Taking Up Your Cross*, p. 80.
2. Anonymous, "Thy Mercy and Thy Truth, O Lord," *The Psalter Hymnal* (Grand Rapids, MI: Publication Committee of the Christian Reformed Church, Inc., Publishers, 1959), 62.
3. Piper, *Desiring God*, p. 238.
4. Ryken, Wilhoit and Longman, *Dictionary of Biblical Imagery*, p. 420.
5. Spurgeon, *Treasury of David,* 3, 2:325.
6. Irish hymn, tr. by Mary Byrne, "Be Thou My Vision," *Hymns of the Christian Life,* 254.

Week forty-Nine

1. Words found on the walls of a Cologne cellar where Jews were hidden during World War II. Information taken from The Bard Project program folder on "Arts on Persecution," September 7-8, 2001.
2. J. Ramsey Michaels, *Revelation* (Downers Grove, IL: InterVarsity Press, 1997), p. 217.
3. Spurgeon, *Treasury of David,* 2, 2:195.

4. Fanny Crosby, "I Am Thine, O Lord," *Hymns for the Family of God*, 455.

Week Fifty

1. Spurgeon, *Treasury of David,* 2, 1:41.
2. Ryken, Wilhoit and Longman, *Dictionary of Biblical Imagery,* p. 849.

Week Fifty-One

1. Day, *Borrowed Glow*, p. 13.
2. Piper, *Desiring God*, p. 26. Excerpted from *Desiring God* © 1986, 1996 by John Piper. Used by permission of Multnomah Publishers, Inc.

Week Fifty-Two

1. *American Heritage Dictionary*, p. 92.
2. Spurgeon, *Treasury of David*, 1, 1:385-6.
3. Piper, *Desiring God*, p. 84.